# PSALMS

# FOR

# CAREGIVERS

(Revised Edition)

# PSALMS

# FOR

# CAREGIVERS

## (Revised Edition)

### MEDITATIONS FOR CAREGIVERS FROM THE PSALMS

## DARLENE SAUNDERS

### AMAZONCREATESPACE

AUCTOREM
HOUSE

Auctorem House
276 5th Ave, Ste 704-2591
New York, NY 10001
www.auctoremhouse.com
Phone: 1 888-332-7718

All scripture quotations, unless otherwise indicated, are taken from the New King James Version. Copyright ©1982 by Thomas Nelson, Inc. Used by permission. All rights reserved.

Published by Auctorem House: 10/24/2024

ISBN: 978-1-965687-02-4(sc)
ISBN: 978-1-965687-03-1(e)

Library of Congress Control Number: 2024919236

Any people depicted in stock imagery provided by iStock are models, and such images are being used for illustrative purposes only.

Certain stock imagery © iStock.

# INTRODUCTION

IN THE INTEREST of keeping this devotional small enough to handle easily, I have elected to leave out the whole psalms, including only the verses referred to. However, I highly recommend that the reader take time to read the entire psalm from which I quote before reading the verses and comments. My chosen scripture version is New King James.

# WALKING IN GOD'S COUNSEL

*Blessed is the man*

*Who walks not in the counsel of the ungodly,*

*Nor stands in the path of sinners,*

*Nor sits in the seat of the scornful;*

--Psalm 1:1

WHERE DO WE as caregivers get our advice? We are constantly in need of answers to the hard questions about the best ways to minister to our loved ones. The world has many suggestions. How do we know what is the right thing to do in each instance?

After I placed my husband in a care facility, many friends and even family members questioned my decision. He didn't seem that bad. He still had his sense of humor. They could sometimes carry on conversations with him. He no longer drove a car, so he wasn't a danger to anyone. What they didn't know about were the months of sleepless nights when Larry kept me awake with rummaging and questions and then wandered off during the day when I fell asleep in my chair. They did not hear the insistent accusations of strange things his mind told him I had done. They did not have to fend off physical attacks when I tried to stop him from abusive behavior to a child or animal. Alzheimer's Disease (AD) patients cover their behavior well when in the presence of someone other than the spouse or other caregiver.

We must make placement decisions with God's help, determining how much God expects us to give and where the patient can get the best care, and that isn't always at our hands.

One day, shortly after I had placed my husband in a nursing home, a younger family member counseled me about the time I spent visiting him and providing for his needs.

"You know, no one would blame you if you divorced him," she said. "After all, he doesn't even know you. You don't need to throw your own life away for him."

I admit I was shocked. I could only answer, "A vow is a vow. He may not be the same man I married but I love the man he was and I will do what is right for him."

God deals with His children individually. Our job is to be sure we are doing what He tells us to – not what the wisdom of the world says.

*Lord, alert me to ungodly counsel. Lead me to people with right answers to my many questions. Bring Your word to my mind as I need it. Thank You for teaching me as I make this journey. In Jesus' name, amen.*

# SPENDING TIME WITH GOD

*But his delight is in the law of the Lord,*

*And in His law he meditates day and night.*

--Psalm 1:2

EARLY IN THE care of my mother, I was introduced to the classic caregivers' book: *The Thirty-Six Hour Day.* What a revelation! Before that I thought I was the only one who felt like a caregiver's day was at least half again as long and twice as difficult as the "normal" person's is.

We are often drained at the end of these long days of giving on top of giving. We encounter spiritually dry seasons because we don't have time to refill our own tanks at the springs of living water. Where can we find the time to refresh spiritually?

You have made lifestyle changes since you began your caregiver journey. I gave up most of my writing time and, for at least a year, I gave up all my service in a local church. Some parts of my life were put on temporary hold, but my physical and spiritual health remained important enough to nurture.

It's not too late to remember what Jesus said in John chapter 4: His Word would be in us, living water springing up to life eternal. Now is the time to meditate on God's Word, whatever we have read and memorized in the past. However short the passages, when we feel overwhelmed, thinking about Scripture brings calm and refreshment. If all you remember are parts of Psalm 23, meditate on those words and think about what they mean to you in your present situation.

Beyond that, take time for yourself to add to your personal storehouse of living water. We may feel we don't have enough time to read God's Word. We may think we need large blocks of time to do it. It's more important to establish a habit of reading just a few verses a day than to try to read whole chapters. A page in a short devotional book may be all you have time for, but meditating on those verses throughout the day will refresh and strengthen you.

*Father, refresh me now with Your words, however long ago I read them. Bring the right words to my mind to calm or give me wisdom. Help me use Your words to calm my loved one too. Thank You for the storehouse of Scripture already in my mind. Help me add to it and use it. In Jesus' name, amen.*

# PLANTED

*He shall be like a tree*

*Planted by the rivers of water,*

*That brings forth its fruit in its season,*

*Whose leaf also shall not wither;*

*And whatever he does shall prosper.*

--Psalm 1:3

DAILY CARE FOR another can leave us feeling weak and vulnerable. Uncertainties crowd in and make us feel wishy-washy. One doctor tells us one thing; another says the opposite. Family members encourage us one time and criticize us the next. Friends may seem to understand our decisions, while others condemn them. Everyone has an opinion to offer and a remedy to try. How we want to be able to stand against all this! We want our choices vindicated. We want results: fruit, if you please.

God says all those wants are fulfilled through meditating on His word, standing with Him, and finding godly counselors. He probably will not lead you to do this job alone, even though there is a limit to how much someone else can help you. Make it a priority to build a network of godly people who can offer good advice and support.

When we moved back to my hometown so that we could be close to good medical and care facilities, we immediately got involved in a local church. I felt my first responsibility was to tell the church leaders about our situation and that, although I had been very involved in ministry formerly, I would not be able to do anything but "sit and soak" for as long as my husband needed my undivided care. That congregation took us in and cared for us without expecting anything in return for a whole year. The members who had been through similar situations offered their encouragement and advice, and those who were just beginning a similar journey learned from us. We are the body of Christ.

Find that local body where you fit. Put down your roots where God can nourish you. God will lead you and you will be able to stand and be fruitful for Him.

*Lord, thank You for Your promises to prosper us. Thank You for caring for our loved ones even more than we do. Thank You for using Your people in our lives and using us in their lives, even when we don't realize it. Thank You for being You. In Jesus' name, amen.*

# OUR ALL KNOWING GOD

*He who sits in the heavens shall laugh:*
*The Lord shall hold them in derision.*

--Psalm 2:4

HOW WELL I remember the confusion I felt after nearly every doctor's appointment with Larry, particularly when he was first diagnosed with Alzheimer's Disease. His family practice physician sent him for an MRI and then to a neurologist. The MRI was inconclusive, except that the doctors who read it suggested Larry's brain might have shrunk. They had no former scans with which to compare it, so I wondered how they could know that. Those were the days when the only sure AD diagnosis was through an autopsy.

Our family doctor suggested B vitamins and maybe ginkgo biloba. The neurologist said B vitamins wouldn't help. He also thought that the fact that Larry had tripped and fallen downstairs might indicate he had Parkinson's Disease. He checked it by observing Larry as he walked down a short hallway. They he moved Larry's arms back and forth. He was sure more signs of Parkinson's would develop. They did not. I was not surprised.

Psalm 2 pictures God in the heavens laughing at our puny efforts. I don't think our loving heavenly Father laughs at us in our quandaries, but he is probably shaking His head at our strange conclusions while He waits for us to come to Him for the answers.

Life is not simple. We don't have all the answers. Some days we don't have any of the answers. But if we have the Savior, we have the One who does have the answers and we can depend on Him to meet our needs. We can lean on Him as He leads us, stretches us, and teaches us the lessons He knows we need to learn.

There is no greater comfort for the caregiver than knowing we are on God's side.

*Heavenly Father, thank You for watching over my loved one's needs – and mine. Help me depend on You to give me the answers I need when I need them. In Jesus' name, amen.*

# WHOM TO TRUST

*Blessed are all those who put their trust in Him.*

--Psalm 2:12

I LIKE THE Amplified Version's translation of "blessed." It is "blessed, happy, to be envied." How many days do you feel blessed, happy, and to be envied? Those are pretty rare feelings when we are in the midst of long days of caregiving. Yet God says that's what we are – if we have our trust in Him.

Larry spent the last three years of his life in Meadow View Manor, a loving care home, now known as Crystal Ridge. I visited him at noon almost every day that he was there. I became acquainted with many other families who experienced circumstances similar to ours. If a family shared our lunch table, I usually got to know them and promised to pray for them. No one ever rejected that statement from me and I honored it by actually praying for them.

Larry outlived most of the patients we lunched with. On several occasions family members returned to tell me I had blessed their lives by expressing care for their loved one and to thank me for praying for them, especially during the loved one's final days. This happened so frequently during Larry's last, lingering weeks that I asked the Lord to relieve me of that ministry if it was the reason that God was keeping Larry on earth.

After Larry had been gone for several months, a nurse's aide who worked at Meadow View Manor told me my testimony was still talked about there. I am known for being blessed, and smiling (happy!). I am envied for my faithfulness and calm in the midst of some of the most trying times of my life. I can assure you that testimony is not my natural personality. Only God could have brought that out of the suffering we went through, because my trust is in Him.

*Lord, it's often hard to let go and trust in You. Help me just relax and let You use me in my loved one's life. Whether there are by-products of blessing to others because of that, or if there are none, let me just trust You and give You the praise for however You choose to use me. In the name of Your Son Jesus, amen.*

# CONTROL OF THE TROUBLEMAKERS

*Lord, how they have increased who trouble me!*

*Many are they who rise up against me.*

*Many are they who say of me,*

*"There is no help for him in God." Selah.*

*But You, O Lord, are a shield for me,*

*My glory and the One who lifts up my head.*

*I cried to the Lord with my voice,*

*And He heard me from His holy hill. Selah.*

--Psalm 3:1-4

WHEN THE DOCTOR advised my sister Joanne and me to find a care home for our mother, I felt overwhelmed with the responsibility. I determined to share all decisions about Mother with Joanne. She had worked many years in a nursing home. Surely she would be able to make wise choices for us.

Sadly, I soon realized Joanne's alcoholism had destroyed any ability to make good decisions. Whenever we discussed the next step needed for Mother's care, she passed it off with, "You decide. You know more about that kind of thing than I do." I soon realized she just did not want to deal with the problems, while I would have welcomed suggestions.

Phone calls to adult care sources resulted in conflicting answers. Instead of helping, they added to our trouble. We hired an attorney who ultimately helped but also relieved us of all the money Mother had put aside for us. We had decided to use that money for Mother's care, as needed. We did not expect it all to go to an attorney in order to sort out her problems!

Many times my heart cried out to God about what appeared to be a multitude of troubles. It seemed those who should have been helping were rising against us.

Yet I cried to the Lord and He did hear and answer. Mother's doctor was a godly many who offered good advice. I didn't have to look for him. God had already put him in our situation. He helped us through the hard choices.

Were there observers who thought there was no help for me from God? If so, He proved to be my shield. He lifted my head. He got us through it.


*Father God, You are my shield at all times. Help me continually trust in You. You will make a way to get me through all the tough times. In Jesus' name, amen.*

# BLESSED SLEEP

*I lay down and slept;*

*I awoke for the Lord sustained me.*

--Psalm 3:5

MANY THINGS KEEP us from a good night's sleep. We may deal with worry (bills, finances someone's health, children), changed schedules, a sleep-denying environment (noise or light), or any number of deterrents.

When my children were babies, I learned to sleep soundly even though I often got up in the middle of the night to change or feed them. Sometimes I would remark in the morning about what a blessing it was that our baby had slept through the night. My husband would laugh and tell me how many times I had been up to care for the little one's needs, while I apparently slept through it all.

But my ability to sleep soundly disappeared when my husband entered the "sun-downers" stage of Alzheimer's Disease. His evening agitation made it hard for him to settle down at bedtime. By the time I got him settled I was too "wound up" to sleep, so I would read until I got sleepy. Shortly after I'd turn out the light, Larry would wake up and begin his usual pattern of getting up to use the bathroom and wandering from room to room to find something he thought he had lost or more likely accused someone of stealing. By then I had to get up and either help him find it or convince him to look for it in the morning. He would settle back into bed but in less than an hour he was up again.

My logical mind told me that he must be as tired as I was so he would surely take a nap during the day. I would be tired enough to fall asleep any time of day, so I kept busy until he dozed off after lunch. Then I would lie down. But Larry only catnapped. Then he would wake up and wander off down the road to the mailbox. Sometimes he remembered where it was and sometimes he didn't. Increasingly, he didn't remember why he had left the house in the first place. On the day he made it out to the highway before I found him, I determined this could no longer continue. I obviously could not keep him from danger. I made the decision to place him in a care home.

The first night Larry was at High Gate Senior Living, I thought it might be strange to sleep alone in the house. I did not stay awake long enough to find out. I awoke in the morning, refreshed, and realized it had been at least two months since I had slept more than an hour at a time.

God gives us sleep to replenish our bodies. If we allow anything to disturb that rhythm, we are asking for trouble: physical, mental, and spiritual trouble. If you are experiencing sleep deprivation, ask God what you should do about it. You cannot be the best help for your loved one when you are sleep deprived.

*Father God, thank You for the gift of sleep. Thank You for giving us bodies that repair themselves if we take care of them. In these trying times, help us take care of ourselves so we can take care of the ones You gave us. In Jesus' name, amen.*

# ANGER

*Be angry, and do not sin.*
*Meditate within your heart on your bed, and be still. Selah*
*Offer the sacrifices of righteousness,*
*And put your trust in the Lord.*

*--Psalm 4:4-5*

FEAR MAKES US angry. Things are not going the way we planned. We have little to no control. Can we trust God to care for us? If we can't control the situation and we don't trust God to, we become angry.

The loved one we care for makes us angry. He does not cooperate. She does not understand why certain procedures have to be done. He argues with us, maybe even attacks us. These are big changes from how it used to be.

Loss of the man/woman he/she was makes us angry.

Dealing with medical personnel makes us angry. We may lose our appointment time because a loved one moved too slowly. At other times we arrive early and have to wait for well past the appointment time because the doctor is late. We mentally acknowledge why this has to be, but it still makes us angry that our time and effort are not considered as important as theirs.

Ephesians 4:26-27 says, "Be angry, and do not sin: do not let the sun go down on your wrath, nor give place to the devil." So bedtime, when we're mulling over the day's frustrations, is a good time to give that anger to God.

Lack of trust leads to fear which leads to anger. What to do?

In Psalm 4:5 God gives a solution: sacrifices of righteousness and trust in Him.

We confess. God forgives. We ask God's help to live more righteously tomorrow. Simple to say; hard to do. It's part of the daily struggle as a caregiver.

Forgiveness and trust: they calm our hearts so that we can rest.

*Father, God, you know our hearts. It does no good to pretend we are not angry when we are. Help us acknowledge anger for what it is, forgive those who have triggered anger in our hearts, and choose righteousness and trust in You. Thank You for Your grace. In Jesus' name, amen.*

# JOY AND GLADNESS

*You have put gladness in my heart,*
*More than in the season that their grain and wine increased.*

--Psalm 4:7

THERE IS A slight difference between happiness and joy. The root word for "happy" is the same as for "happen." How happy we are depends on what has happened to us. So my happiness can be up one hour and down the next – not very stable, for the caregiver's life is not very stable.

On the other hand I read in Galatians 5:22 that "joy" is a fruit of the Spirit of God. Joy is an automatic result of our yielding to the Holy Spirit. It does not depend on our circumstances. It depends on our obedience to God.

Many times in my days of caregiving I was stopped by observers who asked how I could be so joyous during what appeared to be extremely difficult circumstances. In the midst of my duties to my loved one, how I appeared to others did not matter to me, so the question always surprised me. The only answer: it had to be a God thing.

David said it well: "You (God) have put gladness in my heart, more than..." any circumstances or prosperity.

Are you longing for joy to return? Just do what you know God wants you to do – however hard or easy it may be. It's not our job to look for happiness. It's God's job to give us joy. As the old hymn says, "Trust and obey, for there's no other way to be happy in Jesus."

Granted, it's not an easy answer but, if you obey what you know God wants you to do, the joy will follow.

*Heavenly Father, strengthen me to do the hard work You have shared with me. Give me an obedient, servant's heart. Thank You for taking care of the joy part. In Jesus' name, amen.*

# REST IN SAFETY

*I will both lie down in peace, and sleep;*
*For You alone, O Lord, make me dwell in safety.*

--Psalm 4:8

LARRY'S DOCTOR FINISHED examining him and turned to me.

"How are you managing with all of this? You look exhausted," he said.

"I'm tired. I'm awake most of the night. It's like sleeping with a newborn baby. The least sound wakes me."

The doctor nodded. "That's a natural response. You have to be alert for his safety – and for your own."

I thought back to when my grandmother would get up in the middle of the night and put a kettle of water on the range for tea. Then she would go back to bed. Often the smell of the hot, dry kettle awakened my mother – just in time.

I remembered stories of my great-grandmother getting up to go downtown to look for something in the middle of the night. Only her daughter's light sleeping prevented her wandering away.

The doctor prescribed something to help Larry sleep better and so that I could sleep too. That was good, but the best thing I took from that doctor's visit was the realization that God causes us to adapt to our needs for our own protection. Think what might have happened on any night if I had slept through Larry's activities!

I longed for the times when I could again sleep all night. And they finally came. Meanwhile I lay down in peace and slept as well as I could, knowing God would keep us safe.

*Thank You, Father, for Your promise to watch over us day and night. Show me ways to rest so that I am alert when I especially need to be. I trust You to care for us. In Jesus' name, amen.*

# FIRST THINGS FIRST

*Give ear to my words, O Lord,*
*Consider my meditation.*
*Give heed to the voice of my cry,*
*My King and my God,*
*For to You I will pray.*
*My voice You shall hear in the morning, O Lord;*
*In the morning I will direct it to You,*
*And I will look up.*

*--Psalm 5:1-3*

IF YOU'VE READ my book, *Life Lessons for Caregivers,* you know I usually begin my day talking to God even before I get out of bed. Before Larry developed this terrible disease, I occasionally took a few minutes to ask God to direct my day before I arose. But after he began showing symptoms of Alzheimer's, it became my daily habit. I dared not face the day without asking for divine help.

When I taught school, with a family of five to care for, I found it difficult to have a morning devotional time. I reasoned that I would profit from going to sleep at the end of the day after reading the Bible and praying. However, I would usually be too tired to follow through with that idea.

With the children grown and my first husband gone to heaven, I developed the habit of reading my Bible while I ate breakfast. When Larry entered my life, I set Bible reading aside until after breakfast. However I do it, I've found my days go better when I begin them by asking God to take over, This is especially true for a caregiver. We need that extra contact with the heavenly Father from the very beginning of each day.

Maybe you think you don't have time for the devotional life you feel you need, but there are things you can do to draw closer to God. Breathe that prayer for help – short as it may have to be – even before you get up in the morning. Claim quiet moments for prayer or Bible reading at any time throughout the day. Install a Bible ap on your phone to read while you wait in doctors' offices. Fine someone to stay with your loved one so that you can take part in a Bible study or church service.

Until Larry was confined to a skilled care facility, he loved to accompany me to church. Use your best judgment about doing this. Your loved one may or may not benefit from the effort. The really important thing is to provide for your own spiritual nourishment.

*Heavenly Father, reveal to me the times and places I can communicate with You. Thank You for taking care of me and my loved one even on those days when there just isn't opportunity to connect with You. I love You, Lord. In Jesus' name, amen.*

# GOD HEARS OUR VOICE OF WEEPING

*Have mercy on me, O Lord, for I am weak;*
*O Lord, heal me, for my bones are troubled.*
*My soul also is greatly troubled;*
*But You, O Lord – how long?*
*Return, O Lord, deliver me!*
*Oh, save me for Your mercies' sake!*
*For in death there is no remembrance of You;*
*In the grave who will give You thanks?*
*I am weary with my groaning;*
*All night I make my bed swim;*
*I drench my couch with my tears.*

                                                    --Psalm 6:2-6

IT DOESN'T TAKE much to get the tears started. Why is that? We may cry out of sadness, realizing our loved one will never be the person we knew formerly.

We may cry out of frustration, dealing with care issues, financial issues, well-meaning advice-givers, and any number of obstacles.

We may cry out of anger, the injustice of it all.

We my cry out of sympathy. The hardest part of visiting my mother in her later years was to find her in tears and not be able to do anything to alleviate her sadness.

We may just cry because we are physically exhausted and have not taken care of our own needs, so our bodies are out of balance. The very act of crying may deplete us even further.

But God…

Verses 8 and 9 say the Lord has heard the voice of my weeping. He has heard my supplication; and He will receive my prayer. We may not be able to control the tears. But God knows … and cares … and will answer.

*Father, You know everything about me. You know what causes my tears even when I don't know. Thank you for loving me and caring for me and my loved one. Help me rest in the assurance that You know and care and will answer in Your best time. In Jesus' name, amen.*

# FEELING POWERLESS?

*When I consider Your heavens, the work of Your fingers,*
*The moon and the stars, which You have ordained,*
*What is man that You are mindful of him,*
*And the son of man that You visit him?*
*For You have made him a little lower than the angels,*
*And You have crowned him with glory and honor.*

--Psalm 8:3-5

IT WAS ONE of those days when nothing seemed to go right. In the morning my sister Joanne and I dealt with a social worker who told us our mother had too many resources to qualify for Medi-Cal benefits. I calculated the cost of her care and knew her resources would be depleted long before her "spend down" time came to an end.

Frustration. In the hope of leaving small bank accounts for Joanne and me, Mother had put off house repairs that would have been a wiser use of her money. Had she used her funds that way, she would have qualified much earlier for Medi-Cal. Instead, those accounts were used for attorney fees and nursing home care – and the house (where my sister continued to live) still needed repair.

We spent most of the afternoon trying to find a good elder law attorney and convincing Mother to sign financial and health care directives. In the evening we went back to visit an angry mother who was incapable of understanding why she could not go "home" and blamed us for her situation. Joanne was no help. She tossed all the decision-making back into my lap.

Joanne and I commiserated over a late dinner. Then I began the two-hour trip home. The weather had been rainy most of the day, adding to my dampened mood. As I got in my car, I looked up to see what kind of weather I would be driving in and gasped at the wonder of a clear, moonlit, starry sky. It was a though God said, "I'm still here. I made all this by My power and I can take care of you with that same power."

Sometimes just a view of God's creation reveals a little of God Himself.

*Lord God, even though the problems don't seem to be resolved, help me trust You and Your awesome power to get us through these tough times. Thank You for the wonderful displays You give us of Your greatness, as well as Your Word that tells us You love us and will not forsake us. In Jesus' name, amen.*

# REJOICE FIRST

*I will praise You, O Lord, with my whole heart;*
*I will tell of all Your marvelous works.*
*I will be glad and rejoice in You;*
*I will sing praise to Your name, O Most High.*

--Psalm 9:1-2

IT'S NO SURPRISE that the weight of caregiving often overburdens us. Somewhere in the stress of being "on call" 24/7 our joy disappears, along with our stamina. When Larry still lived at home, we would occasionally visit family members overnight. When it became too stressful for Larry to deal with all the activity of a noisy house full of children, we would retire to a motel room. It seemed like the more I did to lighten the frustration for Larry, the more it increased for me.

Once we had to return to a motel to retrieve his suitcase. I should have checked to see that he put it in the car, but I didn't. On the way back to the motel, all I could think about was that it was enough for me to have to take care of my own things. It was unreasonable to expect me to do everything for two of us. But that's what caregivers do, and I had to learn to think double-time.

Double time. Double worry. But not double joy. We think we have to be in good circumstances to rejoice. But our thinking is not like God's. In Proverbs 16:3, God says, "Commit your works to the Lord, and your thoughts will be established."

Frustrated? Angry? Exhausted? Recommit your purpose to pleasing God through your job as caregiver. That opens the way for God to return joy to your life. It may not sound logical, but praising God fills our hearts with joy, whatever the circumstances.

*Father God, thank You for enabling me to think for two. Help me do what I should even when I don't feel like it, for Your glory and my loved one's comfort. Give me a rejoicing heart to share with others. In Jesus' name, amen.*

# OUR REFUGE

*The Lord also will be a refuge for the oppressed,*
*A refuge in times of trouble.*
*And those who know Your name will put their trust in You;*
*For You, Lord, have not forsaken those who seek You.*

--Psalm 9:9-10

WHEN MY MOTHER was diagnosed with Alzheimer's Disease and all decisions for her care fell on me, I learned about needing a refuge. I would spend a day or two taking care of Mother's affairs and then I would drive home to unload my concerns and frustrations on my husband, Larry. How I appreciated a quiet man who just let me pour out my heart without trying to fix the unfixable, often just holding me and letting me cry. What a blessing!

Not many years later, Larry himself began to show the same symptoms as Mother. I listened to his sermons (Larry was a pastor) and realized he couldn't find a stopping place. His confused thinking mirrored Mother's. Terrified, I asked myself, "Who will be my refuge as I try to cope with this terrible disease in the life of the very one who has been my refuge?"

But God has not left us comfortless. I know the Lord walked me through many of the lessons I would need when caring for Larry. He taught me step by step what I had to know to deal with my husband and his doctors and care providers. I am also thankful for many years of baby steps, learning to lean on God. All the little problems that I saw God answer became faith-builders as I depended on God to solve the big problems.

Yes, the Lord is a refuge for the oppressed. Trust in God does not come naturally – but it allows God to work in our lives.

*Lord, Jesus, I need You. I not only need Your help, intervention, and comfort, I need You, Yourself. Thank You for loving and sustaining me. Thank You that I can trust You to continue to be my refuge. In Your own name, amen.*

# ALONE

*Why do You stand afar off, O Lord?*
*Why do You hide in times of trouble?*
*Arise, O Lord!*
*O God, Lift up Your hand!*
*Do not forget the humble.*
*But You have seen, for You observe trouble and grief,*
*To repay it by Your hand.*
*The helpless commits himself to You;*
*You are the helper of the fatherless.*

--Psalm 10:1, 12, 14

IT WAS TIME for Larry to give up driving. He endangered anyone who rode with him and anyone who happened to be out on the roads at the same time he was. We could be liable for any damage or injury he might cause. In his right mind, he would have agreed that he did not want to cause anyone harm. But now giving up driving was a closed subject.

Larry's children urged me to "do something about his driving." Friends cautioned that we could be sued. It was up to me to "do something." But how?

Son Roger suggested talking to Larry's doctor. He said the doctor would forward the information to the Department of Motor Vehicles. Good idea. I just didn't want it coming back on me because Larry could be very cruel and relentless when angered – and this would surely anger him.

The decision was mine alone. I wrote a note to the doctor and passed it silently to the receptionist at Larry's next doctor's visit. I prayed and hoped the doctor would quietly and authoritatively tell Larry to stop driving. To my horror, with both Larry and me in the examining room, the doctor pulled the note out of his pocket and announced, "Your wife is concerned about your driving. You'll have to stop driving. I'm going to notify the DMV that I recommend your license be revoked."

I have never felt so naked and alone in my life: totally exposed, abandoned by the doctor, family, friends, and even God. I dreaded the repercussions, especially on the drive home.

But God had not abandoned me. Larry simply asked me why I was worried about him. Then he turned his anger toward the doctor (whom we'd left safely back in his office) instead of toward me. Later, when Larry rebelled against losing his license, Roger effectively got his cooperation through a phone call. God had not hidden Himself from me nor left me alone after all.

*Lord, I don't always see You working, but I need to learn to trust You anyway. Help me remember past answers to prayer to strengthen my confidence in You. In Jesus' name, amen.*

# FLEE AS A BIRD

*In the Lord I put my trust;*
*How can you say to my soul, "Flee as a bird to your mountain"?*
*For look! The wicked bend their bow.*
*They make ready their arrow on the string,*
*That they may shoot secretly at the upright in heart.*
*If the foundations are destroyed,*
*What can the righteous do?*

--Psalm 11:1-3

I AM IMAGINING the cartoon characters Sylvester Cat and Tweety Bird. Sylvester is always stalking Tweety Bird, and Tweety can't get away because he's a captive in his cage. Fortunately, Sylvester's paws aren't quite long enough to reach Tweety, but there's always the fear that he just might be able to. If only Tweety could escape the cage. But then he would be out in the big scary world. Poor Tweety.

I've felt like Tweety: vulnerable and in jeopardy, fearing that any way I turned would be the wrong way. I've felt caged, afraid of my surroundings, but even more afraid of making a change – into the big, scary world.

God says we can flee as a bird to the mountain. If we *are* caged (confined, not able to change our situation), God is right there with us. He says He will never leave us nor forsake us. (Hebrews 13:5). And our souls are not caged. We can flee to God's loving arms in an instant.

If our circumstances change and we find ourselves in new and frightening places, God is there too. He remains our stability. Whenever we need to, wherever we are, whatever our circumstances, we can flee to him.

*Lord Jesus, thank You for Your promise that no one can snatch me out of Your hand or the Father's hand (John 10:28-29). Remind me to flee to You early, before I am overcome with my circumstances. Calm my fluttering, fearful heart. May I rest in You. In Your own name I pray, amen.*

# GOD'S TESTS

*The Lord is in His holy temple,*
*The Lord's throne is in heaven;*
*His eyes behold,*
*His eyelids test the sons of men.*
*The Lord tests the righteous,*
*But the wicked and the one who loves violence His soul hates.*
*For the Lord is righteous,*
*He loves righteousness;*
*His countenance beholds the upright.*

--Psalm 11:4-5, 7

AN OLD ADAGE says, "Life is a hard teacher. It gives you the tests first and the lessons afterward." How true is this?

I wonder if we don't simply miss the lesson until the test is given. For instance, I had no idea that I was learning anything I would need in the future when I heard the stories of how my grandmother cared for my "senile" great-grandmother. And I was busy raising my children when my mother took care of my grandmother. But I must have absorbed something from watching because, when I had to take care of Mother, I remembered what she had said about getting financial and medical help and care. I used those bits of memory to direct me to the help I needed.

The mental/emotional/spiritual lessons are even more important. The decision about if and when to place a loved one in a care home – especially if they have always spoken against such a move – takes great wisdom and spiritual understanding. I needed to be sure God was leading me to do this. That's when a lifetime of leaning on God, even when I was hardly aware that I was leaning on

Him, resulted in not only the right choices, but quiet confidence that I was doing the right thing.

We can't make up for lost time in God's presence, but we can develop that relationship going forward. It's the lesson most needed for the inevitable tests to come.

*Heavenly Father, thank You for the tests. They reveal to us – and those who may be watching – how close we are to You, our source of wisdom and peace. Show us where and when we can spend more time with You to learn all You have for us. In Jesus' name, amen.*

# THE SIGHING OF THE NEEDY

*"For the oppressions of the poor, for the sighing of the needy,*

*Now I will arise," says the Lord;*

*"I will set him in the safety for which he yearns."*

*The words of the Lord are pure words...*

*You shall keep them, O Lord,*

*You shall preserve them from this generation forever.*

--Psalm 12:5-7

TRAVELING WITH A mentally impaired loved one can be frightening. My mind would nearly explode with thoughts of all the things that could go wrong, especially when flying. I am not a "white-knuckle" flyer for myself, but I needed God's special control when flying with Larry.

What to do about: visiting the bathroom? meals? his wanderlust? sleeplessness? crowded airports? checking luggage? carry-on luggage? strangers? scammers? appropriate clothing? inappropriate behavior? his fears?

God called me to be a teacher, and teachers are planners. It helped to imagine as many scenarios as possible. My needy heart sent many sighs to God. And I'm sure it was God who gave the answers that worked for us.

A bathroom visit. I couldn't accompany him to the men's room in an airport, nor could I leave him alone while I used the ladies' room. Solution: use that tiny facility on the plane. He's not going anywhere while you're in there and he's reassured it's all right for him to use it after he sees you come out.

Meals? Pack favorite snacks. Have him sit near the venders "guarding our stuff" while you buy drinks. For short times, that took care of the need to wander as well – as long as I could retain eye contact.

Unwillingness to check his luggage? Let him carry it to and through the line. He'll be glad to give it up!

Carry-ons? Give him something that won't matter if he loses it, and will provide entertainment (like puzzle books).

Sleeplessness? God gives strength.

Crowds? He was comfortable holding my sleeve. That also eliminated fear of strangers, scammers and inappropriate behavior. Acting like I knew what I was doing kept him calm – and me too, for the most part.

Yes, God kept us in the safety for which we yearned.

*Father God, You got us through. Help me remember that You are with us every step of the journey and to give You praise. In Jesus' name, amen.*

# HOW LONG, O LORD?

*How long, O Lord?*

*Will You forget me forever?*

*How long will You hide Your face from me?*

*How long shall I take counsel in my soul,*

*Having sorrow in my heart daily?*

*But I have trusted in Your mercy;*

*My heart shall rejoice in Your salvation.*

*I will sing to the Lord,*

*Because He has dealt bountifully with me.*

--Psalm 13:1-2, 5-6

THERE WERE DAYS when it seemed God had forgotten me. I was tired. I noted the gradual decline of my loved one, and my heart agonized for his comfort. He wanted to go Home – home to heaven, home where he'd no longer suffer, home where he would be able to think more clearly than he had ever thought before. And although I knew I would miss him, I could not pray to hold him here in his misery. How long? How long?

Had God forgotten us? He says, "Can a mother forget her nursing child, and not have compassion on the son of her womb? Yet I will not forget you" (Isaiah 49:15). Trust that God has not forgotten you. It is only your own tears that hide His face from you.

We cannot know the reasons God has for these hard, long, sorrowful times. Sometimes we get hints of God's purposes. After God mercifully took Larry to heaven, I realized that long, dry time had allowed me to grieve. Knowing we both had trusted Christ for salvation, I rejoice in the hope of seeing both my Lord and my husband at the end of my life. Although I miss him, relief far outweighs grief. Yes, I can sing to the Lord, who deals bountifully with me.

*Once again, Lord, we acknowledge that Your ways are far above ours. We don't understand Your purposes. Help us trust You to work out Your perfect plan in our lives. Help us learn the lessons we need to learn as You stretch and mold us. In Jesus' name, amen.*

# KEEPING A PROMISE

*Lord, who may abide in Your tabernacle?*

*Who may dwell in Your holy hill?*

*He who walks uprightly,*

*And works righteousness,*

*And speaks the truth in his heart...*

*But he honors those who fear the Lord;*

*He who swears to his own hurt and does not change...*

*He who does these things shall never be moved.*

*--Psalm 15:1-2, 4-5*

LARRY AND I wrote our own wedding vows. I promised to love, honor, and enhance the ministry of my pastor husband. Love and honor were there, but I particularly worked at being the best pastor's wife I could be – for him and for God.

So I was devastated when Larry developed Alzheimer's Disease and I realized we would not be growing old serving the Lord together. I certainly questioned God about what He was doing with the life of one whose sole desire was to minister God's Word to his church. It made no sense to me. When Larry resigned as pastor, I no longer had a ministry to enhance. My ministry changed: no longer *with* Larry, but now *to* Larry.

That's when the other vows came into sharper focus: love and honor. The man I married became a stranger. As time went on he became less and less like the person I knew and loved.

Leaving him never entered my mind. This was part of "for better or worse" (who knew how "worse" it could get?), "for richer, for poorer" (we'd never be financially rich, anyway), and "in sickness and in health" (whether it was mental or physical sickness). Even though the vow might be to my personal detriment (verse 4 "hurt"), I could not change. Only God could give me that kind of resolve – and He did.

*Lord God, thank You for enabling me to keep the vows I've made. Help me make all my promises carefully, knowing You expect me to keep them. It's easy to glibly say, "I'll pray for you," or "I'll help you," and then forget the request. Help me be careful only to promise what I know You want me to do and follow through on those promises. In Jesus' name, amen.*

# THE TRUST ISSUE

*Preserve me, O God, for in You I put my trust.*

--Psalm 16:1

SOMETIMES WE THINK we are trusting in God, but then He sends an event that opens our eyes to the fact that we were really trusting in something else. I like Evangelism Explosion's illustration of what it means to trust God. They use an empty chair and ask, "Do you see the chair?" "Do you think it will hold you up?" "Why isn't it holding you up right now?"

Of course the answer is, "Because I'm not sitting in it."

Then the questioner sits in the chair, an illustration of putting total trust in that chair to hold him up. The obvious application is to totally trust God's Son, Jesus Christ, for eternal life. And we can totally trust Him to get us through our earthly life as well.

But we tend to go back to old habits. We've learned to rely on other sources besides God. For instance, we trust our finances to get us through each month. We planned to use the money our mother left us to take care of her. God had to show us another way when the attorney and court fees used up our funds.

I expected family, my sister in particular, to help make decisions concerning Mother's care. Sister proved incapable and unwilling to help. My prayer life increased tremendously during that time.

I expected friends in our congregation to be understanding when Larry began to fail. Instead they became vicious, pushing us out of the ministry as soon as they could. "What a Friend We Have in Jesus," became my theme song.

I expected doctors to diagnose and prescribe knowledgeably. Instead I had to research and decide the best course of medications. Back to more prayer time!

I expected government resources when Mother needed help. God gave me the strength, discernment, and tenacity to get what she needed.

I expected an "elder care" attorney to care about the client. I learned to trust God to meet our needs as I watched her reduce our financial resources to nothing.

*Heavenly Father, there are many sidetracks on life's road. Thank You for showing me where my real trust needs to rest – in You. I trust You for this life and the next. Alert me early when I start to leaning anywhere else but on You. In Jesus' name, amen.*

# HANGING OUT WITH THE SAINTS

*O my soul, you have said to the Lord,*

*"You are my Lord,*

*My goodness is nothing apart from You."*

*As for the saints who are on the earth,*

*"They are the excellent ones, in whom is all my delight."*

--Psalm 16:2-3

MOM, YOU'RE A saint." I've heard that many times, usually when I've rescued a daughter from a financial problem or time crunch. I decline, feeling anything but saintly. On the other hand, I really am a saint. According to 1 Corinthians 1:2, believers in Christ are all saints. The word "saint" means someone who is set apart to serve God. That's me!

That's not what we usually mean when we think of being saintly. We mean someone who is above and beyond the normal – someone who acts the way we think a Christian should – someone who is like Christ.

I remember feeling dread when a certain family member showed up on my doorstep. I knew it would be a day of complaint and criticisms. She was, by the 1 Corinthians definition, a saint. She even lived a pure life. But her mouth cancelled out any good she might have done. By the time she left I was exhausted and in a negative mood myself.

Here in Psalm 16, David says he delights in the saints. How fitting! Remember when you spent a day with negative people and became negative yourself? Better yet, think about the last time you spent time with godly people who encouraged you. Didn't you become just a little more like them?

As caregivers we may be limited in our interactions with others. That makes it even more important to choose saintly people for our friends and confidants – people who are saints, not just in name, but in word and deed.

*Heavenly Father, I want to hang out with Your people, true believers who pass on to me the encouragement You have given them. Send me that kind of friends. Then let me be one who passes the joy on to others even in the limited sphere You have given me right now. In Jesus' name, amen.*

# YOUR GOOD INHERITANCE

*O Lord, You are the portion of my inheritance and my cup;*

*You maintain my lot.*

*The lines have fallen to me in pleasant places;*

*Yes, I have a good inheritance.*

--Psalm 16:5-6

IT WAS ONE of those thirty-six hour days. Larry had challenged me on every request. How do you deal with a two-year-old personality in a seventy-five-year-old body? Even constant silent prayer did not keep my patience from running out by evening.

Something on the television reminded him he'd had his driver's license taken from him. He raged for hours, demanding answers that I couldn't give. How can a mind that cannot stay on task for more than a few minutes park on a complaint for hours? Nothing would distract him, not even a bedtime snack.

Then I faced the bedtime challenges – and complaints. This wasn't his bed. He'd already brushed his teeth today. There was no reason to put his clothes in the hamper: he'd only worn them a day – or two at the most. Why wasn't I coming to bed too? I spent too much time on the computer. He needed a drink of water. He needed to check on his wallet. Somebody must have stolen his pocketknife because he couldn't find it.

The harangue about his missing pocketknife was the proverbial straw on my camel's back. I retreated to my bedroom in tears, shaking my fist toward God, demanding to know "Why me? Why him?"

In a few minutes my sobbing stopped and I felt God's comfort, like a hug around me. "You have Me," He seemed to say. "Right here with you. This is My will for you to take care of My servant. It's all right to be angry with Me but you'll see in the long run that I have you in a pleasant place. I am your inheritance – whatever I lead you through in this life."

Strengthened by God's comfort. I returned to Larry's bedroom and found his pocketknife in the pants I had thrown into the hamper for him. Satisfied, he settled into his bed for a few hours of sleep. I did the same.


*Father, I am safe with You. You understand my frustrations and allow me to vent my anger with You. Forgive me for doubting Your tender care for both my loved one and myself. You have chosen what is best for us. Help me trust You when I can't see that. In Jesus' name, amen.*

# THE BEST ADVICE

*I will bless the Lord who has given me counsel;*

*My heart also instructs me in the night seasons.*

*I have set the Lord always before me;*

*Because He is at my right hand I shall not be moved.*

--Psalm 16:7-9

WHEN I BEGAN experiencing homesickness each time I drove home from my daughter's house and realized we needed to move from the remote location we lived, my mind filled with worries about how to solve the problem. I had obligated myself to the families involved in our one-room school by promising I would be with them as long as they needed me. Should I break that promise? Should we just move closer to medical facilities and commute to work? Should we stay where we were and hope my husband would not get worse until such time as the school no longer needed me?

The nights were the worst. I retired most evenings with a burden of worry that even prayer didn't always lift. One night, after returning from my old hometown, all those questions flooded my mind as I tried to relax enough to sleep. I wracked my mind for answers, but none came. I prayed, but my mind was too full to listen to God's answers. However, with the morning sun came assurance in my heart that God knew and had already prepared the answer.

That very day the first parent told me her children would not be returning next year because her husband, who had been out of work for many months, had finally found work across the state. Immediately, I recognized God's hand, but He would have to move most of the rest of the families to make the school no longer a viable option.

That wasn't a problem for God. By the end of the school year we were down to one family, and they were willing to go back to home schooling if our school closed. I had not shared my dilemma with anyone, so we set a deadline and advertised for students for the next year. By then I dared to hope that this was all God's doing, so I was not surprised when no new students applied.

God's assurance became reality as He led us back to my hometown, where we found ample medical and care facilities from which to choose.

Sleep on it! How many times I've been told to "sleep on it" when I had a decision to make. And how many times I've gone to bed with a befuddled mind, contriving some involved and complicated solution to a problem, only to wake up with the simple answer already on my mind. God instructs us in the night seasons.

*Thank You, Father, for speaking to my mind even when I am asleep. May I remember always to set You and Your ways before me. You cannot be moved, and neither can I if I stay by Your side. Hold me close. In Jesus' name, amen.*

# A BRIGHTER FUTURE

*Therefore my heart is glad, and my glory rejoices;*

*My flesh also will rest in hope.*

*For You will not leave my soul in Sheol,*

*Nor will You allow Your Holy One to see corruption.*

*You will show me the path of life;*

*In Your presence is fullness of joy;*

*At Your right had are pleasures forevermore.*

--Psalm 16:9-11

I REALLY DON'T know how a person without faith is able to cope with life as a caregiver. In my visits to the convalescent homes where various family members have spent their final years, I witnessed many hurting people.

Sometimes guilt takes over and adult children want "nothing but the best" for a parent they have ignored or even treated shabbily most of their lives. Or they really love the person and are overcome with grief and anger as they see their parent or spouse failing. They may want heroic measures taken to keep their loved one here as long as possible when the patient may be miserable and just want to go.

Faith isn't a medicine to be taken as needed. It's more of a bed that is built up quilt by quilt. We learn to rest on God in each stage of life, using what we have learned from past experiences to help us trust Him in the present.

Early in Larry's disease I recognized that God had equipped me to deal with it through lessons learned in the care of my parents and in watching and hearing about the care of grandparents and even great-grandparents. I thanked God for those lessons.

More important than that, God had taught me to walk close to him, trusting Him to meet my needs. I knew from experience that He would either enable me to make wise decisions or overrule my foolish ones. He led me to find comfort and direction in His Word. I learned to take my problems to Him in prayer and attempt, with varying success, to leave them there. He didn't *give* me hope: He *is* my hope.

That isn't to say it's ever too late to start the walk of faith. God is always ready to take us from where we are to where He has planned for us to be. When we get off the track, He's ready to take us back. As the old song says, I'm "learning to lean on Jesus."

*Heavenly Father, thank You for giving me the hope of eternal life for my loved one and myself. Thank You for leading me on the path of life. Thank You for the joy I find in Your presence even on the tough days. Thank You for the promise of pleasures forevermore. Remind me of Your presence on the difficult days. May my faith in You be an encouragement to other caregivers I meet. In Jesus' name, amen.*

# MOUTH CONTROL

*You have tested my heart;*

*You have visited me in the night;*

*You have tried me and have found nothing;*

*I have purposed that my mouth shall not transgress.*

--Psalm 17:3

AS A CHILD, every report card I brought home said some variation of this: "Darlene is a good student but she needs to control her talking." I know the teachers were noting the quantity of my words, but the older I've gotten, the more I realize I also need to control the quality. Nothing gets me into more trouble than my mouth.

My friend Vivian is frustrated because she can never think of a clever retort until she has left the conversation. For me that would be a good thing. I not only immediately think of a searing answer, but too often I blurt it out, to the hurt of myself and all who hear it.

I can vow to control my mouth, but that's just another mouthy offense. It is "easier said than done." Where do all those bad words and harmful phrases come from anyway?

Jesus said, "Out of the abundance of the heart the mouth speaks." (Matthew 12:34) It's not a mouth issue: it's a heart issue.

Caring for my husband Larry taught me the futility of argument. One evening his son Tracy argued with him about a theological issue for several hours. No matter how Tracy approached the subject, Larry just kept repeating what he knew to be true from a lifetime of study and preaching. Tracy became frustrated and I became increasingly irritated. I finally took Tracy aside and asked, "Would you argue with a five-year-old?" Then why are you pursuing this with a man who has Alzheimer's Disease? Think about it!"

The lesson was good for me too. My natural inclination, enhanced by years in the classroom, is to present arguments until the other person "gets it." I've learned it isn't always important for the other person to "get it." It's certainly not important that I win the argument.

*Lord Jesus, help me control my tongue. Help me analyze what causes me to speak as I do. I give you my anger and frustration, which often parade through my words. Show me what's important to say and what is not necessary – before I spew out verbal poison. Keep my heart tender so my words are tender. Then I won't have to "eat them." In Jesus' name, amen.*

# THE APPLE OF HIS EYE

*I have called upon You, for You will hear me, O God;*

*Incline Your ear to me, and hear my speech.*

*Show Your marvelous lovingkindness by Your right hand,*

*O You who save those who trust in You*

*From those who rise up against them.*

*Keep me as the apple of Your eye;*

*Hide me under the shadow of Your wings.*

--Psalm 17:6-8

MY FIRST HUSBAND, Bud, was absolutely entranced when our first child, Debbie, was born. She was faultless – perfect – to him. He just wanted to hold her and gaze on her beautiful face, commenting on her peaches and cream complexion. He wondered from whom had she inherited her button nose, her green eyes, or the ability to raise a single eyebrow. Truly she was the apple of his eye.

Do you think there was anything Bud would not have done for Debbie as she was growing up? When I told him we had another child coming, he fretted about how he would ever be able to love another child as much as his firstborn. Amazingly, he found he had enough love for both of them and even a third child later!

Our heavenly Father is like that. You are the apple of His eye. And so am I. And so is each child who has come into His family. He loves us and sees us as perfect in His Son Jesus.

Bud could not protect Debbie or her siblings from troubles, illnesses, insults, or any of the other problems children experience. He had limited control, however much his heart may have wanted to keep them safe.

Our heavenly Father has total control. We can trust Him to allow into our lives only what is best for us. We can hide under the shadow of His wings and know He not only wants the best for us, He is able to orchestrate it. How sweet to rest in that promise, especially during tough times of caregiving.

*Father, thank You for Your promises to care for me and my loved one. Remind me of how You have worked for our good in the past. Help me encourage others by sharing what You have done and are doing even now. In Jesus' name, amen.*

# MY STRENGTH ... ROCK ... FORTRESS ... DELIVERER ... SHIELD

*I will love You, O Lord, my strength.*

*The Lord is my rock and my fortress and my deliverer;*

*My God, my strength, in whom I will trust;*

*My shield and the horn of my salvation, my stronghold.*

*So shall I be saved from my enemies.*

*--Psalm 18:1-3*

WE HAD MOVED back to my hometown and I accepted it must be true that "you can't go home again." Much had changed in my forty-eight-year absence. Street names were familiar but most of the businesses on those streets were not. I called on my daughter Laura for directions many times because she had moved into Mother's house several years before so she knew the area much better than I. I often felt alone, disoriented, confused, and vulnerable.

My top priority was to find a church home where my husband Larry and I would both be comfortable. I had been an active teacher, Sunday school superintendent, choir director, and pianist/organist before the move. Now I realized Larry's care would be my ministry. From my teens I had taught children and been part of the music ministry wherever we fellowshipped, so I felt strange coming to a church with nothing to offer. I intended to "shop around" to find a church that was a good fit for our worship needs.

I started with the church Laura and her family had been attending. The people were friendly and did not look strangely at Larry when he exhibited signs of dementia. The pastor made a point of greeting me after the morning worship service. I explained our situation and apologized that I would not be able to serve as long as I had Larry's care. Pastor Sam encouraged us to just come and let the congregation minister to us.

I no longer felt led to "shop" for another church. God used that congregation to be my rock, my fortress, my deliverer, my strength, and my stronghold. We could not know the difficult days that would follow, but the wise children of God that He put in our lives met all of our needs. In just a few weeks I realized I no longer felt alone, disoriented, confused or vulnerable. God had brought me "home" among His children.

*Father God, You work in so many diverse ways. Sometimes You alone show Yourself to be my stronghold. Sometimes You strengthen Your people to help hold me up. Lord, strengthen me so that I can be a wall in Your fortress for someone else. In Jesus' name, amen.*

# DYING GRACE

*The pangs of death surrounded me,*

*And the floods of ungodliness made me afraid.*

*The sorrows of Sheol surrounded me;*

*The snares of death confronted me.*

*In my distress I called upon the Lord,*

*And cried out to my God;*

*He heard my voice from His temple,*

*And my cry came before Him, even to His ears.*

--Psalm 18:4-6

NO ONE LIKES to talk about it. We pretend it won't happen but it happens to every person on this earth. Our minds may dwell on the "what-ifs" of it but words don't leave our mouths.

There *is* fear in death. We fear the unknown. Even those of us who have placed our trust in Christ have some fear, because we've not gone there before. Or we may fear the pain and debility that comes before the golden door opens. Yet we should talk about it. Many times a loved one may be hoping someone else will bring up the dreaded subject, whether for comfort and assurance or for the practical aspects of that loved one's wishes for aftercare and dispersal of properties.

The few times I attempted to talk about arrangements with my mother she became defensive, assuring me she had taken care of everything. She hadn't, and I was forced to make many decisions that should have been hers to make. There could have been an easier way, but God led me to good advisers.

At least I knew Mother had placed her eternal life in God's hands. She did not fear where she was going. Several times I have met patients whose uncertainty exhibited itself in extreme restlessness. Talking to them about God's provision for their eternal life brought assurance of their final destiny, and the restlessness disappeared.

*Father in Heaven, You know us better than we know ourselves. You have placed a yearning in our hearts for You. When thoughts of death for myself or my loved one bring anxiety, fear, and sorrow, remind me to cry out to You for the comfort and assurance that only You can give. Let our very presence relieve our distress. In Jesus' name, amen.*

# THE SAVIOR OF THE HUMBLE

*With the merciful You will show Yourself merciful;*

*With a blameless man You will show Yourself blameless;*

*With the pure You will show Yourself pure;*

*And with the devious You will show Yourself shrewd.*

*For You will save the humble people,*

*But will bring down haughty looks.*

--Psalm 18:25-27

CARING FOR A loved one is a humbling task. Think of all the undignified activities in which you must be involved. The hardest thing for me to do at the beginning of Larry's dementia was to separate myself from his inappropriate behavior.

My friend Mary cared for her mother, who also had Alzheimer's Disease, at home. As long as she could she involved her mother in daily activities. Often, when grocery shopping, her mother would become annoyed with her clothing. Mary learned to carry sanitary gloves and an opaque bag with her so that she could retrieve her mother's underwear when she stepped out of it in the grocery store. Embarrassing, yes. But she did it with as much dignity as possible.

Crowds and noise caused Larry to react with anger, cruelty, and stubbornness. If I insisted we leave, he yelled or struck out at me. I learned to suggest he come aside with me to a quiet place so I could rest. If it was for me, he would gladly follow me away from the source of agitation.

Proverbs 15:1 says, "A soft answer turns away wrath, but a harsh word stirs up anger." Nowhere is that more true than when dealing with someone who suffers from dementia. Although my first reaction to confrontation is anger, God has taught me to think before I speak, and then to speak calmly and kindly. The more time we spend with God, the more we become like Him: merciful, blameless, pure, and wise. He truly does save the humble.

*Father, thank You for teaching me and shaping me to be more like You. I still have a long way to go, but You've brought me a long way already. Remind me of the "soft answer" rule. May I be a calming influence to my loved one. In Jesus' name, amen.*

# THE PERFECT WAY

*As for God, His way is perfect;*

*The word of the Lord is proven;*

*He is a shield to all who trust in Him.*

--Psalm 18:30

I LOVE TO quilt, and I give most of my quilts away to friends and family members. I belong to a quilting guild and a sewing group, where I often do hand quilting. Of course, my fellow quilters want to see what I'm making, and I always feel compelled to tell them, and those who receive one as a gift, not to look too closely because my work is not perfect.

It's the same with my piano playing. I'm comfortable accompanying a soloist or group, but I don't enjoy piano solos. Mistakes stand out when I play alone. My performance is never perfect.

I have looked for perfect days as a caregiver. The morning may go well and I'll think maybe today there will be no glitches. But problems will come before the day is over. My loved one will find some reason to blame me for his frustration. I'll not be able to schedule the appointment I need to make or connect with the doctor who needs to answer my question. There's never a perfect day.

But "as for God, His way is perfect." I think that means that even in my imperfect world, as I trust in God the overall picture is going to be perfect. At the end of a disappointing day it's good to rest in the fact that my perfect Savior is taking care of my imperfect world.

*Lord God, Your Word is proven and Your way is proven. Thank You for Your Word that tells me You have everything under control – even my restless heart. Even my loved one's mind and body. I trust You to be my shield. In Jesus' name, amen.*

# SECRET FAULTS

*Who can understand his errors?*

*Cleanse me from secret faults.*

*Keep back Your servant also from presumptuous sins;*

*Let them not have dominion over me.*

*Then I shall be blameless,*

*And I shall be innocent of great transgression.*

*Let the words of my mouth and the meditation of my heart*

*Be acceptable in Your sight,*

*O Lord, my strength and my Redeemer.*

--Psalm 19:12-14

SHORTLY AFTER MY first husband passed away, I had a neighbor who decided he should harass me about my son Jim's behavior. Admittedly Jim was not a model teenager. However this was not a new thing and I never understood why the neighbor waited until I was dealing with widowhood to make my life even more miserable.

Most of the harassment was verbal – over the fence or over the phone. But one day I came home to a sack of beer bottles and a note accusing Jim and his friends of tossing them into his yard. My anger was elevated, but I decided I would gently return the sack to the neighbor and explain that Jim and his friends were not responsible, and ask him to leave us alone. A soft answer turns away wrath. I had it under control.

Unfortunately, instead of remaining calm, my anger simply escalated. By the time I reached his front door I was furious. My soft answer became a screaming tirade and my gentle return of the bottles turned into slamming them onto his concrete steps. I returned to my home ashamed of my response, knowing I would never have an opportunity to demonstrate Christian grace to that man.

What went wrong? Proverbs 16:3 says, "Commit your works to the Lord, and your thoughts will be established." Thoughts and actions are intertwined. They build on each other. I have learned to take time to bring my thoughts and motives to God in prayer before responding to annoying circumstances. (At least I hope I have.)


*Lord, help me to remember to ask You for help in keeping the words of my mouth and the meditation of my heart acceptable in Your sight. You are my strength and my Redeemer. I don't always understand my errors. But I ask You to cleanse me from my faults and guide me away from great transgressions. In Jesus' name, amen.*

# ANSWERS IN A DAY OF TROUBLE

*May the Lord answer you in the day of trouble;*

*May the name of the God of Jacob defend you;*

*May He send you help from the sanctuary,*

*And strengthen you out of Zion ...*

*May He grant you according to your heart's desire,*

*And fulfill all your purpose.*

--Psalm 20:1-2, 4

OUR MINISTRY IN Vallecito was finished. We had resigned as associate missionaries with American Missionary Fellowship. Larry's confusion both in the pulpit and out of it was obvious to everyone except Larry. He did not understand why the Vallecito church membership declined, and he thought he should find another small church to minister to. I envisioned trouble and heartache and I prayed constantly about our situation.

Staying in Vallecito, our home within fifty feet of the church building, would cause continual frustration and sadness to both of us. We needed to sell our house and move. But where? We could not sell until we had a place to go.

We visited a small work in Paskenta, where a pastor/friend was retiring. Larry was interested but did not pursue it to the point of becoming a candidate. Our Paskenta friend also suggested a ministry in Eureka, and for two days I helped Larry work on a resume' to send them. But although he talked about it, he did not seem to know how to send it and I did not offer to help.

While we waited for God's leading, we attended worship services in Rail Road Flat, a little town about forty miles from our home. One day the women of that church resurrected a ladies' Bible study that had been dormant for a year because of the illness of the leader's mother. Now the mother had passed away and Elaine was again available to lead the study. Starving for fellowship, I went to the first meeting, and it was there that I found the perfect house for Larry and me.

When Larry saw the house, he agreed it was perfect for us: room for all of his books, parking space for my father's trailer, fenced yard for our dog, spacious, and homey. He immediately agreed to selling our Vallecito home and moving there, and he never again talked about pursuing a ministry elsewhere. It was as though once he felt at home, God gave him peace with retirement. When God moves, He does it thoroughly. Our house sold within six weeks and we moved into the Rail road Flat home seven weeks from the time I first saw it.

*Lord God, controller of all things, help me remember past answers to my prayers. Continue to give me hints of how You are taking care of my loved one and myself. Let me just rest on You in all the troublesome days. In Jesus' name, amen.*

# THE ONE-SIZE-FITS-ALL PSALM

*The Lord is my shepherd; I shall not want.*

*He makes me to lie down in green pastures;*

*He restores my soul;*

*He leads me in the paths of righteousness for His name's sake.*

*Yea, though I walk through the valley of the shadow of death,*

*I will fear no evil; For You are with me;*

*Your rod and Your staff, they comfort me.*

*You prepare a table before me in the presence of my enemies;*

*You anoint my head with oil. My cup runs over.*

*Surely goodness and mercy shall follow me all the days of my live;*

*And I will dwell in the house of the Lord forever.*

--Psalm 23:1-6

GO BACK AND read it again. Read it several times. Let the words of Psalm 23 wash over you and bring you peace.

When Larry pastored the Vallecito church and I began my new life as a pastor's wife, I wondered why he invariable quoted Psalm 23 at every funeral and frequently when we visited hospitalized church members. Was it the only psalm he knew? Were there not other psalms that would bring comfort: I did not voice my opinions, but I thought he could have been more creative than that. There was a whole Bible from which to choose comforting passages.

When Mother passed away, we held a memorial service in the denominational church she had remained loyal to for her whole life. The only Scripture the pastor used was Psalm 23. Later our friend Pastor Henry Sweeney officiated at the graveside service we had for her. In preparing an order of service, Pastor Sweeney suggested we quote the same psalm. He explained, "We use the shepherd's psalm because it is familiar to many people, as well as comforting."

So now I get it. The psalm I memorized as a child in Sunday school is coming back to sustain me during my times of loss as an adult. As a teacher I often explained to the children that we memorized Scripture to put it in our heads (and hearts) so God could use it later to share with others or to counterattack Satan's temptations. But assuring passages, like Psalm 23, are probably used even more often than that.

So read it again or quote it if you can. Let its promises encourage you: provision, rest, peace, restoration, righteousness, fearlessness, abundance, anointing, superabundance, goodness, mercy, and eternal life. Pick what you need for today and come back again and again for comfort and strength.

*Blessed Shepherd, thank You for Your beautiful words of comfort and encouragement. Bring my mind back to dwell on them frequently to counteract the busyness and frustrations of the life I now live. Bring them to my loved one's mind for comfort and assurance. I nestle in Your arms, my Shepherd. In Your precious name, amen.*

# WHEN YOUR WORLD TUMBLES OUT OF CONTROL

*The earth is the Lord's, and all its fullness,*

*The world and those who dwell therein.*

*For He has founded it upon the seas,*

*And established it upon the waters.*

*Who may ascend into the hill of the Lord?*

*Or who may stand in His holy place?*

*He who has clean hands and a pure heart,*

*Who has not lifted up his soul to an idol,*

*Nor sworn deceitfully.*

*He shall receive blessing from the Lord,*

*And righteousness from the God of his salvation.*

*This is Jacob, the generation of those who seek Him,*

*Who seek Your face. Selah*

--Psalm 24:1-6

IT WAS A year of turmoil. The doctor diagnosed Larry's Alzheimer's Disease. His symptoms were becoming more obvious every day, but he was in denial and very argumentative. Both of my parents were in care homes. Mother's body was breaking down, literally, and Dad's anger made it hard to visit him. I needed to continue working for financial reasons. I enjoyed the time away from home, thankful for the God-given ability to live in the moment and put family problems aside.

However, as I returned home at the end of each day, my mind reverted to fear of what would manifest itself as the "problem of the day." I would hear a neighbor's alarming report about Larry's activities, or get a phone call about another medical need of one of my parents. One day Dad's care home called to tell me he was becoming too dangerous. I had to find him another home. My world was tumbling out of control. How much worry could I carry? I had no recourse except God, but I found that God was all I needed.

I looked for care homes for Dad. There were none nearby that took violent patients. All I could do was pray and extend my circle of search. My own calmness baffled me as the deadline loomed, until that phone call in the middle of the night. Dad suffered another stroke and passed into eternity. God already knew that would happen and calmed my heart.

Then God provided a loving caregiver for Larry on my teaching days. Once again I could return in peace at the end of a workday.


*Father, help me remember to seek Your face when my world is tumbling out of control. Help me know that the earth is Yours — all of it — even what looks like my world. I rest in the assurance that You will not give me more than You and I can handle together. In Jesus' name, amen.*

,

# PRAISE BRINGS JOY

*Lift up your heads, O you gates!*

*And be lifted up, you everlasting doors!*

*And King of glory shall come in.*

*Who is this King of glory?*

*The Lord strong and mighty,*

*The Lord mighty in battle.*

*Lift up your heads, O you gates!*

*Lift up, you everlasting doors!*

*And the King of glory shall come in.*

*Who is this King of glory:*

*The Lord of hosts,*

*He is the King of glory. Selah*

--Psalm 24:7-10

SUNDAY MORNING BEGAN dreary with threatening rain clouds. Exhausted from weeks of sleep-deprived nights and the increasing frustrations of dealing with Larry, I dragged myself from bed. If it were not for decades of habit and the will to provide as much normalcy as possible for him, I would have crawled back under the covers and skipped the worship service.

I constantly struggled to learn how to allow for Larry's slowness. It now took nearly two hours for him to get dressed and have breakfast. He refused my help and snapped at me when I reminded him of the next steps in dressing or where to find the garment he needed. So once again we arrived late at the morning service. I made a mental note that promptness must not be nearly as important as I had always considered it.

The singing time of worship had already begun. Smiling greeters asked our welfare and found us good seats, treating Larry with as much respect as they did me. Larry sat and listened which I stood and joined in the singing, praising God for His attributes as Creator, Savior, and Sustainer of my life and my future. Before long I had to wipe away tears of joy and gratitude.

I don't remember the sermon, but I do remember more tears. Larry slept through much of it, but he rallied at the end and interacted with brothers and sisters who made a point of welcoming us. My heart overflowed with God's love through them.

Lessons learned:

1. Praising God lifts the heaviest burden.
2. Fellowship with God's people brings comfort.
3. The weather and life's frustrations don't have to influence my joy.
4. God cares.

*Lord Jesus, help me remember it's worth the effort to gather with Your people and sing Your praises. You made us and You know that praising You brings us joy. Give me a joyful heart in the midst of trial. In Your own name, amen.*

# YOU HAVE ENEMIES

*To You, O Lord, I lift up my soul.*

*O my God, I trust in You;*

*Let me not be ashamed;*

*Let not my enemies triumph over me.*

*Indeed, let no one who waits on You be ashamed;*

*Let those be ashamed who deal treacherously without cause.*

*--Psalm 25:1-3*

WHEN DEALING WITH an illness, whether physical or mental, you are fighting many battles. As a child, I hated confrontations. I remember when I was about five years old I went home crying because a playmate had deliberately thrown sand in my face in the sandbox. My father was furious. He wanted me to go back and repay the offender. Fortunately, mother's cool head prevailed and we decided I should just stay away from the bully.

Some battles are best handled just that way. Walk away, avoid the offender. On the other hand, many battles against Satan, who want you to fail in living an exemplary life for God, need to be met head on. Battles to get the right diagnoses and care for your loved one cannot be side-stepped. It is important to stand your ground against well-meaning friends and family who continually push their ideas about how to treat your ill loved one, whether it's the latest medication on the market or old wives' tales and remedies.

Like me, you have probably experienced days of tactfully thanking people for their suggestions and wondering how much explaining you needed to do to alleviate their fears that you are not caring for your loved one to the best of your ability. Maybe that same day you had to spend hours on the phone trying to convince health care providers of the validity of your claim or the need for an appointment or to change a medication. The list goes on and on, and it's all up to you.

By the end of such a day, your patience is thin, and then Satan throws in a new symptom (or intensifies an old one) causing you to feel abandoned by your heavenly Father. Whatever you do, don't go to bed feeling forsaken. Spend even a little time at Jesus' feet lifting up your soul to God, reaffirming your trust in Him. He's on your side. The enemy can't win the fight. Don't let him win even one battle.

*Lord Jesus, thank You for the many psalms that remind me You are right there with me in every battle. I trust in You even when the way seems dark and I am so very tired. I know the enemy cannot triumph over me because I am in the palm of Your hand. Thank You, Jesus. Amen*

# HIS WAYS ARE BETTER

*Show me Your ways, O Lord;*

*Teach me Your paths.*

*Lead me in Your truth and teach me,*

*For You are the God of my salvation;*

*On You I wait all the day.*

--Psalm 25:4-5

MOTHER GREW UP in a household of tight finances. She married a shoe salesman who gambled away most of their income. A couple of years later he succumbed to a meningitis epidemic and, after several years, Mother remarried; this time to a man who faithfully paid off his bar bill every payday, but left our family little to live on. So when Mother gained her independence, she wanted to pass on her earnings to her two daughters. She set up bank accounts for us and added to them regularly.

Then Mother became ill with Alzheimer's Disease. After a stay in an acute care hospital her doctor urged us to place her in a care home, knowing neither of us would be able to meet her needs. We took his advice and began researching how we would pay the nursing home. We withdrew the money she had set aside for us, put it into a joint account, and used much of it to pay for Mother's care. We had to set up an irrevocable trust for her, and the attorney was expensive. We decided to use the rest of the bank money to make needed house and yard repairs.

In a few months my sister (who lived in Mother's home) called me to say she thought her repairmen and yard people had been cheating her. Sure enough, I detected double and even triple billing on all the repair and maintenance bills. But she had paid them in cash (at their request) and they were no longer in the area. All the money Mother had set aside for us had disappeared.

I could have been angry, but I stopped to consider. Mother would have been sad to see the money she had put aside for us used for her own care and for making the repairs she had put off. But God is in control. The money was used for her care, and the attorney we needed. I was sorry my sister had been cheated out of the rest of it, but I could rejoice that there had been enough to cover Mother's expenses. We had no bills to pay out of our own pockets.

*Thank You, Father, that I can trust You to take care of every part of my life. Lead me in Your path. Help me wait on You all day, every day. In Jesus' name, amen.*

# IT'S NOT YOUR FAULT

*Remember, O Lord, Your tender mercies and Your loving kindnesses,*

*For they are from of old.*

*Do not remember the sins of my youth, nor my transgressions;*

*According to Your mercy remember me,*

*For Your goodness' sake, O Lord.*

--Psalm 25:6-7

IT HAD BEEN a difficult day caring for my father. When he first moved in with us (an RV on our property), he tried very hard to get along with my husband, whom he despised. Now he was getting tired of pretending, and it seemed like every time I visited him he had a complaint to make about my "holier than thou" husband Larry. That evening I again took Dad his dinner and once more he began berating Larry. This could not continue, so I interrupted him mid-sentence.

"Dad, I'm not going to listen to you putting Larry down," I said, my anger rising. "He's done nothing but good to you and, although he is a preacher, he certainly never acts 'holier than thou' as you put it."

My voice was now rising with my anger. "As a matter of fact if you don't like the care we're giving you, you can just expect us to leave you on your own. Think about it and let me know."

With that I slammed the door on his trailer and stomped back to my own house, already ashamed of my angry reaction.

Months later, Dad went from his trailer to an acute care hospital and then to a convalescent home. Almost daily I received phone calls from the home reporting on Dad's destructive behavior. Many nights I went to bed worrying about his care and asking God, "What did I do to deserve this?" The door-slamming incident would come to mind. Was God punishing me for my angry responses?

First John 1:9 says, "If we confess our sins, He is faithful and just to forgive us our sins, and to cleanse us from all unrighteousness." I had certainly confessed and been forgiven. God reminded me of His forgiveness. Troubles would come, but I was not their cause. What peace!

*Father God, We are so prone to blame ourselves for everything that goes wrong. Help me not to resort to "Why me?" when I face trouble. May I rest in Your forgiveness and trust You to get me through the difficulties. Why not me, Lord? "I can do all things through Christ who strengthens me" (Philippians 4:13). Praise Your name, amen.*

# THE BENEFITS OF HUMILITY

*Good and upright is the Lord;*

*Therefore He teaches sinners in the way.*

*The humble He guides in justice,*

*And the humble He teaches His way.*

*All the paths of the Lord are mercy and truth,*

*To such as keep His covenant and His testimonies.*

*For Your name's sake, O Lord,*

*Pardon my iniquity, for it is great.*

--Psalm 25:8-11

I CAN THINK of so many times when a little humility on my part would have greatly helped my situation. Like when I insisted the spelling of mnemonic was pneumonic – in a school faculty meeting, no less. Or when I was accompanying a violinist at a wedding and congratulating myself on how well I was playing – right before someone opened the door and the wind scattered my sheet music all over the front of the sanctuary, leaving me to play nothing but simple (and sometimes non-harmonic) chords for the rest of the prelude.

Maturity should teach humility, but that isn't always the case. Dona, a fellow teacher, could rarely bring herself to ask help from anyone, particularly someone younger. When she once complained to me that she did not know how to properly apply make-up, I referred to my daughter, who seemed to do that well.

Dona became indignant at the very suggestion. A student wouldn't be able to teach her anything! And she was right, but only because she was not willing to learn.

I have even heard arrogance in some people's prayers – thanking God for their good sense to recognize God's offer of salvation as a good thing or demanding that God take care of a problem their way. Our stubborn refusal to step out on faith when God calls us to do something is certainly another demonstration that we think our way is better than God's

But God says He guides the humble in justice and teaches them His way. I want that guidance and teaching. I used to pray for humility, but I've found I don't need to do that. I just need to remember how embarrassed I felt when my music went flying.

*Savior, You who left heaven's glory to live a humble life on earth, help me exhibit Your humility in my life too. Give me a clear understanding of who I am. Give me a servant's heart, even during the exhausting times of caregiving. In Your own name, amen.*

# GOD'S PRESERVATION

*Turn Yourself to me, and have mercy on me,*

*For I am desolate and afflicted.*

*The troubles of my heart have enlarged;*

*Bring me out of my distresses!*

*Look on my affliction and my pain,*

*And forgive all my sins.*

*Consider my enemies, for they are many;*

*And they hate me with cruel hatred.*

*Keep my soul, and deliver me;*

*Let me not be ashamed, for I put my trust in You.*

*Let integrity and uprightness preserve me,*

*For I wait for You.*

--Psalm 25:16-21

HOW MANY TIMES have you prayed, "Lord, just get us through this"? You are dealing with feeling abandoned (desolate) and afflicted. Your heart is more troubled about your loved one every day. You are distressed to the point of tears. You are not only concerned about your loved one's afflictions and pain, but also that you know caregiving is taking a toll on your own health. Sometimes you wonder if there is something in your past for which you are being punished. It even seems as if the people who should be helping you have turned against you and become your enemies.

Jesus said, "Come to Me, all you who labor and are heavy laden, and I will give you rest." (Matthew 11:28). What a precious promise! He will keep your soul and deliver you and the loved one for whom you care. He will take away shame when we trust in Him. His integrity and uprightness (not ours) will preserve us. What a blessing to rest in Him.

I suggest days of respite from the care of your loved one. On those days it is good to spend at least some time reading God's promises and talking to Him about your feelings. He cares. He wants to hold you up. Let Him.

*Father, thank You for Your promises to preserve me even in the midst of overwhelming days. Help me rest in You, trust You, and praise You for Your integrity and uprightness that preserve me. In Jesus' name, amen.*

# WALKING IN INTEGRITY

*Vindicate me, O Lord,*

*For I have walked in my integrity.*

*I have also trusted in the Lord;*

*I shall not slip.*

*Examine me, O Lord, and prove me;*

*Try my mind and my heart.*

*For Your lovingkindness is before my eyes,*

*And I have walked in Your truth.*

*But as for me,*

*I will walk in my integrity;*

*Redeem me and be merciful to me.*

*My foot stands in an even place;*

*In the congregations I will bless the Lord.*

--Psalm 26:1-3, 11-12

THE ADVERTISER ON TV says he can't speak for others who claim integrity but he guarantees you'll like the way you look in his suits. My friend ran a company named Integrity Construction. I would swear to his honesty, but I have known other companies who sullied that name.

I would love to be able to claim, like David, that I have walked in integrity. But wait a minute? This is the same David who had an adulterous affair with Bathsheba, which he tried to cover up by murdering her husband. What kind of integrity is that?

What kind? The kind that acknowledges sin and forsakes it so that God can cleanse the soul (Psalm 32, 51). The kind that hour by hour leans on God, receives and emulates His lovingkindness, and walks in His truth.

As a caregiver, you probably don't have many perfect days. I certainly didn't. But, like me, you can daily ask for God's strength and help to walk in His integrity. At the end of each day you can drop all the errors you've made at His feet, find His forgiveness, and be ready for a new day in the morning. He has promised His mercies are new every morning (Lamentations 3:23). Rest in that.

*Father God, I cannot live a perfect life, much as I want to. Thank You for Your forgiveness and grace. Give me this day my daily strength. Help me walk in integrity in order to care for my loved one and honor Your name. In that name I pray, amen.*

# RENEWAL THROUGH WORSHIP

*I will wash my hands in innocence;*

*So I will go about Your altar, O Lord,*

*That I may proclaim with the voice of thanksgiving.*

*And tell of all Your wondrous works.*

*Lord, I have loved the habitation of Your house,*

*And the place where Your glory dwells.*

--Psalm 26:6-8

IN THE MIDST of caring for my husband Larry, there were many Sunday mornings when I awoke too tired to begin the struggle needed to get both us of ready for church. Often I thought it would not matter if we didn't go. Larry didn't know what day of the week it was even though I knew he enjoyed attending church more than just about any other activity we did. It took great effort, prayer, and a lifelong habit of church attendance to get us to church on those Sundays.

However, once we got there, even if we came in late (as Larry became slower and slower in his ability to get ready), soon I entered wholeheartedly into the worship service. Many times I could not sing because the words were too poignant to our situation. The chorus "Suffering children are safe in His arms" would always make me cry as I pictured my husband returned to a childlike state and God hugging him to His breast.  Other worship songs often had me in tears as well.

I could not count the number of times the sermon seemed aimed right at me – usually for my comfort. Larry was safe at church. He did not attempt to wander as was his habit in other places. He often slept through the sermon and afterward beamed with obvious pleasure as folks greeted us on the way out. They were strangers to him, but he seemed to sense they were the family of God.

Before that time, as a pastor's wife, I often encouraged people to come to church even when they didn't feel like it. I heard other people say they were glad they had come although it had been a struggle to get there. Now I knew it for myself. It was always worth the effort for both Larry and me.

*Lord, You promised that where two or three are gathered in Your name, You are there too. I know You are with me "one-on-one" but You specially bless us when we meet together to sing Your praises and hear Your Word preached. Help me remember it's worth the effort on those days when it doesn't seem like it. Make me a blessing to the people with whom I worship. In Jesus' name, amen.*

# MY LIGHT ... SALVATION ... STRENGTH ... CONFIDENCE

*The Lord is my light and my salvation;*

*Whom shall I fear?*

*The Lord is the strength of my life;*

*Of whom shall I be afraid?*

*When the wicked came against me*

*To eat up my flesh,*

*My enemies and foes,*

*They stumbled and fell.*

*Though an army may encamp against me,*

*My heart shall not fear;*

*Though war may rise against me,*

*In this I will be confident.*

--Psalm 27:1-3

SO MANY THINGS can happen in your day as a caregiver that would make you think you are in a war. I remember days when I retired exhausted from all the conflicts I'd dealt with. Sometimes it was fighting for entitlements: insurance or benefits. Other days it was standing up to the medical profession, either refusing to give a suggested but suspect prescription or demanding further testing or care. Maybe it was a day spent in the emergency room because a loved one took a fall.

Or it might have been one of those days when he would not cooperate, maybe even attacked me. It is no wonder caregivers often suffer from post-traumatic stress disorder.

Where do we find relief from the battle? The psalmist says, "The Lord is my light and my salvation. Whom shall I fear?" I love those words set to music in the old church anthem. Just listening to that music soothes my soul. Meditation on the words — how God not only provides our light, salvation, strength, and confidence, but He Himself is that light, salvation, strength, and confidence. All these assets and many more!

Stay close to God. He dispels the fears.

*Heavenly Father, help me remember that You are with me all the time. You are here to light up my path, You are my Savior. In You I find strength. I have confidence, which is found only in You. Banish my fears, Lord, as I rest in You. In Jesus' name, amen.*

# IN GOD'S HOUSE

One thing I have desired of the Lord,

That will I seek:

That I may dwell in the house of the Lord

All the days of my life,

To behold the beauty of the Lord,

And to inquire in His temple.

For in the time of trouble

He shall hide me in His pavilion;

In the secret place of His tabernacle

He shall hide me;

He shall set me high upon a rock.

And now my head shall be lifted up above my enemies all around me;

Therefore I will offer sacrifices of joy in His tabernacle;

I will sing, yes, I will sing praises to the Lord.

--Psalm 27:4-6

MY GRANDDAUGHTER WAS complaining about her recent troubles in the classroom. I remarked that she reminded me very much of myself at that age, hoping to comfort her with the fact that this too will pass and she really will grow up to be a productive citizen.

"You mean I'm going to grow up to be like Grandma?" she asked her mother, with definite alarm in her voice.

"What's wrong with that?" her mother answered.

"I just can't imagine myself wanting to be in church all the time like Grandma is," she answered.

I laughed. "No, I can't imagine you wanting to do that either – now. But hopefully the day will come when you will find as much joy in church people and activities as I do. I can't imagine being more content."

Look at what the psalm says are major benefits of "dwelling" in God's house: beholding God's beauty; inquiring in His temple (and surely getting His answers); and being hidden, safely, set up high out of reach of any enemy. Caregivers need to stop and see His beauty – and all the beautiful things He has created. We need ready access to His answers for the many dilemmas we face. And we definitely need to rest in His protection.

*Father, thank You for the privilege of spending time with Your people, joining them in worship and fellowship, upholding one another with Your love. Thank You for the comfort of Your very presence in my life. May my loved ones see Your effect in my life and desire those same benefits. In Jesus' name, amen.*

# SEEKING THE FACE OF GOD

*Hear, O Lord, when I cry with my voice!*

*Have mercy also upon me, and answer me.*

*When You said, "Seek My face,"*

*My heart said to You, "Your face, Lord, I will seek."*

*Do not turn Your servant away in anger;*

*You have been my help;*

*Do not leave me nor forsake me,*

*O God of my salvation.*

*When my father and my mother forsake me,*

*Then the Lord will take care of me.*

--Psalm 27:7-10

"CAREGIVING IS SUCH a lonely job. I don't know where to turn for help." My new friend wept on my shoulder outside her mother's room. I wanted to barge right in and tell her how God had filled my life so that I no longer experienced those lonely times, but she wasn't ready to hear that yet. She just needed someone to hear her, and I became that person. She hugged me when I promised to pray for her and her mother.

Gradually, over weeks, she began asking why I never seemed to have those same meltdown moments. Then I was able to share my walk of faith. When I told how I came to realize God had put me in my husband's life for just this difficult time, she began to accept that she was there for the same reason for her mother.

The switching of roles is difficult for both parent and child (or husband and wife). Suddenly you find you must make the decisions for the one who made all your decisions years before. It's not usually sudden, but it seems that it is as we fail to recognize a parent's (or spouse's) lessening abilities. You feel alone and forsaken – and you are. But not by God.

What a promise! When my very parents forsake me (for whatever reason), God Himself is there to take care of me. He says to seek His face. May our response always be, "Your face, Lord, I will seek." Then He can help us. Then we will know for sure we are not forsaken.

*Father God, I seek Your face. I thank You that You are there for me, waiting for me to surrender my struggles so that I can rest in You. In Jesus' name, amen.*

# THE ANITDOTE FOR LOSING HEART

*I would have lost heart, unless I had believed*

*That I would see the goodness of the Lord*

*In the land of the living.*

*Wait on the Lord;*

*Be of good courage,*

*And He shall strengthen your heart;*

*Wait, I say, on the Lord!*

--Psalm 27:13-14

I SAY, "I can't do this, Lord!"

He says, "We can do it together."

"Why me, Lord?"

"Why not you?" He answers.

"It's too hard!"

"Without Me you can do nothing," and "I can do all things through Christ who strengthens me."

--John 15:5; Philippians 4:13

"You promised You would not give me more than I can carry, but I think my bucket is too big!"

"Take My yoke upon you and learn from me … for My yoke is easy and My burden is light."

--Matthew 11:29-30

In my classroom each spring, we would grow young plants on the science table. Usually someone brought in the pupa of a butterfly or moth, and the children and I anxiously waited for the creature to emerge from its cocoon. The hardest part of that science lesson was to keep the children from helping the butterfly come out. It struggled so hard. Every year the children worried that it was never going to make it without our help.

What would have happened if we had "helped" the creature by clipping the cocoon away? Instead of a beautiful butterfly, it would have emerged a bloated, undeveloped freak, unable to fly or care for itself, doomed to an early death.

It helps to know God's words, for He uses them to answer the complaints of our hearts. He promises to sustain us in our dark hours. He tells us to wait on Him. His timing is obviously not ours, but He wants us to be beautiful butterflies, not helpless freaks.

*Help me wait on Your timing, Lord. And while I'm waiting, remind me to read more of Your Word to hear Your answers. Develop me into the beautiful person You intend. In Jesus' name, amen.*

# ASSURANCE OF PRAYERS HEARD

*To You I will cry, O Lord my Rock:*

*Do not be silent to me ...*

*Hear the voice of my supplications*

*When I cry to You,*

*When I lift up my hands toward Your holy sanctuary.*

*Blessed be the Lord,*

*Because He has heard the voice of my supplications!*

*The Lord is my strength and my shield;*

*My heart trusted in Him, and I am helped;*

*Therefore my heart greatly rejoices,*

*And with my song I will praise Him.*

--Psalm 28:1-2, 6-7

CHILD OF GOD, you can cry to God and know He will hear you. Like David, you can depend on Him to be your strength and shield. Your heart can trust in Him and be helped. So why do we so often feel abandoned? What's going on?

As a parent, did you always give your children what they wanted as soon as they asked? My son wanted a motorcycle when he was two years old. Do you think I gave it to him? Of course not. We got him a Big Wheel. At four he still wanted a motorcycle. We gave him a tricycle. At six? Same request. Answer: bicycle – with training wheels.

A bicycle would be more like a motorcycle without the training wheels. He wanted them off. Did we comply? Not right away. He finally took them off himself and wobbled away, crashing frequently until he finally "got the hang of it."

Did he ever get that motorcycle? Yes – I cosigned for it in his last year of high school. He was ready.

God is that kind of parent with us. We can't see the pitfalls of what we ask for, even the things that seem like they must be the best solutions for our loved ones and ourselves. We don't know what kind of growing we need to do before we are ready for God's "Yes!" We just need to concentrate on learning to ride with what He's given us here and now.

Look at it this way: we can bless the Lord because He has heard us. The answer is already in the works and will come at the perfect time. Rejoice and praise Him!

*Thank You, God, for being a perfect parent, not only willing to give us all we need but able to do so. Help us wait on Your perfect answers and Your perfect time. Give us patience, for waiting is the hardest part of all. Help us see our world through Your eyes, Lord. In Jesus' name, amen.*

# CAN'T SEE THE FOREST FOR THE TREES

*The voice of the Lord is over the waters;*

*The God of glory thunders;*

*The Lord is over many waters.*

*The voice of the Lord is powerful;*

*The voice of the Lord is full of majesty.*

*The voice of the Lord breaks the cedars,*

*Yes, the Lord splinters the cedars of Lebanon ...*

*The voice of the Lord divides the flames of fire.*

*The voice of the Lord shakes the wilderness;*

*The Lord shakes the Wilderness of Kadesh.*

*The voice of the Lord makes the deer give birth,*

*And strips the forests bare ...*

--Psalm 29:3-9

THERE ARE TIMES when we are overwhelmed with the elements of the care of our loved ones. That confusing time of diagnosis and adjusting medicines, changing diet, and reorganizing schedules befuddles the mind. I remember my thoughts whirling as I drove home from a time of overseeing my mother's care. Prayer brought perspective and helped me prioritize the details. I prayed, "Lord, I need help. I can't see the forest for the trees."

Look what David said God does to those trees (in Psalm 29). According to verse 5, God only has to speak and those mighty trees are turned into toothpicks. (I know, it says splinters, but what do you think they used for toothpicks in those days?)

Remember Elijah? (Read about him in 1 Kings 18 and 19.) Talk about overwhelmed! He was ready to give up when Queen Jezebel issued an APB for his arrest. So he hid in a cave and God came to him. He had to listen for God's voice. He thought it would be loud, like in a wild wind or a rumbling earthquake or crackling fire. But God spoke to him in a quiet voice.

Look what God's gentle voice can do. Besides making toothpicks of the forest, He thunders over the waters, shows His majesty, divides fire, shakes the wilderness, causes the wild animals to give birth, and completely controls nature. With all that power, can we doubt He will get us through the details of our forests?

*Lord, You are the Almighty God. You created all things by just speaking the Word. I am trusting You to speak the words that will turn the wilderness of my life into manageable pieces. Thank You for Your still, small, calming voice that leads me in the right direction. In Jesus, name, amen.*

# JOY COMES IN THE MORNING

*Weeping may endure for a night,*

*But joy comes in the morning ...*

*You have turned for me my mourning into dancing;*

*You have put off my sackcloth and clothed me with gladness,*

*To the end that my glory may sing praise to You and not be silent.*

*O Lord my God,*

*I will give thanks to You forever.*

--Psalm 30:5, 11-12

I HAD THE privilege of writing the biography of missionary Carol Hastings. In an early chapter she tells how God directed and comforted her in the loss of a dream.

On the morning before her wedding date, Carol's Bible reading schedule took her to Psalm 30. Verse 5 caught her attention. She wondered why God gave her such a verse the day before her wedding. "Weeping may endure for a night, but joy cometh in the morning" (KJV). She meditated on that thought, and then spent her usual time in prayer.

When Carol returned from running errands, she found her roommate Louise in tears. She had received a telegram from Carol's fiancé.

"Is it to me?" Carol asked, picking up the telegram.

"No, he sent it to me," Louise answered. Then, angrily: "He says to tell you the wedding is postponed."

Carol dropped into a chair, crumbling the telegram. "Well, why didn't he send it to me?" Then, "I guess he didn't know how."

"Oh, Carol, I am so sorry," Louise wailed, hugging her. "This must hurt you so much."

"Why, I'm not crying!" Carol said, surprised at her own composure. "I think I'm disappointed. I'm sure I love Warren, but I love Jesus more. I've been asking Him to stop this wedding if it isn't His will. Why cry when God has done what I asked?"

Louise shook her head and her sobs continued. She could not speak. Instead of comforting Carole, Carol comforted her by sharing with her the verse that God had given her that morning.

"How good to be sure of the leading of the Lord," she said, and that confidence continued to uphold her when the tears did come. (From *To India with Love,* copyright 1992, by Darlene Saunders.)

Caregiving brings on much weeping. Our dreams are shattered and we grieve over their loss. Trust that it is only "for a night" and joy will come in the morning.

If you are trusting God, even the most disappointing events will turn to joy. Sorrows happen, but God surprises us with joy.

*Lord Jesus, I know there will always be tough times. I thank You for going through them with me and then for surprising me with joy and confidence. Help me dwell on the joyful times. Thank You for friends and family who share both the weeping and the laughter. In Your own precious name, amen.*

# DELIVERANCE

*In You, O Lord, I put my trust;*

*Let me never be ashamed;*

*Deliver me in Your righteousness,*

*Bow down Your ear to me,*

*Deliver me speedily;*

*Be my rock of refuge,*

*A fortress of defense to save me.*

--Psalm 31:1-2

I WAS STILL taking care of both of my parents when my husband Larry began showing symptoms of Alzheimer's Disease. I remember thinking (asking God) how I would ever get through this period of our lives. I wanted nothing so much as deliverance from my burden of caregiving.

Reflecting on my mother's care of my grandmother and their stories about caring for my great-grandmother, I realized that there was no way around this situation. God doesn't promise to take us around our problems or even to get us over them. He promises to get us through them.

Furthermore, He promised to go with us through them. In Hebrews 13:5 He says, "I will never leave you nor forsake you." I learned that verse as a new believer. As a teenager it did not seem as important to me as it became in my caregiving years.

Another observation: David (the psalmist) pled for God to deliver him speedily. I don't know what David's immediate problem was, or whether God acted speedily for him. I do know God never promises a speedy deliverance. God's timing is not ours. We don't understand the delays, but we can rest in Him, knowing His way and His timing are perfect and will result in the goal He has planned for our lives. Rest assured that He will be with us, sustain us, support us, comfort us, meet all of our needs, and teach us – all the way.

*Heavenly father, what a blessing Your promises are. Help me rest on them, knowing You are with me even when I am too tired or stressed out to recognize Your presence. Help me convey that calm assurance to my loved one. Get us through it, Lord, as You said You would. In Jesus' name, amen.*

# A COMMITTED SPIRIT

*For You are my rock and my fortress;*

*Therefore, for Your name's sake,*

*Lead me and guide me.*

*Pull me out of the net which they have secretly laid for me,*

*For You are my strength.*

*Into Your hand I commit my spirit;*

*O Lord God of truth.*

--Psalm 31:3-5

WE USUALLY THINK of the phrase "into Your hand I commit my spirit" in the context of our Lord's final moments on the cross, for He quoted these very words. It was His final act of obedience to the Father.

I doubt that David had death in mind when he penned that phrase. He was talking about the day-to-day life experiences where he found wisdom in submission to God's leading. He mentions God's strength and protection, His leadership and guidance, and His redemption. If you read the life of David (1 and 2 Samuel) you will be impressed with the way God answered his prayers, rescuing him through numerous trials and difficulties. Can we depend on God in the same way David did? Will He lead us, protect us, and be our Redeemer?

I am a goal-oriented person. I really don't like it when someone or something interrupts my set schedule. I find my patience short when I am deterred from my agenda. But lately, instead of fussing about the redirection in plans, I have tried to see changes as God's intervention with a better plan. Taking it a step further, I now frequently end my morning prayer journal with, "It's Your agenda, Lord, not mine" and "bless others through me." That's my way of committing my spirit into God's hand.

That said, or written, I go on with my prayed-over plans, but I find myself much less likely to be disturbed by the changes God drops into my day. Sometimes I even get a glimpse of what God is trying to accomplish through me. What an awesome privilege!

Disappointment? God's appointment!

*Father God, I am overawed at the very thought that You would allow me to serve You. Thank You for reappointing my days and hours to serve You better. Help me be more flexible, more responsive to your leading. Into Your hands today I commit my spirit. In Jesus' name and for His glory, amen.*

# WHAT DOES IT TAKE?

*Oh, love the Lord, all you His saints!*

*For the Lord preserves the faithful,*

*And fully repays the proud person.*

*Be of good courage,*

*And He shall strengthen your heart,*

*All you who hope in the Lord.*

--Psalm 31:23-24

FROM THE STANDPOINT of nearly eighty years I look at my grandchildren and see much of myself in them. One child in particular tends to go from trouble to trouble, usually because she is fighting too hard for what she considers her rights. No one should get away with calling her a bad name. Her reputation has been smudged and she doesn't understand why. Her teachers think she is a "loud mouth" with anger-management issues.

I have gently tried to counsel her on numerous occasions, with little result. While praying for her this morning, God reminded me that He defends His children. If we are doing His will, we can expect Him to defend us, and His defense is far greater than any we can do on our own.

This isn't just a young person's problem. I have a couple of other family members whose lives are constantly upset because they feel they must set the record straight for every real or imagined slight. I can't even visualize living with the constant adrenaline rush that causes.

However, in the midst of caregiving, I too have often felt I needed to defend myself or my loved one. Yet David says (Psalm 31) that the Lord preserves the faithful; He fully repays the proud person (who opposes you) and strengthens your heart.

Does life require our retaliation? No. Just love the Lord and let Him take care of it. What a relief!

*Father God, help me to remember that You will defend and protect me if I am obeying You. Give me the courage and tact to live and tell this truth to my family members. Thank You for making me Your child. I hide from trouble in Your arms. In Jesus' name, amen.*

# CONFIDENT PRAYER

*I acknowledged my sin to You,*

*And my iniquity I have not hidden.*

*I said, "I will confess my transgressions to the Lord,"*

*And You forgave the iniquity of my sin. Selah*

*For this cause everyone who is godly shall pray to You*

*In a time when You may be found;*

*Surely in a flood of great waters*

*They shall not come near him.*

*You are my hiding place;*

*You shall preserve me from trouble;*

*You shall surround me with songs of deliverance. Selah*

--Psalm 32:5-7

ALL MIKEY WANTS is for Dad to fix his bike. He's done it in the past. All Mikey has to do is ask. But there is a problem. Dad told Mikey to ask for help next time the bike needed to be fixed. Mikey decided to do it himself instead. Now the bike is worse, some parts are missing, and Mikey even damaged one of Dad's tools. Mikey is understandably afraid to ask Dad for help.

Sometimes we're like that with God. We know He wants us to ask Him for help. We may try to fix the problem ourselves. We make it worse. But God will still help us. We just don't have the confidence to ask. Our sin comes between us and God.

David went through this in a *big* way. Psalm 32 is a journal of that event. How did David regain the confidence to ask God's help? Verse 5 says, "I acknowledged my sin to You, and my iniquity I have not hidden. I said, 'I will confess my transgressions to the Lord,' and You forgave the iniquity of my sin."

As caregivers we always need God's help. It takes a lifetime of learning to trust God to work in our behalf, and the first step is always to keep short accounts with Him. Like the toddler in close fellowship with his father, we can crawl up into our Father God's lap and confidently ask Him anything.

*Lord, Your ways are not our ways but I trust You to do what's best and in Your own perfect time. Help me confess and forsake the sin that would get between us. Thank You for going with us through this difficult period of our lives. In Jesus' name, amen.*

# GUIDED BY GOD'S EYE

*I will instruct you and teach you in the way you should go;*

*I will guide you with My eye …*

*Many sorrows shall be to the wicked;*

*But he who trusts in the Lord,*

*Mercy shall surround him.*

*Be glad in the Lord and rejoice, you righteous;*

*And shout for joy, all you upright in heart!*

--Psalm 32:8, 10-11

WE WERE IN a strange town on the way to a funeral parlor for my brother-in-law's memorial service. We thought we heard the directions clearly, but they didn't make sense after our exit from the freeway. So we made our way down what looked like a logical street and were soon hopelessly lost.

We could have wandered around and finally found our destination. Or we could have driven until we found a store or gas station and asked for help. But our driver had a better idea. He simply pushed the GPS button, gave the name of the funeral parlor, and we received directions immediately. Amazing! It was like having an eye in the sky to guide us.

GPS is a fairly new technology. But we have always had a spiritual "eye in the sky." God Himself promised to instruct us and teach us the way we should go. How often I felt I needed divine direction in making decision for my ailing loved one. God knew that. He waited for me to ask, for He could not answer until I pushed the prayer button, acknowledging I needed help and was willing to go the way He showed me.

*Father God, what a comfort to know that You see me. You know my needs. You have the answers. Your timing is perfect. Give me the wisdom to want Your directions, for it is far superior to any solution I could devise. Keep me close to You, in Your* Word. *Guide me with Your eye. In Jesus' name, amen.*

# LET MUSIC HELP

*Rejoice in the Lord, O you righteous!*

*For praise from the upright is beautiful.*

*Praise the Lord with the harp;*

*Make melody to Him with an instrument of ten strings.*

*Sing to Him a new song;*

*Play skillfully with a shout of joy.*

--Psalm 33:1-3

LARRY WAS PRETTY narrow-minded about his music. He thought all modern songs and rhythms were from the devil. He grew up in a community that frowned on dancing so he became very uncomfortable when I danced around the house to whatever music I might be listening to. Before the onset of Alzheimer's Disease, he just tolerated my choices and movements, but he really liked it when I would sit at the piano and play and sing hymns and country gospel songs.

However, as the Alzheimer's Disease developed he became less and less tolerant of my music choices, eventually exhibiting anger whenever any recorded music played, particularly if he were trying to read, work a word-search puzzle, or talk to someone. I believe the addition of music brought just too much stimulation for his brain to handle.

So Larry wanted less (meaning none) music at a time when I needed the comfort of more. To me it was a dilemma for which I desperately needed a solution. This may not work for everyone but it worked for us:

First: Larry was losing his hearing and mine was very acute. Easy solution, especially if we were in different rooms or if he were resting: play whatever I wanted to listen to at the low level I could appreciate at least as background music.

Second: I paid attention to the times when Larry became agitated. I turned the music down or off when visitors came or when we were having a "conversation." I could actually see the tension drain from his stance when I did that.

Third: I noticed instrumental music caused agitation. During quiet times I played familiar hymns or gospel music in which the words were understandable. Sometimes he would even fall asleep with these favorites playing.

Music can be soothing or stimulating. It is a gift from God. I admit I worked hard at finding solutions to this problem because I myself needed the comfort of God's Word set to melodies. I am sure God showed me how to use His gift of music to bless us both.

*Creator of all that's beautiful, thank You for Your gift of music. Help me use it to encourage, comfort, and admonish myself and whoever You send my way. In Jesus' name, amen.*

# WILL NOT THE JUDGE OF ALL THE EARTH DO RIGHT?

*For the word of the Lord is right.*

*And all His work is done in truth.*

*He loves righteousness and justice;*

*The earth is full of the goodness of the Lord.*

--Psalm 33:4-5

I HAD A dear pastor friend whom the Lord used to minister to my heart through the years of Larry's dementia. During that time I also experienced and grieved over the death of my father, and a few months later, my mother. The school where I taught disbanded, so I was without a job, and I went through several disappointing job interviews that left me feeling that God must have abandoned me. Through it all, Pastor Sweeney would quote Genesis 18:25, "Shall not the Judge of all the earth do right?"

Sometimes he would call to ask how the battle was going. After I complained about the newest problems, he would gently remind me of 1 Samuel 17:47, "The battle is the Lord's."

Those are not just pat answers to gripe sessions. The battle really is the Lord's, and the longer we are involved in it the more we see His hand working for us.

If we have placed our trust in Christ to get us through this life and into the next, we know for certain that He is the judge of all the earth, and He not only wants to do right, He is the only One who can completely accomplish what is right.

We need to remind ourselves of these facts on the days we are not overwhelmed. That keeps them near the surface of our brains on those many days when we feel we are about to drown in troubles. Thank you, Pastor Sweeney, for that calm assurance.

*Lord Jesus, You are the Judge of the Universe. I am Your child. I trust You to do what is right for my loved one and myself. I am overawed with the thought that You allow me to have a part in Your war for truth and righteousness. Help me keep my place in proper perspective and watch You bring us through the battles. In Your own precious name, amen.*

# WAITING

*Our soul waits for the Lord;*

*He is our help and our shield.*

*For our heart shall rejoice in Him,*

*Because we have trusted in His holy name.*

*Let Your mercy, O Lord, be upon us,*

*Just as we hope in You.*

--Psalm 33:20-22

ONE OF MY favorite scriptures is Isaiah 40:31, "But those who wait on the Lord shall renew their strength; they shall mount up with wings like eagles, they shall run and not be weary, they shall walk and not faint." I like that concept so much that I have even made it into two counted cross-stitch wall hangings, one for myself and one for my daughter.

Enjoying the wall hanging or even meditating on the principle is one thing; actually waiting on the Lord goes much further. As caregivers, we spend a lot of time waiting. And whether it's in the doctor's office, or at a bedside, or in line at the pharmacy, ultimately it's all about waiting on the Lord, for He controls our times and seasons, small and great.

Finally, we must endure the frustration of waiting for God to take our loved one home. We wrestle with whether or not it is wrong to ask Him to relieve the suffering through death. We fear the separation; the grieving we know will follow, often without realizing that we are already grieving. We weep with the one who despairs of this life, feeling useless and incapable of caring for him/her, who just "wants to go home." A lifetime of training results in guilt feelings when we wish the battle were over. This waiting is the hardest of all.

The last few months of Larry's life exhausted me. I came home from the care home in tears most afternoons. I knew he wanted nothing more than to graduate on to see the Savior he had served all his life. His misery became my misery. Daily I asked God why He was leaving him here on earth.

When the parting day finally came, I had the answer. The relief was so great that I hardly grieved at all. I almost felt guilty that I was not sad, until I realized I had done my grieving in those months before his death. There were moments of sadness, but mostly joy, as I pictured my healed and restored husband dancing and singing around the throne and embracing His Lord.

*Yes, Lord. Let Your mercy be upon us as we wait and hope in You. Help us remember always that You are our help and shield. In Jesus' name, amen.*

# TAKE A PRAISE BREAK

*I will bless the Lord at all times;*

*His praise shall continually be in my mouth.*

*My soul shall make its boast in the Lord;*

*The humble shall hear of it and be glad.*

*Oh, magnify the Lord with me,*

*And let us exalt His name together.*

--Psalm 34:1-3

MEDICAL SCIENCE FREQUENTLY corroborates what the Bible has been teaching through the centuries. A recent secular news article extolled the virtues of smiling. Researchers had discovered that just making the facial muscles work to create a smile results in a better mood, as exhibited by elevated endorphins actually recordable in the laboratory. Depressed patients are learning to make themselves happy by pasting on a happy face.

I don't know how long the pretend euphoria lasts, but I do know God tells us to give thanks in everything, for this is His will. And from experience, I know that thanking God in the midst of trials brings joy.

We heard this before, and our natural inclination is to think that God could not have meant for us to be thankful in the depths of tribulation where we find ourselves. But even on the hardest days there are things for which we may genuinely thank God. He did not tell us to be thankful for the trial. We could not honestly do that. But we can thank Him that He is right there with us and that He has our best interests at heart and that He will see us through it. We can thank Him for stretching us and increasing our faith, however small or large that stretch may seem at the time. Depending on the circumstances, we can thank Him for other caregivers and prayer warriors and friends on whose shoulders we may cry.

As a child, when I faced things I didn't like, my mother would tell me to grin and bear it. I had no idea she spoke cutting edge psychology! Add a thankful heart to the happy face and your joy will get you through another day.

*Father God, thank You for encouraging us to do the hard things, for being thankful when we'd rather complain is a hard thing. You made us. You know what makes us work. Help me do what You say so that I may honor Your name and reap the blessing You promise. In Jesus' name, amen.*

# MISPLACED FEAR

*I sought the Lord, and He heard me,*

*And delivered me from all my fears.*

*They looked to Him and were radiant,*

*And their faces were not ashamed.*

*This poor man cried out, and the Lord heard him,*

*And saved him out of all his troubles.*

*The angel of the Lord encamps all around those who fear Him,*

*And delivers them ...*

*Oh, fear the Lord, you His saints!*

*There is no want to those who fear Him ...*

*Come you children, listen to me;*

*I will teach you the fear of the Lord.*

--Psalm 34:4-7, 9, 11

MANY ARE THE fears of the caregiver. When a loved one is diagnosed with a debilitating disease, worry doesn't just creep in – it pounces. Fortunate is the child of God who has developed a lifetime of running to God with fears. We need to bring all the "what ifs?" and "what nows?" to our heavenly Father – over and over, as often as they raise their monstrous heads.

First Peter 5:7 says, "Casting all your care upon Him, for He cares for you." We cast, but we drag the line back and have to cast again. He tells us to "fear not" and we want to be fearless, but here we are again, worry beads in hand.

There is a fear we are told to embrace – the fear of God Himself. Now I know we've been taught that's not the same thing, and it certainly isn't the same as worrying. But the great, awesome creator and sustainer God of the universe *is* a fearsome Being. We *should* fear Him, for ultimately He is the only power who has the final say about anything touching our lives. Those who have not become part of His family by trusting in Christ's finished work on the cross should fear His judgment. But those who are trusting in Him only fear displeasing Him because of mutual love.

So, what are you afraid of? The unknown trials and decisions in front of You? Your loving, all-powerful Father God has them totally under His control. Fear Him, instead.

*God of all peace, thank You for being my peace even when I don't feel it. Help me trust You in every hour ahead of me – or give me grace to bear the burdens and wisdom to make decisions. Stretch my faith. Make me a trophy of Your grace. In Jesus' name, amen.*

# TOTAL DELIVERANCE

*The eyes of the Lord are on the righteous,*

*And His ears are open to their cry.*

*The face of the Lord is against those who do evil,*

*To cut off the remembrance of them from the earth,*

*The righteous cry out, and the Lord hears,*

*And delivers them out of all their troubles.*

*The Lord is near to those who have a broken heart,*

*And saves such as have a contrite spirit.*

*Many are the afflictions of the righteous,*

*But the Lord delivers him out of them all.*

--Psalm 34:15-19

THE BOOK OF Psalms is a reassuring place to go when we are overwhelmed with trials of grief. Somewhere in my training I adopted the idea that it was ungodly to complain. It showed a great lack of faith. No matter what life sent my way, I must stay positive.

Then I began reading in the Psalms and I realized how many times David and the other psalmists cried out, complaining to God. God knows our hearts. Why try to hide our feelings from Him?"

David is a good example of how to deal with our complaints. He cries. However, he knows God not only hears, but He is already answering. David feels alienated, yet He acknowledges that God is near to the brokenhearted. The psalmist suffers multiple afflictions, but he is confident God is delivering him out of *all* of them.

I remember one frustrating evening when I retreated to my bedroom sobbing, shaking my fist toward heaven, barely muffling my cry of, "Why me, Lord? Why me? Where can I go to resign?

My first reaction to my own outburst was dismay that I could yell at God. But as I cried before him, I realized He already knew how I felt. He wanted me to be honest with Him. It was as though He spoke to me, "I know. It's not fair. But it's my plan for you and Larry, and I'm here. It won't always be this way. You can trust me in this too."

*Loving Father, You know my heart. Thank You that I am not the first person to go through this kind of trial. Thank You for psalm writers who recorded their experiences with You so that we who read, centuries later, can understand Your care for us. Help me rest in Your care, knowing You will deliver at just the right time. Thank You for Your grace, in Jesus' name, amen.*

# LIKE EAGLETS

*Your mercy, O Lord, is in the heavens;*

*Your righteousness reaches to the clouds.*

*Your righteousness is like the great mountains;*

*Your judgments are a great deep;*

*O Lord, You preserve man and beast.*

*How precious is Your lovingkindness, O God!*

*Therefore the children of men put their trust under the shadow of Your wings.*

*They are abundantly satisfied with the fullness of Your house,*

*For with You is the fountain of life;*

*In Your light we see light.*

--Psalm 36:5-9

I LIVE IN the Sierra foothills of California. Although the town I grew up in has expanded, I am still surrounded by beautiful mountain flora and fauna. Deer wander through yards, and we have endured warnings about bear and mountain lion sightings in the past year. Small birds abound, and I can drive half an hour into the mountains and come upon giant nests built by vultures or eagles.

A popular pastime around here is to relax at one of the nearby rivers. I like to cool off in the water for a few minutes then just lie on my back in the sun, watching eagles soar and drift in the air above me. I am always reminded of a passage in one of Andrew Murray's books, where he describes how the mother eagle teaches her young to fly. She starts by encouraging verbally, but eventually must push her frightened eaglet out of the nest.

Imagine the terror as that little bird begins to plummet toward earth. Then it starts to flap its wings, and after several tries it gets the hang of it. Always the mother flies below, encouraging with her "words" and her presence, but ready to scoop him up on her back if he tires.

I see myself like that eaglet. God encourages me to step out for Him, but sometimes He has to push me out of my comfortable nest. Like the eaglet, I am not abandoned to fly on my own. He continues to encourage me and be there for me to land on when I can go no further.

*Lord, the shadow of Your wings causes me to trust in You. Open my eyes to see You. You satisfy me with Your fullness – Your sufficiency – even when I feel empty. I look forward to drinking from the river of Your pleasures. You have given me the fountain of life. I don't always feel these truths, so remind me often of Your care – especially on the hard days. In Jesus' name, amen.*

# FEEDING ON HIS FAITHFULNESS

*Do not fret because of evildoers,*

*Nor be envious of the workers of iniquity ...*

*Trust in the Lord, and do good;*

*Dwell in the land, and feed on His faithfulness.*

*Delight yourself also in the Lord,*

*And He shall give you the desires of your heart.*

*Commit you way to the Lord, trust also in Him,*

*And He shall bring it to pass.*

*He shall bring forth your righteousness as the light,*

*And your justice as the noonday.*

--Psalm 37:2-6

THE COMFORTING HUSTLE and bustle of life in my daughter's house played out as unbearable confusion to my husband Larry. When we visited, I had to watch for signs of his agitation, especially in the evening. Then we would retreat to a motel for the night. The added work and expense were necessary so that both of us could rest.

Sometimes I grumbled to myself because I now had to pack two suitcases instead of just my own. Larry would not allow me to put his personal items in my suitcase, although I did sometimes sneak in last-minute things. On one occasion I prayerfully determined that I understood my role was to look after his possessions, and grumbling was inappropriate. This was my job.

We managed to get everything Larry needed in his suitcase this time. He slept fairly well, with only a couple of confused awakenings in the night when he tried to go outside to figure out where he was. We had no set agenda the next morning, so there was no need to hurry him. He was no more than normally insistent that he be in charge of his own "stuff," including carrying his own suitcase.

We met family for breakfast. Then we intended to drive the 100 miles to our home. After eating, Larry wanted his dental floss. I opened the back of the car to get out his suitcase, hoping the floss had been packed. But there was no suitcase. I should have watched him more carefully to make sure he put his suitcase in the car, but I obviously had not. Now I was beyond grumbling. I scolded him angrily for insisting on doing something he then neglected to do, causing us to have to drive back to the motel, waste time, money, etc.

I would really like to be consistent. One day I handle setbacks well. The next day they upset me. My faithfulness is spotty at best. But God says just to dwell in the land and feed on His faithfulness. So that's what I will have to do, hoping I'll become more like Him as He takes care of us.

*Father, thank You for Your faithfulness. Forgive me for my lack of consistency. Help me rest in You. In Jesus' name, amen.*

# WILL I EVER FEEL RESTED AGAIN?

*Rest in the Lord, and wait patiently for Him;*

*Do not fret because of him who prospers in his way,*

*Because of the man who brings wicked schemes to pass.*

*Cease from anger, and forsake wrath;*

*Do not fret – it only causes harm ...*

*The Lord knows the days of the upright,*

*And their inheritance shall be forever.*

*They shall not be ashamed in the evil time,*

*And in the days of famine they shall be satisfied.*

--Psalm 37:7-8, 18-19

MY FRIEND JAN took care of her terminally ill husband for what seemed an interminably long time. Night after night she would be up with him as he battled the cancer that finally took his life. Day after day she made the rounds of doctor's appointments and did all the errand running that is involved in caregiving, added to "normal" life. As the days and weeks wore on, she began to wonder how she could continue to function with the small amount of sleep she was able to get per night.

She was learning to rest in the Lord. A catnap here and a quick forty winks there sufficed to get her through each day. Obviously, she was not running on her own strength, but on God's.

We wish circumstances would be better, but they are not. The psalmist says not to fret. It only causes harm. We may think each day is the most important, but God says our inheritance will be forever. That helps to put events in proper perspective. I was often asked to sing the song "One Day at a Time" at the church we attended when my husband was beginning to exhibit symptoms of Alzheimer's Disease. The congregation knew I sang from my heart.

Take each day as God gives it. Don't fret. Wait on God's timing and rest in Him. Know your inheritance will be forever. No matter what happens, you will be satisfied. What wonderful promises in this psalm!

*"One day at a time, Sweet, Jesus! That's all You're asking from me." Help me remember that and just rest and watch You work in our lives. In Your own precious name, amen.*

# YOU ARE NOT FORSAKEN

*The steps of a good man are ordered by the Lord,*

*And He delights in his way.*

*Though he fall, he shall not be utterly cast down;*

*For the Lord upholds him with His hand.*

*I have been young, and now am old;*

*Yet I have not seen the righteous forsaken,*

*Nor his descendants begging bread ...*

*Depart from evil, and do good;*

*And dwell forevermore.*

*For the Lord loves justice,*

*And does not forsake His saints;*

*They are preserved forever.*

--Psalm 37:23-25, 27-28

AFTER OUR FEW years of ministry in Vallecito, God moved us to a miniscule rural town. We always laughed when away from home and someone would ask where we were from. We'd say, "Rail Road Flat," and inevitably they would ask, "Where's that?" Larry usually described the town as "where there ain't no railroad and it sure ain't flat."

We loved the remoteness of our home. We had a small church nearby and neighbors "within shoutin' distance," but few cars, only one small general store, a post office, and an elementary school in town. The quiet nights were occasionally broken by mountain lion screams or coyote yips. We enjoyed watching our neighbor's bison herd crash through the trees on the other side of our fence. Only once did they break through that fence and lumber down to our pond.

Rural life is wonderful when you are in good health. However, as Larry became more and more afflicted with symptoms of Alzheimer's Disease and we began making more frequent visits to doctors and medical testing facilities, that half-hour car trip began to concern me. I had done some research to find a care facility when my father needed one, so I knew we would be extremely limited when such care became necessary for Larry. Suddenly, I felt forsaken. We lived too far from the help we might need.

But God had not forsaken us and He did not allow us to feel like He had. Through definite leading, He brought us back to the town where I grew up, where we found many excellent doctors and a choice of excellent nursing homes. When Larry broke his hip ten months after our move, we had already established the care network we needed. God knew. His timing is always perfect.

*Thank You, Father, that You walk with us, before us, and behind us, preparing the way, guiding us, and even picking up after us! My heart rests in Your care and perfect timing even when my mind feels forsaken. Help me remember You are there and have my best interests at heart.*

# SINS OF THE TONGUE

*I said, "I will guard my ways,*

*Lest I sin with my tongue;*

*I will restrain my mouth with a muzzle,*

*While the wicked are before me."*

*I was mute with silence,*

*I held my peace even from good;*

*And my sorrow was stirred up.*

*My heart was hot within me;*

*While I was musing, the fire burned.*

*Then I spoke with my tongue:*

*Lord, make me to know my end,*

*And what is the measure of my days,*

*That I may know how frail I am.*

*Indeed, You have made my days as handbreadths,*

*And my age is as nothing before You;*

*Certainly every man at his best state is but vapor. Selah*

*--Psalm 39:1-5*

MY NINETY-YEAR-OLD FRIEND Betty frankly admitted that nothing got her into trouble except her tongue. Now I might think that by ninety she would have learned to control that little offender, but obviously it still gave her trouble. I must admit it is my tongue that has gotten me into most of my self-inflicted troubles.

I have a record of tongue offenses in my school report cards. Every quarter the teacher would comment about what a good student I might have been if it were not for all the time I wasted talking to my classmates. I considered those words to be just educators' opinions until a Bible verse got my attention. In Matthew 12:3, Jesus said we are accountable to God for every idle word we speak. Ouch! That's a lot of accountability.

Add to that all my angry retorts, put-downs, complaints, and outbursts – I have a lot to answer for. Repentance brings silence, as David said in Psalm 39:2. And in the silence we can better ponder our frailty and dependence on our loving Lord's grace.

*Gracious Father, Your words are true. Ours are so often selfish, idle, or spiteful. As an old children's chorus asks, help us bridle our lips. Help me realize every thought I have is not so wonderful that it has to be expressed. May the words that I allow to come out of my mouth bring blessing and encouragement to all who hear. Fill me with Your words so that I can pass them on. In Jesus' name, amen.*

# HORRIBLE PITS

*I waited patiently for the Lord; and He inclined to me,*

*And heard my cry.*

*He also brought me up out of a horrible pit,*

*Out of the miry clay,*

*And set my feet upon a rock,*

*And established my steps.*

*He has put a new song in my mouth –*

*Praise to our God'*

*Many will see it and fear,*

*And will trust in the Lord.*

--Psalm 40:1-3

A SANDY AREA in the creek near where I grew up had a reputation for being quicksand. Whenever my friends and I walked through that part of the woods we always reminded each other to stay away from the quicksand. I don't know if it really was quicksand, because we knew better than to test it out. Just the thought of falling into it brought visions of capture by a horrible pit from which rescue might be impossible.

As an adult I have known friends who became bogged down in pits: not actual miry clay or quicksand, but emotional pits of depression. Occasionally, I have experienced depression as well. We can enter a descending spiral of sadness from which there seems to be no rescue. Depression is a horrible pit.

Of course there may be physical reasons for depression, so afflicted people need to stay in touch with their doctors. But there may be spiritual reasons as well – or a combination of both. Elijah was depressed to the point of wanting to die. God provided nutrition, rest, and hope, which raised his spirits to continue the work God had for him to do. We can read his story in 1 Kings 10.

Sometimes we have to wait patiently for God to answer, trusting His timing is always best. But if we take care of the bodies God gave us and continue to spend time in His Word and in fellowship with His people, He will bring us up out of the pit, set us on solid ground, and put a new song in our hearts. An added benefit: we will have stories to tell that will cause many others to fear God and trust in Him.

*Wow, God! I am overawed that You would use my life to be a witness for You. Help me remember that might be one of Your purposes when I go through the low places of my journey. Help me to trust You to get me through the hard stuff. Return Your joy to my heart. In Jesus' name, amen.*

# FINDING GOD'S WILL

*Sacrifice and offering You did not desire;*

*My ears You have opened.*

*Burnt offering and sin offering You did not require.*

*Then I said, "Behold, I come;*

*In the scroll of the book it is written of me.*

*I delight to do Your will, O my God,*

*And Your law is within my heart."*

--Psalm 40:6-8

MY DAUGHTER AND I were on a mountain road on our way to grocery shop. My exhaustion and frustration with caregiving showed. I complained to Laura, ending with, "Why me?"

Laura's answer said it all. "I asked God about that, Mom. I asked, 'Why does my mom have to go through this?' And God said, 'I've prepared her to be the one to take care of my servant Larry.' That's your job, Mom. Your God-given job."

I had no answer. I knew she spoke what God had been trying to say to my own heart. All that I had learned before would now be poured into taking care of this man of God until his dying day.

Knowing God's will puts everything in perspective. I won't say I never complained again or asked the "why" questions, but now I knew the answers.

Determining God's will seems difficult. Theologians have written many books about it. But often the answer is right in front of us. Acknowledge that God Himself has placed us where we are. This is His will. He walks beside us all the way.

*Heavenly Father, thank You for leading me to this place, date, time, and experience. Help me trust You to continue to show me the way. Give me delight in doing Your will. In Jesus' name, amen.*

# TELLING YOUR STORY

*I have proclaimed the good news of righteousness*

*In the great assembly;*

*Indeed, I do not restrain my lips,*

*O Lord, You Yourself know.*

*I have not hidden Your righteousness within my heart;*

*I have declared Your faithfulness and Your salvation;*

*I have not concealed Your lovingkindness and Your truth*

*From the great assembly ...*

*Let all those who seek You rejoice and be glad in You;*

*Let such as love Your salvation say continually,*

*"The Lord be magnified!"*

*But I am poor and needy;*

*Yet the Lord thinks upon me.*

*You are my help and my deliverer;*

*Do not delay, O my God.*

--Psalm 40:9-10, 16-17

MY CHRISTIAN HERITAGE includes old-fashioned churches that had "testimony" meetings on Sunday evenings. As a teenager I was too shy to stand up before the

140

congregation and tell what God had been doing in my life, but I found other people's stories interesting and encouraging. I miss that feature of worship.

Apparently David knew something of the testimony meeting, for he frequently talks about proclaiming good news or praising God aloud in the great assembly. It is good to share what God has done when we come together for worship and fellowship.

Today I tell my "God story" one-on-one with my friends. Or sometimes during small group meetings or Bible studies, something God has done in my life relates to what we are studying. I am no longer too shy to speak up about God's work in my life.

Another way I'm telling the story is by writing. I have written my life story (and those of family members who are no longer with us) and given copies to each of my children and grandchildren. The Christmas I did this, everyone stopped opening presents to begin reading.

Not every person may feel competent to write a publishable book, but I believe everyone should write down his/her life story for descendants to read. Audio and video tapes are another way to pass on the story. What God has done for you should be a major part of your offspring's legacy.


*Thank You, Father, for courage to tell Your story. Thank You for the story to tell, even though living it has often been difficult. Use my story to encourage others to cling to You. For Jesus' sake, amen.*

# WHEN ALL THE WORLD'S AGAINST YOU

*Blessed is he who considers the poor;*

*The Lord will deliver him in time of trouble.*

*The Lord will preserve him and keep him alive,*

*And he will be blessed on the earth;*

*You will not deliver him to the will of his enemies.*

*The Lord will strengthen him on his bed of illness;*

*You will sustain him on his sickbed.*

*The Lord will deliver him in time of trouble.*

*The Lord will preserve him and keep him alive,*

*And he will be blessed on the earth;*

*You will not deliver him to the will of his enemies.*

*The Lord will strengthen him on his bed of illness;*

*You will sustain him on his sickbed.*

*I said, "Lord, be merciful to me;*

*Heal my soul, for I have sinned against You."*

--Psalm 41:1-4

IN DEALING WITH dementia patients, it helps to realize they are simply acting according to what their brains tell them. What else do we have to believe but our own minds? How frightening even to suggest that the mind could be sending wrong signals! But it does.

The caregiver is also subject to mental misfirings. Our minds play strange tricks on us, especially when we are exhausted. Sleep deprivation is a major cause of dementia. Paranoia becomes almost normal under wearisome circumstances.

So sometimes it seems as though the whole world is "out to get us." Nothing goes right. We may feel we are being blamed for everything that goes wrong. At such a time the very soul seems sick.

Exhaustion may be the problem, but even that may be exacerbated by guilt for sins we have not confessed. Physical rest is crucial. Spiritual rest is just as necessary. First John 1:9 says, "If we confess our sins, He is faithful and just to forgive us our sins and to cleanse us from all unrighteousness." That's the first step to spiritual rest. Then we can pray like David, "Heal my soul, for I have sinned against You."

*Lord Jesus, I'm tired. I need both rest and Your supernatural power. Show me anything in my thoughts, words, or acts that might keep me from Your power. Help me rest in You. In Your own name I pray, amen.*

# FAMILIAR SONGS

*As the deer pants for the water brooks,*

*So pants my soul for You, O God.*

*My soul thirsts for God. For the living God.*

*When shall I come and appear before God?*

*My tears have been my food day and night.*

*While they continually say to me,*

*"Where is your God?"*

*When I remember these things,*

*I pour out my soul within me.*

*For I used to go with the multitude;*

*I went with them to the house of God,*

*With the voice of joy and praise,*

*With a multitude that kept a pilgrim feast.*

*--Psalm 42:1-4*

LARRY AND I spent a week at family camp at Forward Bible Conference. The camp directors were also American Missionary Fellowship area administrators. Larry had been an AMF volunteer for many years so, even in his declining mental state, he knew them well enough to be comfortable.

He was not, however, comfortable with the camp music. A young camp trainee had been assigned to lead singing and he chose contemporary songs that we had never heard before. As a musician, I found it challenging and fun to learn new songs, but Larry didn't see it that way at all. He wouldn't even try to sing and he complained about the music loud and long.

I wanted Larry to enjoy all of the camp activities as much as I did, so I prayed about how to help him with the music. Then I realized many of the contemporary songs were simply words of Scripture put to music. In our private devotional times, I began to read these Bible passages and then sing the words for which I had heard the melodies. The first verses of Psalm 42 struck the right note with Larry and he began to try to sing them, first with me and then in the group.

I can't say Larry enjoyed all of the music. Some of it just went too fast for his mind to grasp. But by relating the Bible verses to the music, he could enter in to the worship time. Later, when we attended churches that used contemporary music, I rejoiced to see Larry singing along to these now familiar songs.

*Father, thank You for music. Thank You for Your Word. Thank You for men like David and other psalmists who wrote these words and put them to music thousands of years ago. And thank You for musicians today who take the same words and put them to modern music that appeals to today's generation. Help me look for You in the unfamiliar. In Jesus' name, amen.*

# DEALING WITH DISQUIET

*Why are you cast down, O my soul?*

*And why are you disquieted within me?*

*Hope in God, for I shall yet praise Him*

*For the help of His countenance.*

*O my God, my soul is cast down within me ...*

*The Lord will command His lovingkindness in the daytime,*

*And in the night His song shall be with me —*

*A prayer to the God of my life.*

*I will say to God my Rock,*

*"Why have You forgotten me?..."*

*Why are you cast down, O my soul?*

*And why are you disquieted within me?*

*Hope in God;*

*For I shall yet praise Him,*

*The help of my countenance and my God.*

--Psalm 42:5-6, 8-9, 11

WE WERE GOING through a difficult time. Larry was just beginning the Alzheimer's Disease journey and I could not figure out how to partner with him. Some days I needed to make all the decisions. Other days Larry became offended when I even made suggestions. He had resigned from pastoring and we needed to move but we didn't know where. My prayers often seemed ignored. Had God forgotten us?

In a few months God led us to a new home in a new community where I could continue to serve Him in a local church and Larry would be safe – at least for the present. God hadn't forgotten us. Even though the Alzheimer's roller coaster had begun and continually worsened, my heart was once more encouraged.

The weariness of caregiving sometimes makes us feel uneasy and/or depressed. Even when things are going relatively well, we probably feel apprehensive. "Waiting for the other shoe to fall," my father used to say. And when things are not going well, we sometimes feel God has forgotten us.

Apparently the psalmist felt this way too. I like the way he often starts out lamenting his circumstances. Then it seems he takes time to listen for God's answers and end the psalm with encouraging words. Hope in God! Praise Him! He is our help. He is God and He is still on the throne.

*Thank You, Father, that You are a good and loving God who does not forget Your children. Help me remember that Your timing is best and You will not allow anything in our lives that is not the best for us. I love You, Lord. In Jesus' name, amen.*

# LEAVING A LEGACY

*We have heard with our ears, O God,*

*Our fathers have told us,*

*The deeds You did in their days,*

*In days of old ...*

*For they did not gain possession of the land by their own sword,*

*Nor did their own arm save them;*

*But it was Your right hand,*

*Your arm, and the light of Your countenance,*

*Because You favored them.*

--Psalm 44:1, 3

MY DAUGHTER LAURA and I were driving past a forested area near her home. I remarked, "I used to ride horses with my friend Jackie through those fiends and woods."

Laura was amazed. "I didn't know you rode horses."

"Only every weekend and vacation day of my junior-high years," I laughed.

A few days later we attended a band concert in a local park. "This takes me back to when I was in the drum corps at Hennessy Elementary," I commented.

Again, Laura expressed wonder. "There's a lot you haven't told us about your growing up years," she said.

But there's a lot I have told them, too. I've written a book on my life so that my children and grandchildren can know how God has led me to become His child and then to serve Him. Maybe I need to go back and fill in some details – like horseback riding, friendships, and school activities – but the important things are there. How to become God's child and live in His family are spelled out for them.

I believe everyone should leave a written or taped life story for his or her offspring to read. It is our testimony of how God has gotten us through this life. It marks the path for them to follow. Our written testimony may influence our progeny long after we have left this earth.

*Lord, I haven't done anything by myself. It is Your strong arm that has saved me. Thank You for favoring me. Help me pass on my story for the benefit of my children's children. In Jesus' name, amen.*

# MAIDS IN WAITING

*The royal daughter is all glorious within the palace;*

*Her clothing is woven with gold.*

*She shall be brought to the King in robes of many colors;*

*The virgins, her companions who follow her, shall be brought to You.*

*With gladness and rejoicing they shall be brought;*

*They shall enter the King's palace.*

--Psalm 45:13-15

WHEN I FIRST wrote this I was giving myself a respite from my recliner. A couple of months before that I should have been acting my age during vacation Bible school, but I tried to keep up with the kids and ended up with plantar fasciitis. At first I thought it was Achilles tendonitis. I had this once before – decades ago – so I thought I could doctor myself. But two months, two six-hour plane rides, and an active children's ministry training session later, I finally had to take my limping self to a real doctor.

My primary care doctor believed my self-diagnosis and put me in an orthotic boot. That left me housebound and moving slowly, when I moved at all. Pretty humbling, to say the least. I might have been depressed if it were not for passages of the Bible that told me I am a royal daughter. I will be brought to the King as His pure and beautiful bride in robes of "many colors." We will rejoice together at the marriage feast in Heaven. I am a trophy of His grace.

However, my self-diagnosis was incorrect. When I didn't heal, I was sent on to a podiatrist, who determined that I suffered from plantar fasciitis. The first doctor's prescription would have been partly right, if I had been able to follow it. He said "rest" (which I didn't really do). The foot doctor said, "rest and clunky shoes," which I willingly purchased to alleviate the pain. Only then was I on the way to recovery.

Getting out of the boot, even into clunky shoes, was like getting out of prison. I hope I won't be confined to "clunkies" the rest of my life, but dealing with life's frustrations is preparation for our coming wedding to the heavenly Bridegroom. Like an engaged princess going through the frustrations of preparing for the wedding, life can be wearing and challenging to our patience. We need to look beyond the plain image in the mirrors of our life to see the glories that await those who trust the King of kings for eternal life. Hallelujah!

*Thank You, Father, that this earthly life is not all there is. Thank You for drawing us to Yourself and making a home in heaven for us to enjoy eternally. And thank You for getting us through every day of waiting. In Jesus' name, amen.*

# WHEN GOD REPEATS HIMSELF

*God is our refuge and strength,*

*A very present help in trouble.*

*Therefore we will not fear,*

*Even though the mountains be carried into the midst of the sea;*

*Though its waters roar and be troubled,*

*Though the mountains shake with its swelling … Selah*

*The Lord of hosts is with us;*

*The God of Jacob is our refuge … Selah*

*The Lord of hosts is with us;*

*The God of Jacob is our refuge. Selah*

--Psalm 46:1-3, 7, 11

SOMETIMES I JUST don't get it. That's been a lifelong problem. I don't think it's because I'm stupid. In analyzing myself, I think I've figured out that my problem is that I come to the event with my mind already made up. As a child I would have to hear my mother's directions or corrections several times before I realized she was talking about something other than what I "knew" she was going to tell me.

God has had to deal with me the same way as my mother did. But I don't think I am the only one with this problem, because God repeats Himself in the Bible many times. Apparently, approaching God with an already made-up mind is a human fault that we all need to work on.

This is particularly true in the case of our fears. Trouble too often paralyzes us. Fear blinds us and makes us deaf to God's assurances. That's why it helps us immeasurably to spend time reading calming words from the Bible, especially the Psalms. I have marked and dated many passages that spoke to my heart in my troubled times. Each time I read through the Psalms, God reminds me that He is with me.

Hallelujah!

*Father, God, You know I am a slow learner. Yet You take the time to show me over and over how much You love me and that You are with me in the good times and the bad. Help me trust You. Help me pass this assurance on to the people You send my way. In Jesus' name, amen.*

# SING PRAISES!

*Oh, clap your hands, all you peoples!*

*Shout to God with the voice of triumph!*

*For the Lord Most High is awesome;*

*He is a great King over all the earth ...*

*He will choose our inheritance for us,*

*The excellence of Jacob whom He loves. Selah*

*God has gone up with a shout,*

*The Lord with the sound of a trumpet.*

*Sing praises to our King, sing praises!*

*For God is the King of all the earth;*

*Sing praises with understanding.*

--Psalm 47:1-2, 4-8

I'VE BEEN DEALING with some legal matters lately. Fortunately, my daughter Laura is a licensed paralegal and she reads and understands "legalese." I don't. Even when legal options are explained to me, I seldom see their logic. Some of it makes sense, but a lot of it doesn't.

Often it seems that God is like that too. He tells us to be thankful in every situation (Ephesians 5:20). To me, that appears to be not only impossible, but counterproductive. God also tells us our ways are not His ways (Isaiah 55:8), and I can no more explain that than I can the Trinity. (My only explanation for the Trinity is that, if my finite mind could understand it, He would be a pretty small God. And He isn't.)

However, logical or not, experience has taught me that God's way works. On days when I am really upset, or even depressed, thanking Him calms and raises my spirits. Singing His praises works even better. After all, He knows the end from the beginning, and we are winners with Him. He made us, so He knows what our spirit needs. He is the One who chooses our inheritance for us! He is the Great King in charge of all things.

Understand that and how can you not sing His praises?

*Heavenly Father, God of the universe, help me rest in Your care and sing Your praises whatever the circumstances. In Jesus' name, amen.*

# BACKGROUND MUSIC

*Great is the Lord, and greatly to be praised*

*In the city of our God,*

*In His holy mountain.*

*Beautiful is elevation,*

*The joy of the whole earth,*

*Is Mount Zion on the sides of the north,*

*The city of the great King.*

*God is in her palaces;*

*He is known as her refuge.*

--Psalm 48:1-3

MY FRIEND BEGAN reading a psalm out loud at a ladies' Bible study, when she stopped to say, "That sounds like a song!"

And it was. The words had been put to a modern melody that we sing frequently in our worship services. Many of the psalms are like that. I remember learning the first words of Psalm 48 around a summer campfire to the accompaniment of guitars. That scene comes to mind, and the melody wraps around the words every time I read it.

Most of us realize the psalms were actually written to be sung. Imagine David, the shepherd boy, strumming his harp and singing praises to God in order to keep his flock calm. I don't know how many of those early songs made it to the "hymnbook," but I do know David continued writing all his life. Most, but not all, of the psalms are his compositions. I have often wished we had the tunes to go with them, but our modern melodies are right for us.

I like a quiet house. It helps me concentrate when I am writing. But sometimes I need the encouragement of praise music in the background. Some of the most uplifting tunes are Scripture set to music. The psalmists' poetry has been around for centuries and it still calms the flock of God.

*Great Shepherd, You know our hearts. You know our needs and You have provided for them. Thank You for David (and other writers) through whom You penned words of comfort and encouragement. Thank You for the modern writers who have set whose words to music. Thank You for making me one of Your flock. In Jesus' name, amen.*

# WHAT GOD WANTS FROM US

*"Gather My saints together to Me,*

*Those who have made a covenant with Me by sacrifice."*

*Let the heavens declare His righteousness,*

*For God Himself is Judge ... Selah.*

*Offer to God thanksgiving,*

*And pay your vows to the Most High.*

*Call upon Me in the day of trouble;*

*I will deliver you, and you shall glorify Me."...*

*"Whoever offers praise glorifies Me;*

*And to him who orders his conduct aright*

*I will show the salvation of God."*

--Psalm 50:5-6, 14-15, 23

OUR HEARTS TELL us God wants something from us. We fear His judgment and can't imagine that He could love us. That's why every culture has a set of rules meant to appease its deity. Yet the Bible tells us our good works cannot assure us a place with God (see Ephesians 2:8-9; Romans 6:23).

We can be grateful God doesn't leave us in the dark about what pleases Him. Here in Psalm 50, we learn that sacrifice opens the door. In the New Testament we find out it is Christ's sacrifice on the cross that paid the penalty for our sins and made it possible to have a family relationship with God. Paul said, "Believe on the Lord Jesus Christ, and you will be saved" (Acts 16:31).

That settled, the rest follows out of a heart of love. God tells us exactly what will keep us close to Him: thanksgiving, paying our vows (keeping our word), praising Him, and conducting our lives like a King's child should.

Pleasing God isn't so hard after all, and He has even made a way to get back into fellowship with Him whenever we get off track (which, for me, is at least daily). First John 1:9 ways, "If we confess our sins, He is faithful and just to forgive us our sins, and to cleanse us from all unrighteousness."

I am overawed with the fact that God loves me; that He loved me before I even knew Him, in spite of my totally self-absorbed life. What joy to bask in that love and know He is with me through easy times and hard!

*Loving Father God, thank You for loving me and providing the way for me to be in Your family. Thank You for enriching my life and strengthening me for every task. Thank You for Your comforting, instructing Word. Help me spread the awesome good news about Your love and forgiveness. In Jesus' name, amen.*

# WHEN WE REALLY BLOW IT

*Make me hear joy and gladness,*

*That the bones You have broken may rejoice.*

*Hide Your face from my sins,*

*And blot out all my iniquities.*

*Create in me a clean heart, O God,*

*And renew a steadfast spirit within me ...*

*The sacrifices of God are a broken spirit,*

*A broken and a contrite heart –*

*These, O God, You will not despise.*

--Psalm 51:8-10, 17

I WAS TALKING to a woman who told me God could never forgive her: she was too terrible a sinner. I am so glad God didn't leave out the gory details of the sordid lives of those He calls His own. Think of the apostle Paul who persecuted Christians to prison and to death until God got hold of his heart. Go with Christ through the Gospels and be amazed at the sinners Jesus forgave: tax collectors, adulterers, and political zealots.

The Old Testament is filled with changed lives as well. Here in the Psalms, David included several poems written to God, pleading for forgiveness and restoration. What could David have done to bring on this great load of guilt?

Most people know the story. In a low period of David's kingship, he stayed home from the battle and lazed about the palace. One evening, while walking on the cool palace rooftop, he noticed a young woman bathing in her back yard. Immediately, lust took over and he sent for Bathsheba, whose brave and loyal husband Uriah was out fighting the battle David should have been leading. David seduced her. A few weeks later she sent word to David that she was pregnant.

Adultery would be sin enough to bring shame. But David did not stop there. Instead of confessing the sin, he sent for Uriah, expecting that he would go home to his wife, thus covering David's transgression. However, Uriah's loyalty to the troops in the field kept him from indulging himself, so he refused to go to his home. As a result, David had him executed by the enemy's sword. What a burden of guilt David carried for months until he finally responded to his friend Nathan's accusation with proper repentance. Psalms 32 and 51 are two of the songs that came from his breaking heart.

Did God toss David to the side? Maybe David worried that God would take the crown from him as He had taken it from Saul. The difference was that David repented; Saul did not.

Is there something in my life that I think is too bad for God to forgive? Not if I respond to His love with repentance and contrition. No one is too bad -- or too good -- for God's forgiveness.

*Father, thank You for showing Your love for David so that we can be assured of Your love for us too. In Jesus' name, amen.*

# BUT GOD ...

*But I am like a green olive tree in the house of God;*

*I trust in the mercy of God forever and ever.*

*I will praise You forever,*

*Because You have done it;*

*And in the presence of Your saints*

*I will wait on Your name, for it is good.*

--Psalm 52:8-9

I REMEMBER PRAYING, "Lord, I'm stuck. I've promised to conduct this one-room school as long as they need me here, but I feel like I need to move Larry somewhere closer to medical facilities. I am suddenly homesick for the town where I grew up, but there's no way I can move there or anywhere else. All I can do is wait for You to move, and it doesn't look like anything is going to change very soon. So I wait."

Those facts were true, the outlook seemed bleak. There was no way God could answer, but I prayed and waited anyway. Then it happened. It appeared completely negative at the time. We began planning for the next school year and, one by one, families found there were unable to commit to another year. Three families moved. Another found the commute too difficult to continue. A new family could come only if we provided day care. We were finally left with a single family, and they were willing to go back to home-schooling. It was is if God said, "You're finished here. Go home."

Isaiah 59:1 says, "Behold, the Lord's hand is not shortened, that it cannot save; nor His ear heavy, that it cannot hear." God's timing, as always, was perfect – but that's another story.

Remembering how God intervened in that "impossible" situation helps me rest assured that I am not ever really stuck in the place God has me.

*Father, thank You for leading in my life and for showing me that You are there. I am overawed by Your love for me. In Jesus' name, amen.*

# MAKING THE PSALMS PERSONAL

*So I said, "Oh, that I had wings like a dove!*

*I would fly away and be at rest.*

*Indeed, I would wander far off,*

*And remain in the wilderness. Selah*

*I would hasten my escape*

*From the windy storm and tempest ..."*

*As for me, I will call upon God.*

*And the Lord shall save me.*

*Evening and morning and at noon*

*I will pray, and cry aloud,*

*And He shall hear my voice.*

*He has redeemed my soul in peace from the battle that was against me,*

*For there were many against me.*

*--Psalm 55:6-8, 16-18*

I WAS JOURNALING through the Psalms while we waited for a vacancy in a care home. Here are some of my notes:

"Lord, moving Larry may give me real pain of heart. I trust You to get me through it." – Psalm 55:4

"Help me not to be afraid." – Psalm 55:5

"Yes, Lord; I have wanted to escape. But You haven't allowed that. They need me here. So bring me through without the respite." – Psalm 55:66-7

"Some in the family will surely badmouth me, saying I moved him too soon. Protect me from their words, Lord. Give me the right answers to calm their fears." – Psalm 55:9-11

"Here's a good prayer plan: evening, morning, and noon. I've got morning down, as long as I journal." – Psalm 55:17

A quick reading through a psalm may give a little encouragement, but taking time to apply Scripture to your present circumstance is dynamic. The Bible is a living Word that God is able to use for our current needs. How often have you been amazed by how your Bible reading for the day applied to the problems and blessings before you?

Take time to meditate and apply God's Word to your life.

*Holy Father, I don't understand it, but I love how You meet my needs with Your ancient words. Awesome! Thank You. All day long, bring my thoughts back to what I read in the morning. Let me share them with others and watch You use them there too. In Jesus' name, amen.*

# SAD REMEMBRANCES

*You number my wanderings;*

*Put my tears into Your bottle;*

*Are they not in Your book?*

*When I cry out to You,*

*Then my enemies will turn back;*

*This I know, because God is for me.*

*In God (I will praise His word),*

*In the Lord (I will praise His word),*

*In God I have put my trust;*

*I will not be afraid.*

*What can man do to me?*

--Psalm 56:8-11

I AM FASCINATED by manners and customs of Bible times. Understanding more about them often enables me to understand God's Word more easily. One of the strange ones (to me it seems strange) was the carrying of a small vial on a string around the neck. The vial was used to catch and keep the tears of a friend or family member. A woman did this to show her loved one that she shared her pain. David says that God cares for us as deeply as one who carries our tears in his bottle. God keeps a journal of our troubles. He is there for us.

On those times when I could barely see to drive because of the tears I shed from observing Larry's helplessness in his last days, I thought of God's vial filling up with my tears. How precious to know God is pained with my pain and that His journal is filled with my sorrows as well as my triumphs.

Life is filled with tears? Yes. Sorrows? Yes. But fear? That's not necessary. Notice how David repeats himself (verses 4 and 11) that he has put his trust in God. Man can do nothing to us that God does not allow for our benefit. We can trust Him.

*Abba, Father. I have certainly contributed many tears to Your bottle. Thank You for sharing my sorrow, even though You know the beginning from the end and even though You bring into my life only those things that cause me to become more like Your Son. Help me trust and not be afraid. In Jesus' name, amen.*

# KEEPING VOWS

*Vows made to You are binding upon me, O God;*

*I will render praises to You,*

*For You have delivered my soul from death.*

*Have You not kept my feet from falling,*

*That I may walk before God in the light of the living?*

--Psalm 56:12-13

WHEN THE GOING gets tough, some of us just want out. I have seen sad cases where taking care of a loved one became so overwhelming that the able spouse simply disappeared, either through divorce or simply walking away and letting someone else take over. I will admit to shaking my fist toward Heaven and asking where I could go to resign, but that's as far as God ever let me get with the idea of abdicating my responsibility.

My journal through Psalm 56 has been asking God:

"What vows have I made to You? I have vowed to love, honor, and cherish Larry and help his ministry. Help me keep every part of that vow.

"I have vowed to live an exemplary life as Your daughter, Help me watch my words and actions as I seek to keep this vow."

"I have vowed to raise my children to love and serve You. Make me be aware of when and where I can still influence my children and grandchildren for You."

I have vowed to tithe regularly. May I continue to make that a priority."

"If there are other vows I have made, please remind me.  I praise You for helping me to keep my vows to You."

As a teenager I was negatively impressed by the actions of a neighbor. When the wife became terminally ill, the husband hired another neighbor to help with her care. In a few weeks the husband and neighbor became romantically involved and even carried on their tender conversations in front of the dying wife. I am sure the community gossip impressed me concerning marital vows. Determination to do the right thing keeps us from failing when the going gets tough.

*Father, only You can give the stamina it takes to keep a vow — any vow. Thank You for helping us stay true to our word. Use our faithfulness to honor You and to teach the next generation integrity. In Jesus' name, amen.*

# HANDLING CALAMITIES

*Be merciful to me, O God, be merciful to me!*

*For my soul trust in You;*

*And in the shadow of Your wings I will make my refuge,*

*Until these calamities have passed by.*

*I will cry out to God Most High,*

*To God who performs all things for me.*

*He shall send from heaven and save me;*

*He reproaches the one who would swallow me up. Selah.*

*God shall send forth His mercy and His truth.*

--Psalm 57:1-3

CALAMITY. THAT'S AN old-fashioned word I had to look up. It means "an event that brings destruction and/or loss." A synonym is "disaster."

Our worst calamity was when Larry had to give up driving his pickup. There were other calamities leading up to the loss of his driver's license – frightening times when he pulled out in front of other vehicles; shouting matches as he turned left when I had directed him to go right; scary times when he couldn't find his way home; reports from neighbors who had pulled his pickup out of the ditch while I was at work.

Then there were the arguments when family members suggested it was time for him to give up driving. The worst for Larry was when he got the DMV notice in the mail that his doctor had reported his diagnosis and he must surrender his driver's license to their office within twenty-four hours.

Fortunately I had already gotten beyond being embarrassed by his behavior. When he railed at the DMV clerk, I stepped back and let the clerk handle it. He was told he could protest the ruling and be re-evaluated, and I cooperated, providing transportation to the office for the interview and what comfort I could when the result changed nothing.

When he drove his pickup without a license, I praised God for tattletale neighbors who let me know. When he wouldn't listen to my warnings, God prompted me to call his son, to whom he did listen. I convinced him to sell his pickup, and a friend bought it from him for cash, which satisfied him, at least long enough to remove the pickup from our home. I traded my car for an unfamiliar vehicle that he did not know how to drive.

All of this happened while I prayed for God's direction and refuge. The calamities did pass. We were in the shadow of His wings. God performed all things for us — all the way from Heaven to save us!

*Father, we can't handle calamities. Only You can. What a lesson! Help us remember Your great power when the next calamity falls. In Jesus' name, amen.*

# LONG DISTANCE PRAYERS

*Hear my cry, O God;*

*Attend to my prayer.*

*From the end of the earth I will cry to You,*

*When my heart is overwhelmed;*

*Lead me to the rock that is higher than I.*

*For You have been a shelter for me,*

*A strong tower from the enemy.*

*I will abide in Your tabernacle forever;*

*I will trust in the shelter of Your wings. Selah.*

*--Psalm 61:1-4*

MOTHER SPENT THE Christmas holiday with me, caught a cold, and wanted to go home earlier than we had planned. I drove her home (three hours, one way) and left her in the care of my sister, Joanne. At least I thought I had. A few days later, Joanne called to tell me Mother's cold had turned to pneumonia and Joanne had an ambulance take her to the hospital.

I spent a few days visiting Mother, conferring with her doctor, attempting to organize her checkbook and bills, and finally placing her in a long-term-care facility. Mother's Alzheimer's Disease symptoms worsened dramatically during her hospital stay, but I had to return to my own home before I really felt confident that everything that could have been done for her had been. In my few days overseeing Mother's care, I realized Joanne would be no help. I felt abandoned.

Thus began long distance care. I returned to Mother's home for a few days each month, until I had cleaned and sorted the stacks of clutter. I dealt with her bills and bank account disaster. I listened to her complaints, but then I would have to go back to my own home.

Although God led us to a good care home for Mother, her deteriorating condition and pleas to go home broke my heart. This certainly gave me a lot to worry about, but the very fact that I had no way to control the situation forced me to rest in God. Every time I began worrying about the problems, God seemed to say to me, "Am I not just as present at your mother's side as I am at yours? Trust me to care for her."

Yes, there were still frequent trips to oversee Mother's house and affairs. Yes, I made many phone calls to the care facility to assure them I was concerned about their treatment of my mother. But God is the one who sustained me and freed me from worry. Long distance prayer works.

*Heavenly Father, thank You for being omnipotent. Only You, God, can be everywhere at once. Thank You for the comfort of knowing You care for my loved ones even more than I can do. Help me rest in You. In Jesus' name, amen.*

# SILENT TESTIMONY

*Truly my soul silently waits for God;*

*From Him comes my salvation.*

*He only is my rock and my salvation;*

*He is my defense;*

*I shall not be greatly moved ...*

*My soul, wait silently for God alone,*

*For my expectation is from Him ...*

*Trust in Him at all times, you people;*

*Pour out your heart before Him;*

*God is a refuge for us. Selah.*

--Psalm 62:1-2, 5, 8

BILL'S WIFE FRAN spent most of every day at his bedside. When Bill and Larry were placed in the same room, I wondered how much time I should spend at the care home. I prayed about it. How productive was it to sit and watch a man sleep? If Larry had called out for me when he awoke, that would have influenced my decision. He did not. Nor did he know me most of the times I visited. But Fran's faithfulness spoke to my heart.

I did feel I should visit daily, and the noon meal seemed the best time, for then Larry was most alert and most likely to show an interest in any conversation. As his disease progressed, he needed encouragement to eat, and the care home staff was stretched to the limit with patients who needed help with their meals.

I asked the aides how Larry managed at his other meals, and came to the conclusion that he was able to feed himself at breakfast and supper, probably because he had fewer choices on his plate. The noon meal was dinner, and many times he just couldn't decide where to start. He ate for me when I made choices for him. As his ability to feed himself failed, I eventually had to physically feed him, and finally, all I could do was encourage him to drink his fortified meal.

I did this because I loved the man I had married, even though he had drastically changed. And I did it for myself, so that I could feel I had done all I could to help him. However, several times we shared the table with other patients whose family members did the same, and occasionally a son or daughter would stop by to tell me my faithfulness had encouraged them as well. After Larry's passing, many of the aides told me what a testimony my faithfulness to him had been to them. I can only say the strength came from God.

*Lord, You use us in ways we don't expect as we yield our lives to do Your will. Larry's Bible on the table and his wife at his side spoke volumes. Help me continue to quietly encourage others by allowing You to live through me. In Jesus' name, amen.*

# SEEKING GOD EARLY

*O God, You are my God;*

*Early will I seek You;*

*My soul thirsts for You;*

*My flesh longs for You*

*In a dry and thirst land*

*Where there is no water.*

--Psalm 63:1

THE WALK OF faith is a learning process. It begins with spiritual birth, and then growth continues throughout life. That is in the healthy Christian life. We can short-circuit or even stop the growth process by disobedience, but we risk becoming stunted Christians if we make that choice.

As a young believer I had the idea that God was only interested in major events in my life. I thought I could handle the small problems myself, so I should only bring the big things to God. I soon learned I couldn't handle even the little things. They soon became big things and then I'd turn them over to God – not so much in faith as in desperation. There wasn't anything else to do with them.

When it came to caregiving, I repeated those lessons. I considered myself a reasonably intelligent person. I was sure I could make decisions for my parents or disabled sister. What a shock when I realized I couldn't even decipher the "legalese" on documents I had to sign. And I had no idea whom to trust for help.

My inabilities brought on anxiety until I had to just give the problems to God and trust Him to work them out.

By the time I became my husband's caregiver, I had finally learned to pray about matters from the moment I realized a decision needed to be made. I didn't even wait for my formal quiet time at the beginning or ending of the day. I prayed on my way home from whatever meeting brought up the problem. If a situation needed immediate attention, I prayed right there in the office or hospital room. And God honored those early requests.

*Heavenly Father, thank You for taking all _our_ burdens. Thank You for being concerned with _all_ our needs. Thank You for loving us and delighting in our early requests for Your help. In Jesus' name, amen.*

# SPIRITUAL REFRESHMENT

*I have looked for You in the sanctuary,*

*To see Your power and Your glory.*

*Because Your lovingkindness is better than life,*

*My lips shall praise You.*

*Thus I will bless You while I live;*

*I will lift up my hands in Your name.*

*My soul shall be satisfied as with marrow and fatness,*

*And my mouth shall praise You with joyful lips.*

--Psalm 63:2-5

WHEN LARRY AND I ministered in Vallecito, our little congregation persisted in staying very small. The townspeople were not interested in attending a church. Neither were they interested in getting to know newcomers. We had been there several years when I complained about still feeling like an outsider. The one to whom I complained explained, "They won't consider you one of them until about the fourth generation!"

No wonder I felt starved for fellowship with other Christians. What joy when we moved and became part of a church and community that accepted us! I felt like a desert wanderer who had finally found an oasis. The part that satisfied us most was worship with God's people: singing God's praises together and hearing His Word preached. We soaked it up.

We moved again, and once more I felt somewhat like that desert wanderer. I didn't know how social a person I had become until I found my days filled with the care of my husband whom I could not leave unattended for even a few minutes. I craved intelligent conversation, laughter, and time with God's people.

But I had learned how to satisfy that thirst. God led us to a church that took us in, fed us, and poured spiritual water on our souls. Larry's increasing Alzheimer's symptoms only heightened his desire to meet with God's people as well. Among the people of God I could relax and drink in God's goodness. Their hugs sustained us. We looked for God in the sanctuary and found his power and glory.

*Almighty God, I praise You for quenching my spiritual thirst with the music and words of the saints. I praise You for the sense of calm that times of worship bring to Your hurting people. May I never stray from assembling with Your people and reaping the benefits there. In Jesus' name, amen.*

# THOSE SLEEPLESS NIGHTS

*When I remember You on my bed,*

*I meditate on You in the night watches.*

*Because You have been my help,*

*Therefore in the shadow of Your wings I will rejoice.*

*My soul follows close behind You;*

*Your right hand upholds me.*

--Psalm 63:6-8

WHEN MY CHILDREN were babies, I could sleep like the proverbial rock. However, when Larry developed dementia, my sleep pattern changed drastically. In the early months, when he became a night wanderer, I had trouble going to sleep because I worried that he would get up and go outside without my waking. I soon realized that would not happen, because his every movement and sound alerted me.

Occasionally I slept lightly until he got up. If it was just a bathroom trip, I could usually go back to sleep. But if his mind was playing tricks on him and we had to spend time trying to find something he thought had been stolen from him, by the time I got him resettled, my mind was too awake to settle myself down.

I could read, but the light would bother Larry, and reading woke me up even more. So I lay in bed, staring into the dark, wishing for sleep. My thoughts naturally turned to God, first of all asking Him to help me go back to sleep. Sometimes sleep would come, but often I would have a long talk with my Father, something I rarely had time to do during the day. The night watches became precious meeting-with-God times for me.

Nighttime blocks out the cares of the day. In the stillness we can look back and thank God for the way He helped us during the day. We can rejoice in His protection (the shadow of His wings). We can ask Him to show us a better way to handle something that didn't go well. We can ask for help to follow closer to Him. We can rest in the fact that His right hand holds us up.

Larry has been gone for some time now. But those habits formed in years of caregiving remain with me. I still wake up in the middle of the night and, when I don't go right back to sleep, I know what to do with my mind. My Father waits to talk to me.

*Loving Father, thank You for those quiet moments we have together. Help me not to fret, but to spend time with You, knowing that You will give me the rest I need. Help me follow You ever more closely and trust in Your care. In Jesus' name, amen.*

# IT'S NOT ALL ABOUT YOU – OR YOUR LOVED ONE

*Blessed is the man You choose, And cause to approach You,*

*That he may dwell in Your courts.*

*We shall be satisfied with the goodness of Your house,*

*Of Your holy temple.*

*By awesome deeds in righteousness You will answer us,*

*O God of our salvation,*

*You who are the confidence of all the ends of the earth,*

*And of the far-off seas;*

*Who established the mountains by His strength,*

*Being clothed with power;*

*You who still the noise of the seas, The noise of their waves,*

*And the tumult of the peoples.*

*They also who dwell in the farthest parts are afraid of Your signs;*

*You make the outgoings of the morning and evening rejoice.*

--Psalm 65:4-8

THE MORE I deal with family problems, the more frustrated I become. The more I think about my loved one's needs, the more depressed I am. Focusing on the problems, or even the resolution of those problems, brings anxiety. I tend to ask, "Now what?" or "What else can go wrong?"

Those are not helpful questions. I would do better to step back and realize I am just a small part of God's great plan. It's not all about me. It's not even all about the person (or persons) God has given me to care for.

It's really all about God and His program. The wonderful result of this realization is that, when we focus on what God has done and is still doing and will do in the future, those frustrations, depressions, and anxieties fade. No, they don't disappear but, like the blurred background of a sharp close-up photo, they take their rightful place outside the realm of our focus.

The old gospel song said it well: "Turn your eyes upon Jesus; look full in His wonderful face, and the things of earth will grow strangely dim, in the light of His glory and grace." Psalm 65 is a good reminder of our powerful creator and Savior.

*Great God and Father, thank You for this reminder of Your control over all You created – including me and all those people You have put into my life. Help me focus on You, and not on earthly problems. Give me wisdom and discernment, but help me rest in You. In Jesus' name, amen.*

# WHEN WE'RE CORNERED

*Come and see the works of God;*

*He is awesome in His doing toward the sons of men.*

*He turned the sea into dry land;*

*They went through the river on foot.*

*There we will rejoice in Him.*

*He rules by His power forever;*

*His eyes observe the nations;*

*Do not let the rebellious exalt themselves. Selah.*

--Psalm 66:5-7

GOD DELIGHTS TO  work miracles when we are completely helpless. I used to pray with specific solutions in mind to the problems that I faced. Gradually I came to realize God rarely answered the way I thought He would. His way was always infinitely better.

Sometimes I couldn't even think of a way out. When I felt we needed to move to a location that offered more choices for Larry's care, I had no idea how that could come about. I had promised to teach in that one-room school as long as I was needed. The youngest child was in the first grade. That meant at least seven more years.

Yet God put in my heart a yearning to return to my hometown. Seven years to be homesick? Impossible. Seven more years of Alzheimer's Disease? Larry would need more care than I could give him in a much shorter time than that.

All I could pray was, "Help!"

Pray -- then watch: as God dried up the student body just as surely as he dried up the Red Sea. Who would have expected all those families to move before the next school year? Equally amazing to me was the great sorrow I felt every time I returned from a visit to my hometown. It was my first experience with homesickness. As surely as God closed the door on Egypt for the Israelites, he closed the door on Rail Road Flat for us.

I'm just thankful we didn't have to wander around in the wilderness before entering the Promised Land!

*Father, thank You for Your leading. Keep me so in touch with You that I know Your direction for my life every day. Thank You for the miracles that brought me thus far, and the miracles You are going to work for me all the way to heaven. In Jesus' name, amen.*

# GOD'S TESTS

*Oh, bless our God, you peoples!*

*And make the voice of His praise to be heard,*

*Who keeps our soul among the living,*

*And does not allow our feet to be moved.*

*For You, O God, have tested us;*

*You have refined us as silver is refined.*

*You brought us into the net;*

*You laid afflictions on our backs.*

*You have caused men to ride over our heads;*

*We went through fire and through water;*

*But You brought us out to rich fulfillment.*

--Psalm 66:8-12

TESTING AND REFINING: are they the same?

There is an aspect of testing that is used in industry. Psalm 66 says we are tested like silver in the refinery. Precious metals, like silver, are super-heated, and then the impurities that float to the top are skimmed off. The process is repeated until there are no more impurities. In ancient times, the refiner continued the process until the metal was so pure that he could see his reflection in it.

What a picture of God's testing our lives. He wants to see His reflection in us. That won't happen in a life without trials or a life that doesn't give up the impurities that hinder us.

Going through testing? God wants to teach you some important lessons. Pay attention to what you still need to learn. Got trials? That's assurance that you're precious and God wants to make you more like Himself.

*Heavenly Father, I am amazed that You love me so much that You want to purify me and make me like You. Make me willing to be willing to do Your will. Show me what I need to learn. I trust You to be with me through the fire. In Jesus' name, amen.*

# UNANSWERED PRAYERS

*Come and hear, all you who fear God,*

*And I will declare what He has done for my soul.*

*I cried to Him with my mouth,*

*And He was extolled with my tongue.*

*If I regard iniquity in my heart,*

*The Lord will not hear.*

*But certainly God has heard me;*

*He has attended to the voice of my prayer.*

*Blessed be God,*

*Who has not turned away my prayer,*

*Nor His mercy from me!*

--Psalm 66:16-20

I AM A student at heart, so it is easy for me to take time to read and study God's Word. It thrills me to hear Him speak to me through the words of the writers. Reading the Psalms especially brings comfort and encouragement.

However, spending time in prayer has always been a problem for me. I want to read or study and then get up and get busy. I always feel as if I am deficient on the prayer end of my spiritual life.

My answer to this deficit was to do a word study on prayer. Maybe I could find the incentive to pray more. Maybe there was a biblical formula.

I found formulas all right. One of them is right here in Psalm 6. "If I regard iniquity in my heart, the Lord will not hear." As I thought about that, I realized that sometimes unconfessed sin was a root of prayerlessness. When I changed the topics of my conversation with God to adoration... confession... thanksgiving... supplication, I found the amount of time spent in His presence increased.

God wants our conversation: and conversation is a two-way action. We need to hear from Him in His Word, meditate, and tell Him our thoughts. What a promise David gives us: He (God) has heard and has not turned away my prayer.

*Thank You, Father, for loving me so much that You want to spend time with me. Help me set aside more time for prayer. I want to know Your heart. In Jesus' name, amen.*

# YOUR STORY

*God be merciful to us and bless us,*

*And cause His face to shine upon us, Selah*

*That Your way may be known on earth,*

*Your salvation among all nations.*

*Let the peoples praise You, O God;*

*Let all the peoples praise You.*

*Oh, let the nations be glad and sing for joy!*

*For You shall judge the people righteously,*

*And govern the nations on earth. Selah*

*--Psalm 67:1-4*

MY PASTOR TOLD the youth group I belonged to that each person is either a mission field or a missionary. Those who haven't accepted Christ as Savior and Lord are the mission field; those who have, the missionaries.

Someone has said all believers must witness for Jesus — and sometimes we need to use words. I take that to mean my life is a witness (for good or for bad, for other people do keep a critical eye on all who profess to be Christians) and only sometimes do I need to say anything about it.

As a caregiver, you are watched. Witnessing is not your primary purpose. Taking care of your loved one is. Nonetheless, your story is out there for the world to read. As we walk close to God in our daily lives, those without faith may be drawn to our Savior by what they see. Since Larry's passing I have been amazed at the number of people who have mentioned to me how blessed they were by my care of him. I had no idea at the time that I was a blessing to anyone, including Larry. The secret is just to keep walking with God, leaning on Him.

*Father, thank You for allowing me to reflect Your light. I am overawed that You would choose to use this dim lamp. Keep me close so Your light can continue to flow through me. Use our story to draw other people closer to You. In Jesus' name, amen.*

# OUR OWN GOD

*Let the peoples praise You, O God;*

*Let all the peoples praise You.*

*Then the earth shall yield her increase;*

*God, our own God, shall bless us.*

*God shall bless us,*

*And all the ends of the earth shall fear Him.*

--Psalm 67:5-7

LUCILLE TOLD HER hairdresser, Shirley, all the great things God was doing for her lately. She went through a time of suffering – financially, in her marriage, and health-wise. Lucille praised God for the hope she had in him, and told about her many answers to prayers.

After Lucille left the shop, Shirley turned to a fellow hair-dresser and said, "Huh! She must think she's really something if she thinks God would actually do all that for her."

Obviously, Shirley had no concept of the Savior God who wants a relationship with His children. Lucille's humble account of God's blessing sounded like empty bragging to Shirley.

The Bible overflows with instances of God's intervention in the lives of His people. John 3:16 is one of the first verses many of us memorize. It takes us from God's love for the whole world right down to the individual "whoever" who places his/her trust in Christ for eternal salvation.

Throughout the Psalms – the whole Bible, even – God reminds us He loves us each individually. What an encouragement, especially in times of trial, to know that "God, our own God, shall bless us!"

*Father God, I don't understand how You can single out each one of us and suit our blessings and interventions to our own unique needs. But You can and You do because You love us. Thank You for loving me and showing me You are right here with me through all the hard times as well as the easy ones. Remind me of Your presence. In Jesus' name, amen.*

# WIDOWS AND ORPHANS

*Let God arise …*

*A father of the fatherless, a defender of widows,*

*Is God in His holy habitation.*

*God sets the solitary in families;*

*He brings out those who are bound into prosperity;*

*But the rebellious dwell in a dry land.*

--Psalm 68:1, 5-6

I TRIED VERY hard to be a "good Christian wife". I took personally Paul's instruction to wives to be submissive and respectful to their husbands. I actually enjoyed leaving the hard decisions and the responsibility of providing for the family to my husband Bud.

But when Bud passed away, my world was shaken. I remember coming home from the hospital where they had tried unsuccessfully to revive him. I recall going to bed alone and praying, "God, it's just You and me now. I have no one else to take care of me, make my decisions for me, and provide for my needs as well as my children's needs." I realized I had allowed my husband to stand between me and God. Now I had to learn to depend on my heavenly Father for myself.

I was thankful that Bud had turned over the household finances and files to me in the months before his passing. I became aware of the difficulties other widows faced who had not learned how to take care of "paperwork." Praise God for giving me a husband who cared about my life even as his own was ebbing away!

Still there were problems I did not know how to solve. Right away I faced the expense of Bud's funeral arrangements. Although he had set up insurance to cover that, the funds were not available immediately. Besides that, his salary was in transition to retirement, and the state office did not seem to know how to change its status to survivor benefits. The mortuary would not take care of his burial without payment in advance.

Another problem: my son had wrecked my car the night before his father's death. I had no transportation and no money to acquire another car.

Did God know my needs? Could He meet them? Of course. Although God was the only person I told about my lack of finances, He sent a Christian friend who loaned me all I needed to carry me until my own funds were available. This same friend even loaned me his T-Bird, and later another friend loaned me his car until I could buy a replacement.

*Gracious Father, being alone is scary. Thank You for always being with me. Thank You for the seemingly insurmountable problems of life, for they just show off Your great power and love. Increase my faith by reminding me of how You have taken care of me in the past.  In Jesus' name, amen.*

# COUNT YOUR BLESSINGS

*Blessed be the Lord,*

*Who daily loads us with benefits,*

*The God of our salvation! Selah*

*Our God is the God of salvation;*

*And to God the Lord belong escapes from death ...*

*Your God has commanded your strength;*

*Strengthen, O God, what You have done for us ...*

*Sing to God, you kingdoms of the earth;*

*Oh, sing praises to the Lord. Selah*

--Psalm 68:19-20, 28, 32

GOD'S WAYS ARE infinitely different – higher – than our ways. This is especially evident in the way we think. When we are overwhelmed, overburdened, and sad, God says joy will come as we sing His praises and thank Him for our blessings.

We may not think we have anything for which to be thankful, but there are always blessings to be found. Some days I have to start very small with such things as the fact that I'm still breathing or I have a roof over my head. As I thank God for what seems like mundane, general possessions, He brings to mind other blessings for which I can thank Him.

When I am so overwhelmed that I don't know how to pray, I remember God already knows my needs. The Holy Spirit promises to pray for me "with groanings which cannot be uttered" (Romans 8:26). In the midst of the darkest days, I still know how to thank God for His presence and His gifts. That's where I start.

The old hymn writer had it right: "Count your blessings, name them one by one, and it will surprise you what the Lord has done." To raise your spirits, raise your praise.

*Loving Father, thank You for always being there for me and my loved one. Thank You for life, and the awesome responsibilities You are enabling me to undertake. Open my eyes to all Your gifts to me, that I may embrace them and thank You for them. Thank You for ….*

# WHEN I AM WEAK

*To Him who rides on the heaven of heavens, which were of old!*

*Indeed, He sends out His voice, a mighty voice.*

*Ascribe strength to God,*

*His excellence is over Israel,*

*And His strength is in the clouds.*

*O God, You are more awesome than Your holy places.*

*The God of Israel is He who gives strength and power to His people.*

*Blessed be God!*

*--Psalm 68:33-35*

TRUE TO FORM for Alzheimer's Disease patients, Larry vehemently denied he had a problem. He had many excuses for his memory lapses and confusion. When the doctor's diagnosis finally penetrated Larry's thinking, he turned to another way out: God would take away the Alzheimers Disease! A few weeks later he began telling everyone who would listen that God had healed him. He'd prayed about the problem at bedtime, and woke up in the middle of the night to what felt like a sharp whack on the back of his head. Result: he no longer had Alzheimer's Disease!

I certainly wished and prayed that it might be so, but obviously it was not. We talked about how God dealt with illnesses. Larry, after all, was a retired pastor. He'd studied and even preached on these things. I repeatedly brought up the subject of Paul's acceptance of his "thorn in the flesh." I would ask, "Isn't God's grace enough?" (See 2 Corinthians 12:9). Larry would not respond. He just returned to the story of his "miraculous healing."

Eventually, God's grace was enough for Larry. During the process of caring for him, I learned God's grace was enough for both of us – or the whole family – to get through this. Many times I felt powerless. Those were the times God's strength rescued us. With the apostle Paul I learned to say, "When I am weak, then I am strong," for His strength is best observed in our weakness (2 Corinthians 12:9-10).

One of the first new songs we learned at Abundant Life Church was "His Grace is Enough for Me." Singing it, I felt an extra hug from my heavenly Father, who continues to be enough.

*Gracious Father, You are enough. Your strength is made perfect in weakness. Thank You that Larry knows that now, and I'm still seeing it, day by day. Help me continue to lean on You. In Jesus' name, amen.*

# THAT PESKY NIGHTMARE

*Save me, O God! For the waters have come up to my neck.*

*I sink in deep mire, Where there is no standing;*

*I have come into deep waters, Where the floods overflow me.*

*I am weary with my crying; My throat is dry;*

*My eyes fail while I wait for my God ...*

*But as for me, my prayer is to You,*

*O Lord, in the acceptable time;*

*O God, in the multitude of Your mercy,*

*Hear me in the truth of Your salvation.*

*Deliver me out of the mire, And let me not sink;*

*Let me be delivered from those who hate me, And out of the deep waters.*

*Let not the floodwater overflow me, Nor let the deep swallow me up;*

*And let not the pit shut its mouth on me.*

--Psalm 69:1-3, 1-15

WE'VE ALL HAD the nightmare where we are trying to run away from something and our feet won't move. It's as if they are stuck in quicksand or thick mud. I try to run but I wake up gasping and with my heart racing.

In the midst of the most difficult days of caregiving, I felt like I was wide awake in the midst of such a nightmare. There seemed to be no relief. Circumstances kept getting worse. Like the psalmist, I became weary with my crying, my throat dry from calling out to God, and my eyes failing as I waited on God's timing.

But hopeless? Never. Like David, we can rest assured that our prayers are heard and God will act at the right time. He has mercy. He has salvation. He will deliver.

*Thank You, Father, for Your perfect timing, even when it doesn't seem quick enough for me. Help me rest in You and know that even on the days I cannot see You, You are still there. Penetrate the mind of my loved one with that truth. In Jesus' name, amen.*

# THE PRISONER OF THE LORD

*But I am poor and sorrowful;*

*Let Your salvation, O God, set me up on high.*

*I will praise the name of God with a song,*

*And will magnify Him with thanksgiving.*

*This also shall please the Lord better than an ox or bull,*

*Which has horns and hooves.*

*The humble shall see this and be glad;*

*And you who seek God, Your hearts shall live.*

*For the Lord hears the poor,*

*And does not despise His prisoners.*

--Psalm 69:29-33

MANY DAYS I have felt trapped in my home, a virtual prisoner because I had to curtail my activities to take care of my husband's condition. I wanted to socialize, but Larry was not up to it. Or I was not up to dealing with what his words or actions might cause or the resulting agitation that was sure to result. It was easier to stay home.

Not that home was a refuge from conflict. During Larry's agitated times, I often spent whole days and most of the nights trying to calm him. My patience was tortured, to say the least.

In my few quiet moments, I would turn to God's Word for comfort and direction. Often I did word studies on whatever currently troubled me. When I felt imprisoned, I looked up the word "prison" and its derivatives. What an encouragement to read Paul's letters, many of them written from a real prison. The astonishing thing? Although Paul was imprisoned by the Roman government, he called himself the prisoner of the Lord. Paul accepted his confinement as the place in the world where Jesus wanted him to be.

So I too can consider my position as a prisoner of the Lord. I'm doing this – whatever it is – for Jesus. I may be poor and sorrowful, but God's salvation has set me up on high. I can praise and thank Him, for He hears the poor and does not despise His prisoners!

*Lord Jesus, I am Your prisoner. I am honored to serve You. Help me remember that whatever I am asked to do, I am doing it for You. May I feel Your arms around me, especially when I feel poor and sorrowful. If this should be an encouragement to others, I am even more blessed. In Jesus' name, amen.*

# UNWANTED HELP

*Make haste, O God, to deliver me!*

*Make haste to help me, O Lord!*

*Let them be ashamed and confounded*

*Who seek my life;*

*Let them be turned back and confused*

*Who desire my hurt.*

*Let them be turned back because of their shame,*

*Who say, "Aha, aha!"*

--Psalm 70:1-3

WHEN LARRY WAS diagnosed with Alzheimer's Disease, I dreaded telling some of my friends. I knew them well enough to know they would offer us a multitude of "remedies" and insist that I try them. I was right. I determined I would not allow Larry to become a "guinea pig" to test the latest medical guesses.

I spent much time in prayer considering which doctors' and friends' suggestions had worth. God reminded me of simple logic. If the suggested remedy had real value, the newspapers and TV newscasts would be shouting its praises to the world. In most cases I chose not to give him what friends suggested, and I researched as thoroughly as I could the new medications offered by his doctors.

As a result I often had to explain to meddling friends and family why I was not taking care of him the way they thought I should. Sometimes they were convinced. Often they continued to harass me with their strong "suggestions." I began to see them more as our enemies than our friends.

No, I did not pray a curse on them as David does his enemies in Psalm 70; but, when the phone rang and I discovered my caller was one of these well-meaning friends, I often sent up that quick plea for God to make haste to deliver me.

*Loving Father, thank You for my many friends who accept me as I am and do not force their opinions on me. Thank You for giving me wisdom in areas where I have no expertise, and for vindicating my decisions. Thank You for being my true Friend. In Jesus' name, amen.*

# THE ADVANTAGE OF BEING HELPLESS

*Let all those who seek You rejoice and be glad in You;*

*And let those who love Your salvation say continually,*

*"Let God be magnified!"*

*"But I am poor and needy;*

*Make haste to me, O God!*

*You are my help and my deliverer;*

*O Lord, do not delay.*

--Psalm 70:4-5

I NOW RECOGNIZE what an angry person I was in high school. I know I didn't consider the reasons, but frustration ruled my life. I wanted everything to be perfect, and things were far from perfect in my home. So I tried to make everything perfect at school. That worked in the academic classes. It did not work for me in physical education and home economics classes.

One day I failed (again) at a sewing project. My friend Betty belonged to the same home economics class, and she could see that I was frustrated to the point of anger. She tried to calm me by quoting Romans 12:21: "Be not overcome of evil, but overcome evil with good" (KJV). Just pondering the impossibility of that statement calmed me down until the bell rang, ending the class.

However, the words would not go away. I kept thinking about them throughout the week. On Wednesday evening I attended a mid-week prayer meeting with my boyfriend, unconsciously still looking for how to overcome evil with good. The expressions of worship and peace on the hymn singers' faces at that meeting nudged me a step closer to the answer. I went home that evening and got on my knees in my bedroom. "Lord, I can't do this myself. If I'm going to be a Christian, You will have to make it possible."

God can't save us if we don't admit we need to be saved. He can't fill our hands if we keep them full of worthless trinkets. When I think I can "handle this myself," that's when I fail. He is the only One who can help and deliver. No wonder we can say, "Let God be magnified!"

*Lord, thank You for opening my eyes to my need for You. Thank You for allowing me to fail early in life, so that I would learn to depend on You throughout all the hard times that have followed. I trust You and You alone to carry me all the way to Heaven. I praise Your name – in Jesus' name, amen.*

# THE DASH OF LIFE

*In You, O Lord, I put my trust; Let me never be put to shame ...*

*For You are my hope, O Lord God;*

*You are my trust from my youth.*

*By You I have been upheld from birth;*

*You are He who took me out of my mother's womb.*

*My praise shall be continually of You ...*

*Do not cast me off in the time of old age;*

*Do not forsake me when my strength fails ...*

*O God, You have taught me from my youth;*

*And to this day I declare Your wondrous works.*

*Now also when I am old and gray headed,*

*O God, do not forsake me,*

*Until I declare Your strength to this generation,*

*Your power to everyone who is to come.*

*--Psalm 71:1, 5-6, 9, 17-18*

HE WANTED IT simple, so I made it as simple as possible. His headstone reads: Larry E. Saunders, 1926—2008. Observe: Larry's whole life is contained in that dash between the dates 1926 and 2008. The apostle James says we are but a vapor and, compared to eternity, that's accurate.

I have written the story of some of Larry's life. There's no way I could capture all of his eighty-one-and-a-half years. In his early teens he heard about the way to be sure of spending eternity with God, and he put his trust in Christ's work on the cross for him. From then on he knew God's direction in his life. He went first to a Bible institute for training, then to the pastorate, a faithful marriage partner, and secular employment. Then, when he lost his beloved wife, he went on to another marriage, and back again to the pastorate.

I don't know if Larry ever felt the need to pray that God would not cast him off. I know he experienced great loss when Alzheimer's Disease cut short his ability to pastor or teach Bible classes. Yet God had not forsaken him. To the last month of his life he still continued singing God's praises and quoting Scripture to those around him. He bore a testimony for God to the very end.

I want that little dash between my birth and death dates to proclaim God's faithfulness as well.

*Loving Father, You are always faithful. I know You will not forsake me when my strength fails. Like Larry, let my life declare Your strength to this generation and the ones to follow. May they see Your power through me. In Jesus' name, amen.*

# GOD'S ANSWER TO TROUBLES

*Also Your righteousness, O God, is very high,*

*You who have done great things; O God, who is like You?*

*You, who have shown me great and severe troubles,*

*Shall revive me again,*

*And bring me up again from the depths of the earth.*

*You shall increase my greatness,*

*And comfort me on every side ...*

*Also with the lute I will praise You –*

*And Your faithfulness, O my God!*

*To You I will sing with the harp,*

*O Holy One of Israel.*

*My lips shall greatly rejoice when I sing to You,*

*And my soul, which You have redeemed.*

*My tongue also shall talk of Your righteousness all the day long ...*

--Psalm 71:19-24

PSALM 71 REMINDS me of Psalm 23. In Psalm 23 we are told we walk through only the shadow of death. Why fear a mere shadow? Here in Psalm 71 the psalmist says God shows us great and severe troubles. We may think we're in deep trouble, but God says it's only a picture. I'm not afraid of pictures, are you?

However, the picture can take us to great depths – bog us down in the mire, so to speak. Even then, God will bring us up. He promises to increase our greatness – we who never even thought we had any greatness. He comforts us on every side. I take that to mean that even in our emotional life we can become overwhelmed through constant caregiving and lack of sleep. He Himself is our comfort.

No wonder we can praise Him with music and by telling others what He is doing in our lives. When concerned friends and family ask how we are doing, this is our opportunity to share the rejoicing we glean from watching God work in our lives.

*Comforting Father, thank You for being there for me. Remind me daily of Your presence. Keep me praising You on even the hardest days. Help me share the joy. In Jesus' name, amen.*

# THE CRIES OF THE NEEDY

*For He will deliver the needy when he cries,*

*The poor also, and him who has no helper.*

*He will spare the poor and needy,*

*And will save the souls of the needy.*

*He will redeem their life from oppression and violence;*

*And precious shall be their blood in His sight ...*

*Blessed be the Lord God, the God of Israel,*

*Who only does wondrous things!*

*And blessed be His glorious name forever!*

*And let the whole earth be filled with His glory.*

*Amen and amen.*

--Psalm 72:12-14, 18-19

WHAT DO YOU need? When I hear the word "needy," I immediately think of poor people living out of their cars or sleeping under bridges and in parks in my town. That's real physical need.

When I personalize the word, it may mean a need for physical healing for an ailment, either mine or a loved one's. In the caregiver's life, it often means a need for sleep, or respite from the 24/7 grind. (And yes, it is a grind even when done out of love.)

One need can lead to another. Lack of rest leads to lack of time to spend in God's Word. That leads to lack of spiritual direction and feeling alienated from God, who is our source of power. It can also lead to lack of discernment and wisdom in making crucial decisions. Who know what needs those wrong decisions can precipitate?

But David says God will deliver the needy when he cries. He will spare the poor and needy. He will save the souls of the needy. God knows all our needs. He yearns for our fellowship, so He waits on us to cry out to him for help.

*Loving Father, thank You for being able to meet my needs and for wanting to meet them. You know what my needs are this very moment. Give me direction and relief. Help me bless Your name for the wondrous things You are even now doing for my loved one and myself. In Jesus' name, amen.*

# JEALOUSY

*Truly God is good to Israel,*

*To such as are pure in heart.*

*But as for me, my feet had almost stumbled;*

*My steps had nearly slipped.*

*For I was envious of the boastful,*

*When I saw the prosperity of the wicked ...*

*Until I went into the sanctuary of God;*

*Then I understood their end.*

--Psalm 73:1-3, 17

SOMETIMES, SON, THE only thing that makes me think you belong to God is the fact that you don't seem to get away with anything. Your friends don't get caught, but you do. That's a good sign."

Where did I get that idea? I must have been reading Asaph's psalm, where he starts out with how prosperous wicked people seem to be. Here I am, stumbling around, trying to do what's right. Then I look at my neighbor who makes no pretense of following God, and he's winning the lottery or defying the law and getting away with it. It looks like he doesn't have a care in the world. Like, Asaph, I'm confused -- and jealous.

The apostle Paul said, "If in this life only we have hope in Christ, we are of all men the most pitiable: (1 Corinthians 15:19). I tend to focus my mind on the here-and-now, but this life is just the training ground for the next. God is using our trials to grow us to be more like His Son and prepare us for our eternal home. The ungodly don't have anything to prepare for. This is all the heaven they have.

I like what Asaph said about where he was when he began to understand. He went into the sanctuary of the Lord. That's one more reason to make the extra effort to meet with God's people as frequently as we can.

*Bounteous Father, open my eyes to the blessing You have poured out on me. Close them to the things I might worry about. Keep reminding me of Your long-range goal in my life. Keep teaching me and preparing me for my home in heaven. Thank You that the blessings of eternity are forever. In Jesus' name, amen.*

# THERE IS NONE LIKE HIM

*You divided the sea by Your strength;*

*You broke the heads of the sea serpents in the waters.*

*You broke the heads of Leviathan in pieces,*

*And gave him as food to the people inhabiting the wilderness.*

*You broke open the fountain and the flood:*

*You dried up mighty rivers.*

*The day is Yours, the night also is Yours;*

*You have prepared the light and the sun.*

*You have set all the borders of the earth;*

*You have made summer and winter ...*

*Oh, do not let the oppressed return ashamed!*

*Let the poor and needy praise Your name.*

--Psalm 74:13-17, 21

WHERE DO WE get the confidence to know God can and will perform all that we need? He knew we would need that confidence. He inspired the psalmist to tell of His exploits, exhibiting strength and power far greater than that of any human. Picture Him dividing the sea, breaking sea serpent heads, creating the flood, or (on the other hand) drying up mighty rivers. He rules both day and night. He controls the shorelines. He directs the seasons and their climate. No man – no government – can do those things.

We the oppressed who trust in Him will not be sorry we did so. We the poor and needy will praise His name.

*Omnipotent Father, thank You for the assurances from Your own Word that You can and will take care of Your people. Thank You for taking care of my loved one and me. Thank You that we are safe in Your arms – certainly not safe anywhere else. Help me remember that, Lord. In Jesus' name, amen.*

# THANKSGIVING AND HUMILITY

*"I said to the boastful,*

*'Do not deal boastfully,'*

*And to the wicked, 'Do not lift up the horn.*

*Do not lift up your horn on high;*

*Do not speak with a stiff neck.'"*

*For exaltation comes neither from the east*

*Nor from the west nor from the south.*

*But God is the Judge;*

*He puts down one,*

*And exalts another.*

--Psalm 75:4-7

PART OF THE procedure for publishing my book, *Life Lessons for Caregivers,* was to fill out a huge questionnaire about my accomplishments, activities, and awards. In other words it's all about me, me, me. I complained about this to a friend the other day, asking her to pray that I not begin believing my own press.

It is so easy to look at ourselves and think we are something special. Pride moves in at the least opening. Perhaps that is why God never lets me get too far before I fall flat on my face, unless, of course, I am depending on Him for strength and wisdom. With age should come the maturity necessary to realize our only boast is in our connection with God, and we didn't even do that ourselves. He chose us while we were still His enemies.

Stand back and see how God has worked in the world from the very beginning. He is sovereign in the universe. We need not fear the current political situation. God is still on the throne. We need not fear for our own situation or that of the loved ones we care for. God is in charge. Nothing can reach them or us that does not first go through our loving Father. Hallelujah!

Yesterday, my pastor complimented me on my "staying power" as a caregiver. My response was to give God the credit, not out of false humility but because I have analyzed my position and know my natural inclination would be to run and hide. But God has enabled me to stay the course.

*Eternal Father, thank You for giving me all I need. Thank You for growing me in a hard place. Help me always judge my life realistically, giving You the credit for all You accomplish through me. Thank You for choosing me to be Your tool. In Jesus' name, amen.*

# JUDGMENT AND VOWS

*You, Yourself, are to be feared;*

*And who may stand in Your presence*

*When once You are angry?*

*You caused judgment to be heard from heaven;*

*The earth feared and was still,*

*When God arose to judgment,*

*To deliver all the oppressed of the earth. Selah*

*... Make vows to the Lord your God, and pay them;*

*Let all who are around Him bring presents to Him who ought to be feared.*

--Psalm 76:7-9, 11

"GOD, IF YOU'LL just get me out of here safely, I'll serve You forever." We've heard of "foxhole" commitments. Most of us have at some time in our lives made some promise to God that we would live more righteously than we have in the past if only He will rescue us from the present predicament.

It seems to me that God would rather have our steady dependence on Him, but if God has to bring crises into our lives to get our attention, we need to consider carefully what we vow. For God does not take vows lightly and neither should we.

Psalm 77 links vows with judgment. I have known people who vowed in distress and then returned to a sinful lifestyle once they found relief. Only more trouble brought them back to that vow and their need to live right. In at least one case, the forgetful "promiser" lost his life in a tragic accident. It's not my place to judge, but it certainly looked like God's judgment on His wayward child.

In our daily stress we may be tempted to promise anything for relief. It is probably better just to ask God for daily grace. He's with us in the storms. He cares about our cares. He wants us to lean on Him.

*Heavenly Father, omnipotent God, remind me of the vows I have made to You. Help me keep them, to Your glory. Help me lean on You and not try to bargain with You to get through my daily burden. Thank You for walking with me through this dark valley. In Jesus' name, amen.*

# WHAT COMPLAINING DOES

*I cried out to God with my voice –*

*To God with my voice;*

*And He gave ear to me.*

*In the day of my trouble I sought the Lord;*

*My hand was stretched out in the night without ceasing;*

*My soul refused to be comforted.*

*I remembered God, and was troubled;*

*I complained, and my spirit was overwhelmed. Selah*

--Psalm 77:1-3

THE WEEKEND FINALLY ended and our visiting relative departed for her home. I felt greatly relieved and at the same time strangely discouraged. Discussing my feelings with my husband, we immediately identified the problem: negative people leave us exhausted. I felt as if I had been waving pom-poms all weekend, but no one was joining the cheers.

Another time a Sunday sermon actually pinpointed the problem. Joy stealers drain our emotions. That drain even affects us physically. The solution: as much as possible, stay away from joy stealers.

Sometimes we can't avoid negative people. They may be family members with whom we have to contend. It may help to talk to them about your concerns for their discouraged attitude. Or it may not help at all. Fortify yourself with extra time in prayer. Escape as frequently as possible. Keep a thankful attitude in spite of what you hear. I have even made a game of trying to counter every complaint with praise.

After all, Psalm 77 describes the natural result of complaint: becoming overwhelmed. I can't afford to go there, so I need to be the flip side of the joy-stealer coin.

*Father, You tell us the fruit of the Spirit is love, joy, and peace. When I'm tempted to complain, help me stop and thank You instead. I love You, Lord. I want that joy, and I know its result will be peace. Protect me from anything and anyone who would do Satan's work in stealing my joy. In Jesus' name, amen.*

# SLEEPLESS NIGHTS

*You hold my eyelids open;*

*I am so troubled that I cannot speak.*

*I have considered the days of old,*

*The years of ancient times.*

*I call to remembrance my song in the night;*

*I meditate within my heart,*

*And my spirit makes diligent search.*

--Psalm 77:4-6

DID YOU EXPECT to find practical answers to insomnia in the psalms? Here it is.

We have all been there. My mind is filled with trouble. As tired and as ready as I am to drop, I expect to fall asleep the minute I hit the pillow, but my mind won't turn off. The troubles of the day keep cycling in my brain: finances, my loved one's decline, paperwork snags, problems at work, dealing with authorities, family concerns, worries about children – the list goes on.

The psalmist says God holds our eyelids open. We want to close them in peaceful sleep, but God holds them open. And God will win. We are so troubled we can't even put it into words. Does God hold them open so that we will talk to Him about the troubles? Maybe!

There's no pat answer here. I have heard numerous remedies. Sometimes they work and sometimes they don't. But the psalmist says he looked at what worked in the past. Prayer, of course. Songs in the night – out loud, but only if you sleep alone, of course! Remembering words to favorite, appropriate hymns can be comforting and soothing.

Meditation. That's when we mull over those scriptures we have put to memory. That's when we think not about the problems facing us, but how God has shown Himself strong in our behalf in the past.

Maybe God is holding our eyelids open so that we will engage in that diligent quest we haven't had time to do during the day. Maybe we are to search our hearts for anything we should confess and forsake. Perhaps we should be assessing our love for God and planning how to show it. For sure, we should be talking to our heavenly Father about all the people we've promised to pray for and just haven't had time.

I don't know all the answers about insomnia. I still deal with it occasionally. I do know that even though Satan doesn't want us rested, he's apt to leave us alone if we turn our sleeplessness into special times with God.

*Heavenly Father, You know how much rest I need. On those nights I cannot sleep, even then, help me remember to use my wakefulness as an opportunity to get to know You better. Control my mind, Lord. Shut my eyes. In Jesus' name, amen.*

# DEALING WITH THE DISCOURAGED

*Will the Lord cast off forever?*

*And will He be favorable no more?*

*Has His mercy ceased forever?*

*Has His promise failed forevermore?*

*Has God forgotten to be gracious?*

*Has His anger shut up His tender mercies? Selah*

--Psalm 77:7-9

LARRY LOVED TO preach God's Word. He had spent most of his adult life preaching in small home missions churches and teaching Bible classes at a city rescue mission. Shortly after we married, he was offered the pastorate of an American Missionary Fellowship church in Vallecito, a small foothill town. We were thrilled to take on the ministry, commuting every Sunday for three years and then finally moving to the community.

We had followed God's leading to this ministry. So neither of us could understand God's plan when Larry began showing signs of Alzheimer's Disease. I remember praying, "Why, God? Why should this happen to a man who only wants to serve you?"

Larry was confused that he could no longer preach. The hardest thing for him was to give up the pastorate. We then moved to Rail Road Flat and became involved in ministry there, but in a few months it became obvious that he could no longer even follow a manual to teach a class. At that point Larry's discouragement took over. He complained to me and to our pastor that he felt worthless. He might just as well stay home on Sundays. God had deserted him and he did not know why.

Pastor Sweeney talked to Larry about the seasons of life – how circumstances change and it has nothing to do with God's casting us away. He told him that just his smiling greeting on Sunday morning blessed the congregation. He mentioned the things he still could do – like singing in the choir and entering into discussions, especially with the wealth of Scripture that still came readily to his tongue.

I'd like to say that those pep talks improved Larry's outlook, but I don't think they did. Alzheimer's had taken the "old" Larry from us. Sometimes we can't help in all the ways we'd like to – but even then, God has not cast us off forever. He's still there, even in the shadows of our lives.

*Lord of all comfort, help us not be discouraged by the natural results of ageing and disease. Help us remember that You sorrow with us. You are here for us. You will bring us through this. Give us the words we need to encourage our loved ones. In Jesus' name, amen.*

# OUR CONCERNS – HIS CONCERNS

*And I said, "This is my anguish;*

*But I will remember the years of the right hand of the Most High."*

*I will remember the works of the Lord;*

*Surely I will remember Your wonders of old.*

*I will also meditate on all Your work,*

*And talk of Your deeds.*

*Your way, O God, is in the sanctuary;*

*Who is so great a God as our God?*

*You are the God who does wonders;*

*You have declared Your strength among the peoples.*

*You have with Your arm redeemed Your people,*

*The sons of Jacob and Joseph. Selah*

--Psalm 77:10-15

I HAD LUNCH with a lady who complained that her children seemed to have forgotten her. She shared the sad story of how her son told her he doesn't have time to talk when she called him. She lives alone and planned to spend the next holiday by herself. I had just talked to another woman who said she and her husband would be alone for the holiday and wondered if I knew anyone who might like to join them. Of course, I gave my friend's name and phone number to this generous couple.

Beyond that, I reminded her that God was as concerned about her wayward children as she was. We talked about what God had done for her in the past. I tried to encourage her that God's actions on her behalf showed His power and love. What He'd done before, He could and would do again. Think on His works, His wonders, His deeds, His greatness, and His strength. He has redeemed us.

Hallelujah!

We can dwell on the gloomy side of life; or we can move our emotions to view God's past glories. When we talk about the "good old days" we need to remember that God is good all the time.

*Almighty God, thank You for raising me from the pit of despair to the heights of Your glory. On my down days, help me look up into Your face and remember all You have accomplished for me. Then let me lift up others by telling my story. In Jesus' name, amen.*

# IN THE STORM

*The waters saw You, O God;*

*The waters saw You, they were afraid;*

*The depths also trembled.*

*The clouds poured out water;*

*The skies sent out a sound;*

*Your arrows also flashed about.*

*The voice of Your thunder was in the whirlwind;*

*The lightnings lit up the world;*

*The earth trembled and shook.*

*Your way was in the sea,*

*Your path in the great waters,*

*And Your footsteps were not known.*

*You led Your people like a flock*

*By the hand of Moses and Aaron.*

--Psalm 77:16-20

AS LARRY'S DEMENTIA worsened, he became fearful of storms. We lived in an A-frame house, and I loved the sound of rain on the roof. It only agitated Larry. Our walls were mostly bare windows, and I loved to watch the trees sway and the lightning zip through the sky. But the panic I saw in Larry's eyes at the sight of lightning with its thunderous accompaniment sent me scrambling for a way to distract and calm him.

I tried playing music to block out the sounds, but that only agitated him further. Obviously he wanted less noise, not more. The television did not help because he could no longer track story lines. He was not even interested enough to look in that direction. Had he ever been a game player, that might have worked. He wasn't.

So we talked about the storm. He remembered storms from his childhood. Fear remained in his voice. Then we talked about how the storm showed God's power. I found psalms that mentioned storms and related them to God's control – like this seventy-seventh psalm. By the time the storm moved away, Larry had calmed down. He was ready to rest in God once again.

*Almighty God, You are all powerful. Don't let me forget that. In my personal storms remind me how You showed Yourself in control in the physical storms I have witnessed. God, I am so glad I am on Your side. Thank You for bringing me here. In Jesus' name, amen.*

# EVERY MOTHER'S PROVERBS

*Give ear, O my people, to my law;*

*Incline your ears to the words of my mouth.*

*I will open my mouth in a parable;*

*I will utter dark sayings of old,*

*Which we have heard and known,*

*And our fathers have told us.*

*We will not hide them from their children,*

*Telling to the generation to come the praises of the Lord,*

*And His strength and His wonderful works that He has done.*

--Psalm 78:1-4

"YOU KEEP CROSSING your eyes and one day they're going to stay that way."

"No coffee for you. It will stunt your growth."

"An hour of sleep before midnight is worth two hours after."

"Sing before breakfast: cry before supper."

"A penny saved is a penny earned."

"Boys may whistle. Girls must sing."

Your mother probably passed on all these proverbs and more. Some are good advice. Others not so much. I have to stop myself from glibly reciting old sayings to my children and grandchildren. I want to make sure my words are true.

One source of parables and proverbs we can rely on is the Bible. We should pass these on to our children, and encourage them to read them for themselves. There's a whole book of proverbs that address every aspect of life from birth to the grave. Wisdom will be gained by anyone slowly absorbing the multitude of wise sayings found there.

One proverb that I memorized as a young Christian has helped me depend on the Lord through all the difficulties and decisions of my life. "Trust in the Lord with all your heart, and lean not on your own understanding. In all your ways acknowledge Him, and He shall direct your paths." (Proverbs 3:5-6).

You might run into trouble following your mother's proverbs, but you'll never go wrong following God's.

*All wise, all knowing Father, thank You for providing us with Your own wisdom in Your special Book. Help us learn that wisdom and tell Your story to the generations to come. In Jesus' name, amen.*

# RESPONDING TO TROUBLE

*When He slew them then they sought Him;*

*And they returned and sought earnestly for God.*

*Then they remembered that God was their rock,*

*And the Most High God their Redeemer.*

*Nevertheless they flattered Him with their mouth,*

*And they lied to Him with their tongue;*

*For their heart was not steadfast with Him,*

*Nor were they faithful in His covenant.*

*But He, being full of compassion, forgave their iniquity,*

*And did not destroy them.*

*Yes, many a time He turned His anger away,*

*And did not stir up all His wrath;*

*For He remembered that they were but flesh,*

*A breath that passes away and does not come again.*

*--Psalm 78:34-39*

WHEN I WAS younger and life seemed relatively pleasant, I tried to have a devotional life with God. After all, that is what I had been taught to do at church, and I could understand the importance of staying close to my Savior. I will admit that it was not easy.

As a working mom, I had very little spare time. I am not a morning person, so it was not productive to get up before the rest of the family for prayer and Bible reading. I reasoned that I was better at night and I could go to bed thinking about what I had read in the Bible, causing pleasant sleep and influencing my first thoughts the next day. However, after taking care of my family and grading papers or prepping for classes, I usually retired too weary for much more than reading a few verses, if that.

So what was God to do to get my attention? Amazingly, when troubles came, I found more time to spend in prayer and Bible study. Where before I had glibly waltzed through my days, enjoying my successes, now I learned the meaning of "pray without ceasing."

Mostly I learned about God's mercy. He is not waiting to punish us for our unfaithfulness. He is the God of forgiveness, just waiting for us to turn back to Him so that He can forgive and lead us into the delights of fellowship and learning to lean on Him.

*Gracious Father, thank You for drawing me back to Yourself. Thank You for teaching me to forgive by forgiving me. Thank You for remembering that I am but flesh, weak and as frail as a passing breath. Let me lean on You and learn Your ways. In Jesus' name, amen.*

# YOUR JOB: LIKE DAVID

*He also chose David His servant,*

*And took him from the sheepfolds;*

*From following the ewes that had young He brought him,*

*To shepherd Jacob His people,*

*And Israel His inheritance.*

*So He shepherded them according to the integrity of His heart,*

*And guided them by the skillfulness of His hands.*

--Psalm 78:70-72

IT WAS A big shock to me when I realized I now had to be the decision maker and enforcer for my husband, Bud, who was considerably older than I, and who had always made all the major family decisions. Several months of confinement to bed had reduced his strength and ability to think things through, even for his own care. It certainly diminished his stamina to carry out his plans.

As a teacher, I was used to telling children what to do. However, I found it difficult to tell Bud what to do. In our twenty-four years of marriage, I had learned to be a cooperative wife, arguing less and less frequently over trivial issues. In dealing with his illness, at first I didn't even realize I needed to be proactive in his care. Only after he had neglected to follow up on medical appointments did I realize I would have to make the appointments, drive him to them, and sit with him as the doctor examined and talked to him. He had become more like my child than my husband, but I was too overwhelmed with the situation to resent my new position.

Bud was an easy patient to care for at home. He just wanted to be left alone. He did not interrupt my activities to ask for food or water or entertainment. He did not complain. I had to learn to honor his request for solitude while still encouraging him to eat and stay hydrated. Soldier that he was, whenever he had a visitor, he always exerted great effort to appear in better health than he really was. I learned to check on him after the visits and limit other visits accordingly.

God chose me to be my husband's shepherd. It was my job to care for him with integrity and skill. Your caregiving experience will be similar in that you must ascertain your loved one's particular needs and gently meet them as you are able. Let David's gentle shepherding be your example.

*Gentle Shepherd, you pass Your heart on to us. Thank You that You do not give us impossible tasks, but You enable us to fulfill them. Continue to strengthen me and give me wisdom for the work You have for me to do. In Jesus' name, amen.*

# THE VINE AND THE BRANCHES

*Return, we beseech You,*

*O God of hosts;*

*Look down from heaven and see,*

*And visit this vine*

*And the vineyard which Your right hand has planted,*

*And the branch that You made strong for Yourself ...*

*Let Your hand be upon the man of Your right hand,*

*Upon the son of man whom You made strong for Yourself.*

*Then we will not turn back from You;*

*Revive us, and we will call upon Your name.*

*Restore us, O Lord God of hosts;*

*Cause Your face to shine,*

*And we shall be saved!*

--Psalm 80:14-15, 17-19

THE DISCOLORED PAGES of Larry's Bible reveal his favorite passages. One of them was the Lord's last words to His disciples in the upper room on the night of His betrayal. I remember several sermons Larry preached from John 15. He not only preached it: he lived it. He knew Jesus was the vine and he was but a branch that needed to stay connected to the vine. He spent many hours each day reveling in the Scriptures, getting to know God better, and meditating on His teachings.

That time in the Bible sustained Larry even through the horrors of Alzheimer's Disease. In his most confused moments he could still quote favorite memorized Bible verses. As long as he could still talk, the most likely words that would come from his mouth were God's words. Many people have shared with me what a blessing he was to them, even in the care facility where he spent his last months. Familiar hymns and Bible passages blessed others even when he was no longer aware of their effect.

*Lord God, thank You for the wonderful minds You have given us to store Your Word. May we always retain Bible verses and songs that we memorize throughout this life. Fill me with Your Word so that I can be a blessing. Thank You for the assurance that we will be restored in Your presence better than we ever are on earth. In Jesus' name, amen.*

# RELEASE FROM BONDAGE

*"I removed his shoulder from the burden;*

*His hands were freed from the baskets.*

*You called in trouble, and I delivered you;*

*I answered you in the secret place of thunder;*

*I tested you at the waters of Meribah." Selah*

--Psalm 81:6-7

DURING THE TIME of caregiving, most days I felt burdened by my situation. For several months I realized I had chosen to be a slave to this person (my husband Larry) in order to take care of him. That could have become a source of depression for me if I had not emphasized the word "chosen." Yes, it was my choice to serve my God by serving the man I had married.

Did that knowledge keep me from praying for release? I certainly prayed for daily strength and a cheerful attitude, and sometimes the burden seemed so heavy that I did pray for release. But release did not come right away.

When Israel prayed for release from slavery in Egypt, God answered -- but only after they had been there for 400 years. I'm glad He didn't take that long to answer my prayer!

Sometimes it helps to have a sense of humor about life's circumstances. I could see little deliverances, day by day. He answered and sustained me in secret places, in things I could not share with friends and family. He tested me, brought me through the test, and ultimately removed my shoulder from the burden and freed my hands from the work. Sing His praises!

*Loving Father, keep my sense of humor intact. Thank You for answering my prayers, even when I don't yet see the results. Help me rest assured that You will see me through the trials. Thank You for promising the ultimate goal of eternity with You. In Jesus' name, amen.*

# LOVING GOD'S HOUSE

*How lovely is Your tabernacle, O Lord of hosts!*

*My soul longs, yes, even faints*

*For the courts of the Lord;*

*My heart and my flesh cry out for the living God.*

*Even the sparrow has found a home,*

*And the swallow a nest for herself,*

*Where she may lay her young —*

*Even Your altars, O Lord of hosts,*

*My King and my God.*

*Blessed are those who dwell in Your house;*

*They will still be praising You. Selah*

--Psalm 84:1-4

IN THE YEAR before Larry had to move to a care facility, I often wondered how important it was to get us to church on Sundays. I am punctual to a fault, but Alzheimer's Disease really slows down its victims. Although I would have Larry bathe the evening before, it still took us from an hour-and-a-half to two hours to get him dressed and breakfasted. Only when I reminded him that it was Sunday and we were getting ready for church did he really cooperate, and then only for a few minutes until he forgot again why I was pushing him.

I needed reminders too. Because he could no longer preach or teach a class, he complained that there was no reason for him to attend church any more. Still, on Sunday mornings, just the reminder that it was the Lord's Day kept him moving toward that goal. From the moment he walked through the door of the church he beamed with delight and contributed to the congregation with his cheerful smile.

The same thing happened when we moved to our new home. Even though he did not know the people in this congregation (by then he no longer knew most of the people in our former church either), the atmosphere of fellowship with Christian people calmed him and rejoiced his heart. You could see it on his face. Even Alzheimer's Disease can't take away a lifetime of love for God's house.

*Heavenly Father, thank You for putting the love of Your people into our hearts. May I never lose that sense of love and fellowship with Your family. Remind me to reach out to strangers with Your love. In Jesus' name, amen.*

# FROM WEEPING TO SPRINGS OF WATER

*Blessed is the man whose strength is in You,*

*Whose heart is set on pilgrimage,*

*And they pass through the Valley of Baca,*

*They make it a spring;*

*The rain also covers it with pools.*

--Psalm 84:5-6

WHAT A PICTURE! Here is a person traveling through a valley so dry as to cause weeping and fainting. Yet, the psalmist says if that person's strength is in God, if his journey (pilgrimage) is the path God has picked out, his very tears will turn that valley of weeping into a spring – an oasis – a place of refreshment for others.

We go through dry times and valleys of despair and weeping. We don't see the purpose. When we realize we are finally through the valley, it's good to look back and see what was accomplished through all those tears. It's good to give God praise for the lives we have refreshed because we exhibited God's strength when onlookers expected us to faint and give up.

It's not all about us. It's not even all about the loved ones we care for. There's joy in being a tool for God's glory even in sorrow and stress. Know that He is using us and strengthening us so we ourselves can become the very refreshment we need to get through the vale of despair. What a privilege to be useful to Him!

*Gracious God, thank You for the privilege of serving You. Thank You for giving me the strength to do what You ask me to do. May my tears be a blessing and testimony for You. May the Source of my Strength be obvious to any who watch. May it all result in drawing people closer to You. In Jesus' name, amen.*

# GOD'S DOORKEEPER

*For a day in Your courts is better than a thousand.*

*I would rather be a doorkeeper in the house of my God*

*Than to dwell in the tents of wickedness.*

*For the Lord God is a sun and shield;*

*The Lord will give grace and glory;*

*No good thing will He withhold*

*From those who walk uprightly.*

*O Lord of hosts,*

*Blessed is the man who trusts In You!*

--Psalm 84:10-12

LARRY LIVED FOR Sundays, even when he was not preaching. He was truly a man after God's own heart. His greatest delight was to preach. After that came Bible teaching and then fellowship with other believers. Those were all acts of worship for him.

In Vallecito we tried to have Sunday evening services in addition to the morning worship, but the people could not be enticed. So we traveled an hour or more to several different churches to hear God's Word preached and sing His praises.

When we moved to Grass Valley, the congregation we joined did not have a Sunday evening service either. Every Sunday afternoon I had to explain to Larry that this group had chosen to make Sunday evenings a time for family. Larry could not understand that. So once again we drove an hour each Sunday evening to attend a service.

Larry never said Psalm 84:10 was a favorite verse, but he lived it.

*Father God, may I never lose the delight of worshiping with Your people. May I never be tempted to turn from living for You to a life that would in any way bring shame to Your name. Help me contribute what I can to delight Your heart and the hearts of those who worship with me. In Jesus' name, amen.*

# GOD'S GOOD GIFTS

*I will hear what God the Lord will speak,*

*For He will speak peace*

*To His people and to His saints;*

*But let them not turn back to folly.*

*Surely His salvation is near to those who fear Him,*

*That glory may dwell in our land.*

--Psalm 85:8-9

IT IS UPLIFTING just to go through the psalms and find the good things God has promised. Psalm 85 is full of such bounty. Just meditate on:

favor to the land and return from captivity – vs. 1

forgiveness – vs. 2

removing His wrath – vs. 3

restoration and salvation – vs. 4

revival and rejoicing – vs. 6

mercy – vs. 7

peace – vs. 8

salvation and glory in the land – vs. 9

mercy and truth; righteousness and peace – vs. 10

truth and righteousness – vs. 11

goodness and increase – vs. 12

righteousness and direction – vs. 13

In a world of turmoil it's easy to forget that God is in control. We need to retreat to a quiet place where we can hear what God says. There may not be peace in the world but He speaks peace to His people. His salvation is near us who fear Him. His glory dwells in the land wherever His children are living for Him.

*Almighty God, thank You that You are in control. Help me bring Your glory to my corner of the world. Thank You that we can rest on Your promises. May others see mercy and truth, righteousness and peace in my life. Give me that righteous direction that You have promised. In Jesus' name, amen.*

# OUR PRAYER-HEARING GOD

*Bow down Your ear, O Lord, hear me; For I am poor and needy.*

*Preserve my life, for I am holy;*

*You are my God;*

*Save Your servant who trusts in You!*

*Be merciful to me, O Lord, For I cry to You all day long.*

*Rejoice the soul of Your servant, For to You, O Lord, I lift up my soul.*

*For You, Lord, are good, and ready to forgive,*

*And abundant in mercy to all those who call upon You.*

*Give ear, O Lord, to my prayer; And attend to the voice of my supplications.*

*In the day of my trouble I will call upon You,*

*For You will answer me.*

--Psalm 86:1-7

AS A YOUNG Christian I certainly did not spend much time in prayer. For one reason, life was not all that difficult. I had good health, a quick mind, good friends, and family. Although most of my family did not join me in my newfound faith, I did not consider that something to pray about. I rested in God's care, even to the point of presuming upon His grace. In some ways that was good, but it did not develop my awareness of His presence in my personal life.

God develops our faith through the hard seasons of life. Often, we do not turn to Him for help until we realize there is nowhere else to turn. And when we do, because we have not grown in our dependence on Him, we do not have the confidence to trust that He will answer in our behalf – or even hear us, for that matter.

Wayward children bring us to our knees. Spending time reading God's Word assures us His arm is not too short to reach them not His ear dull to our requests (see Isaiah59:1). The more we ask of God, the more we see Him answer. Each difficulty we face strengthens us for the next. God wants to raise strong, fruitful trees of faith, not delicate hothouse plants.

Daily caregiving presents the ultimate test of our faith. Know that God cares even more than you do. Know that He hears your prayers and will provide what is best for you and for your loved one. He is the God who hears and answers prayer.

*Loving Father, thank You for caring for me and for anyone I care for. Help me trust You to do what's best. Nudge me to bring my concerns to You early. Remind me of Your answers in the past. Help me rest in You. In Jesus' name, amen.*

# WALKING IN TRUTH

*Teach me Your way, O Lord;*

*I will walk in Your truth;*

*Unite my heart to fear Your name.*

*I will praise You, O Lord my God, with all my heart,*

*And I will glorify Your name forevermore.*

*For great is Your mercy toward me,*

*And You have delivered my soul from the depths of Sheol.*

*--Psalm 86:11-13*

AS I WRITE this I am in the midst of rehearsals to sing Handel's Messiah. While I sat listening to a solo, waiting for my turn to join in with the chorus of more than eighty voices plus orchestra, my heart thrilled to be part of this celebration of God. I reflected on why I was there.

This is a church/community choral group. I don't attend the church that sponsors it. Most of the singers are from that church and, while they are pleasant, they have their own friends. There are only a couple of people I already knew here, and I have not made any new friends in the weeks we have practiced together. I reflect on the fact that I am not here for the fellowship.

The music is difficult. I have sung it since college days and it still takes diligence, concentration, and musical ability. Nothing else musically challenges me like

Handel's writing. It's just plain hard work. As much as I enjoy the result, I'm not here for fun.

I realize I am here simply to praise God and, by my participation, lead others to praise Him too. As in other years, I find tears blurring my eyes on the Hallelujah and Amen choruses. It's a good thing I have some of this memorized or I would have to quit singing, and that's the last thing I want to do. I want to glorify His name forevermore.

This is a form of respite for me. Maybe you can take advantage of similar activities to find refreshment away from the duties of caregiving. But maybe extenuating circumstances keep you from participating in holiday activities that used to be a part of your life. Attend what you can. Or, if all you can do is sing along with a CD, praise the Lord that way. God's heart is blessed with our praise, individually or as a group. Give Him your best. He will rejoice your heart.

*Eternal Father, thank You for the privilege of singing Your praises, and honoring Your Son. Thank You for the gift of music that we can use to praise You. Thank You for ability and strength and the measure of health You give. May I use them all for You in every opportunity You give me. In Jesus' name, amen.*

# SHUT IN

*O Lord, God of my salvation,*

*I have cried out day and night before You.*

*Let my prayer come before You;*

*Incline Your ear to my cry.*

*For my soul is full of troubles,*

*And my life draws near to the grave ...*

*You have put away my acquaintances far from me;*

*You have made me an abomination to them;*

*I am shut up, and I cannot get out;*

*My eye wastes away because of affliction.*

*Lord, I have called daily upon You;*

*I have stretched out my hands to You.*

--Psalm 88:1-3, 8-9

THE PRAYER LIST had a section called "shut-ins." As a new Christian and a teenager, I had no idea what that meant. Never shy, I asked my friend, the pastor's daughter, what in the world that meant. "Those are the old people who can't leave their homes to get to church," she told me. I knew about old people, but it had never occurred to me that one might become so helpless he or she could not leave home. Weren't all those people in convalescent homes?

Some people on that list were in nursing homes. In a few months I became involved in a ministry of visiting them with songs and a short devotional. What a revelation to see their faces light up when we spoke to them individually. Still, I never realized that one day I might feel "shut in" as there were.

Years later, as my husband's dementia increased, it became harder and harder to take him out into the community. One day I realized his disease had caused both of us to become "shut-in." Even in this day of telephones and email, isolation can be a depressing fact of life. Friends would occasionally phone, and usually encourage me to call on them for help or respite, but most of the time I would valiantly try to handle life by myself, until I recognized a frantic pattern developing.

Our loving God was always there, but God also has His people to do His work. I had to learn to reach out for help, and be blessed by the people God sent to minister to us. I praise the Lord that I have never been "shut up" and not able to get out as the psalmist complains. There have always been those who were ready to help as I stretched out my arms to receive what God had for me through them.

*Father, help me reach out to others – either for the help You will provide through them or to provide them the help You pass on to them through me. We need each other. You made us that way. Thank You. In Jesus' name, amen.*

# WHAT THE GRANDCHILDREN SEE

*I will sing of the mercies of the Lord forever;*

*With my mouth will I make known Your faithfulness to all generations.*

*For I have said, "Mercy shall be built up forever;*

*Your faithfulness You shall establish in the very heavens.*

*'I have made a covenant with My chosen,*

*I have sworn to My servant David:*

*Your seed I will establish forever,*

*And build up your throne to all generations.'"*

*--Psalm 89:1-4*

AS MY FAMILY expands and my income doesn't, each Christmas finds me making more presents and buying fewer. It's easy to make things for the women, much harder for the men. Goodie boxes are always appreciated, but one year I didn't have time or money to do that. So I was shopping for a gift for my son-in-law. My youngest grandchild, Cami, was with me.

The store was crowded with bustling shoppers. In the midst of my fruitless search, seven-year-old Cami said, "Grandma, these people are all spending lots of money for presents. Don't' they know it's better to stay home and make presents?"

Cami and I enjoy making things together, either in the kitchen or at the sewing machine. I hadn't really thought of giving my time and talents as a legacy to her, but her comment made me realize that the most important things I will leave my grandchildren are the memories and skills we develop together.

The same is true of what they learn from us as they watch how we care for other people. Those hours of caregiving are not unnoticed by our offspring. How we respond to the indignities with which we deal will greatly influence how they respond to what life brings their way. That soft answer will travel much further than just to the ears of the loved one who is causing us problems. Thank you, Cami, for the good reminder.

*Gracious Father, thank You for reminding me about the great crowd of witnesses who watch my every move. Thank You that I can leave them the very hints and directions that will bring them to Yourself. Keep me mindful of their tender hearts, and overrule when I forget how sensitive they are to what I say and do. May I do nothing to turn them from the right path. In Jesus' name, amen.*

# GOD'S FAITHFULNESS

*O Lord God of hosts,*

*Who is mighty like You, O Lord?*

*Your faithfulness also surrounds You.*

*You rule the raging of the sea;*

*When its waves rise, You still them.*

*You have broken Rahab in pieces, as one who is slain;*

*You have scattered Your enemies with Your mighty arm.*

--Psalm 89:8-10

IT HAD BEEN a year of continually retightening the belt – so to speak. The economy was floundering, and I was not exempt from the fallout. Although I have a stable income, even that was shaken as I received a letter from PERS (Public Employee Retirement System), my source of survivor benefits. It reminded me that one of my checks had been increased by $400 nearly ten years before, and that amount had been allotted for a ten-year period of time. Gulp! Next January my income would go down by ten percent.

Doom and gloom. First response: prayer. Second response: write my congressmen, encouraging them to reinstate this funding. I trusted in God's ability to provide my needs. However, the letter to the congressman seemed just a formality. Every financial consideration in this state had been drastically cut this year. Every service was greatly underfunded. State workers were furloughed and jobs slashed. Every lawmaker scrambled to enable the state to make ends meet.

So how do you think God answered that prayer of faith? In a few weeks I got a letter from PERS. The legislature voted to continue the allowance on my survivor benefit. In a recession year? From a running-scared legislature? Now, if that's not a miracle, I don't know what is! I never expected God to supply in this way. Praise His name. He loves to surprise us!

*Almighty Father, who is mighty like You? You faithfully fulfill Your promises to take care of us — in ways we cannot imagine. You rule, even where the economy is bottoming out. When waves of fear threaten to swamp me, You calm with your dramatic rescues, just in the nick of time. You delight in Your child. I am so glad I am Yours. Keep me trusting. Remind me often of Your love. In Jesus' name, amen.*

# A THOUSAND YEARS

*Lord, You have been our dwelling place in all generations.*

*Before the mountains were brought forth,*

*Or ever You had formed the earth and the world,*

*Even from everlasting to everlasting, You are God.*

*You say, "Return, O children of men."*

*For a thousand years in Your sight*

*Are like yesterday when it is past,*

*And like a watch in the night.*

*You carry them away like a flood;*

*They are like a sleep.*

*In the morning they are like grass which grows up:*

*In the morning it flourishes and grows up;*

*In the evening it is cut down and withers.*

*--Psalm 90:1-6*

I REMEMBER THOSE long days of caregiving. Larry's dementia progressed slowly, and it seemed every day we faced the same questions, same confusions, same frustrations. Often I arose in the morning after little sleep, to face dealing with a very strong man who now had a toddler's mind. I fell into bed at night, dying to rest, only to be faced with another night of repeatedly coercing Larry back to bed.

The mind turns to mush on such a small amount of sleep. Only the basics can be accomplished, if even those are possible. For ten years I found myself dwelling on the question: "How long, Lord? How long?"

When Larry was in a convalescent hospital, the everyday care of him made it seem like forever. As I look back on it now, I realize he was there for only two and a half years. But for a total of twelve years I learned much about him, myself, patient caregivers, and God's grace.

The psalmist reminds us that the God who is with us has been here from the beginning. He is from everlasting to everlasting. I may think I've been dealing with this problem for 1,000 years. A real 1,000 years is but a watch in the night for our everlasting God. He knows we are like the grass that sprouts, blooms, withers, and dies. Yet He is the God who is always there.


*Father God, thank You for being an everlasting God. Thank You for Your everlasting strength. Thank You that my times are in Your hands. Help me remember lessons I have already learned when I face new trials. In Jesus name, amen.*

# ESTABLISH OUR WORK

*Return, O Lord!*

*How long?*

*And have compassion on Your servants.*

*Oh, satisfy us early with Your mercy,*

*That we may rejoice and be glad all our days!*

*Make us glad according to the days in which You have afflicted us,*

*The years in which we have seen evil.*

*Let Your work appear to Your servants,*

*And Your glory to their children.*

*And let the beauty of the Lord our God be upon us,*

*And establish the work of our hands for us;*

*Yes, establish the work of our hands.*

--Psalm 90:13-17

I ALWAYS WONDERED how my sister Joanne and I ended up in the same family. Even as a child, I could not understand her constant list-making. She had lists of things she wanted to buy for Christmas presents, shoes she wanted to own, classes she wanted to take, places she wanted to go, people she wanted to write to, books she wanted to write – and on and on and on. But I never saw her do any of the things on those lists.

The list-making continued even as she became an adult. I learned to make a few lists myself; but my favorite part about list-making was crossing off the items I completed. Sometimes I even added items after I had accomplished them just so I could cross them off!

In later years Joanne talked to me about her dreams. Friends had told her she would be a good writer. Could I help her get started? We talked. I brought her books that had helped me. She read and she talked. But she never wrote. As time went on she complained about how boring her life was. Yet she had potential – if she would just start.

During confined times of caregiving, I often felt like my days were filled with meaningless activity – meaningless to anyone besides my husband, and often meaningless to him, because he was not concerned with who cared for him or how. I did not have large blocks of time in which to write or accomplish sewing projects. Larry's condition kept me from teaching (probably the most meaningful activity of my life). I bordered on the boredom that my sister complained about.

But God establishes the work of our hands. Reading His Word helped me stay centered in Him and His will for me, which was to care for His servant Larry for that season of our lives. And the mental lists I made during those years? I'm working on crossing those items off now.

*All knowing Father, thank You for taking note of our lives and all that we do for You. Thank You for giving us the desires of our hearts and sustaining us in the dormant times. Thank You for Your grace and love. In Jesus' name, amen.*

# SAFETY

*He who dwells in the secret place of the Most high*

*Shall abide under the shadow of the Almighty.*

*I will say of the Lord, "He is my refuge and my fortress;*

*My God, in Him I will trust." ...*

*"Because he has set his love upon Me, therefore I will deliver him;*

*I will set him on high, because he has known My name.*

*He shall call upon Me, and I will answer him;*

*I will be with him in trouble;*

*I will deliver him and honor him.*

*With long life I will satisfy him,*

*And show him My salvation."*

--Psalm 91:1-2, 14-16

WHAT A POWERFUL psalm where caregivers can rest. It may seem that the entire world is falling apart around you, but when you look at circumstances through God's eyes, you can rest assured that you are safe.

My oldest daughter went through a traumatic time when every day brought new tragedy. Often she would groan, "What next?" I felt like joining her, but feared the answer. Every "next" proved worse than the last. Soon my go-to reply became: "Don't ask what's next. I don't want to know."

How much better to take what we are dealt as from the hand of God. When I went through setbacks with Larry, friends and family worried for me. They would ask, "Now, what are you going to do? How will you handle this?"

Psalm 91 became my hiding place. I could answer, "God is my refuge and fortress. I don't know what's next. I don't have all the answers. He does. All I can do is trust in Him."

I love the way the psalm ends. How is it that we can have such complete confidence in God? Because He has set His love on us. Because we have chosen to be called by His name. Because we have called on Him for help. All He wants is our trust – and that's all we have to offer.

*Abba Father, thank You for loving us. Help me just trust You to take care of all those things over which I have no control. Make us a lesson to all who look on in wonder, a trophy of Your grace. In Jesus' name, amen.*

# WITH HARMONIOUS SOUND

*It is good to give thanks to the Lord,*

*And to sing praises to Your name, O Most High;*

*To declare Your lovingkindness in the morning,*

*And Your faithfulness every night,*

*On an instrument of ten strings,*

*On the lute,*

*And on the harp,*

*With harmonious sound.*

*For You, Lord, have made me glad through Your work;*

*I will triumph in the works of Your hands.*

--Psalm 92:1-4

GOD GAVE US music to express our emotions to Him. I may not have been grateful for piano lessons as a child, but I am thankful for that outlet as an adult.

The seniors group decided we wanted an old-fashioned carol sing in December. I happily agreed to accompany them on the piano. During a refreshment break, several members thanked me for playing, to which I honestly replied, "It's my pleasure." The mother of the class leader went further with her comment. She said, "It's fun to sing with someone who obviously enjoys playing for us." I'm thrilled the singers felt that way about our time together.

Playing joyful music is fun. Playing sad music can be therapeutic. Many times, from my teen years on, I have pounded out my anger with a Chopin polonaise or drowned my sorrows in the Tchaikovsky Pathetique. One of my students told me about making up songs to sing to God as part of private devotions, and now I sometimes do that as well. You might be surprised at how many modern worship songs began this way.

So keep up the music practice. If you don't play an instrument, play CDs. Music enables us to tell God what's on our hearts and the share our worship with others.

*Father, thank You for the creative gift of music. May I always sing Your praises. Be pleased with my love songs. In Jesus' name, amen*

# GOD'S DEEP THROUGHTS

*O Lord, how great are Your works!*

*Your thoughts are very deep.*

*A senseless man does not know,*

*Nor does a fool understand this.*

*When the wicked spring up like grass,*

*And when all the workers of iniquity flourish,*

*It is that they may be destroyed forever.*

*But You, Lord, are on high forevermore.*

*--Psalm 92:5-8*

EARLY IN LIFE I learned how to make other people think I knew a lot more than I do. I'm a quick study with anything that I read, including music, so my piano teacher never knew that I rarely practiced more than once or twice during the week between lessons. In English class I found I could manipulate words to write what the teacher wanted to read, so essay tests brought me A's throughout my high school days.

It was a little harder during college, but I actually learned how to study in classes that were designed for teachers to learn how to teach children study skills. With that added help I managed to keep my scholarship in order to finish college.

Of course, as a teacher, I had to keep up the façade of knowing more than the students. And, being of a curious mind, I really did continue learning. I do like to learn new things all the time, and I do not understand people who think they are through learning when they become adults. They are missing out on so much fun.

However, when it comes to understanding God, that's another matter. Nor can I fool Him as I've fooled so many people in my past (and even today). Before I became a Christian, I despaired of understanding the Bible. It made no sense until I got to know the Author. First Corinthians 2:14 says, "But the natural man does not receive the things of the Spirit of God, for they are foolishness to him; nor can he know them, because they are spiritually discerned."

I'm still trying to fill in the empty spaces in my knowledge, but now God is enlightening me to learn the really important things from His Word: how to put His principles to work in my life. That's a lot more valuable than just looking like I know a lot of "stuff."

*Omniscient God, thank You for showing me each day what I need to know to honor Your name and serve You. What an awesome privilege! Help me share it. In Jesus' name, amen.*

# THE FLOURISHING LIFE

*The righteous shall flourish like a palm tree,*

*He shall grow like a cedar in Lebanon.*

*Those who are planted in the house of the Lord*

*Shall flourish in the courts of our God.*

*They shall still bear fruit in old age;*

*They shall be fresh and flourishing.*

*To declare that the Lord is upright;*

*He is my rock, and there is no unrighteousness in Him.*

--Psalm 92:12-15

A WOMAN WHO felt that every sprouted seed ought to be allowed to live had formerly owner our home in Vallecito. The whole yard flourished. We had quite the eclectic garden, but I wondered what would happen when winter came, especially if we had freezing weather.

Sure enough, the first winter was a cold one. Everyone said it had never been that cold before. I am no gardener, but I assume the reason most of our trees and shrubbery survived the intense cold was that they had become acclimated through the years by winters that were almost as cold. They were prepared.

All but the lemon trees in the back yard and the palm trees in the front. It was especially sad to see those tall palms blackened and split, killed in one sap-solidifying night. We had to clean up their debris quickly, for falling fronds endangered anyone passing on the nearby street.

The climate is different where the psalmist lived. I doubt the palm trees there ever faced freezing weather. In their native habitat God made them tall and bare, able to withstand high winds and rain. You've seen them in newscast videos, bent with the wind, but standing tall again after the storm. Yes, they lose some fronds, but the trees themselves survive – maybe even stronger than before the storms.

God has made His children to bend with the storms like that. I like the idea of the righteous person being planted in the house of the Lord and bearing fruit even in old age. I want to be that kind of tree.

*All-powerful God, I want to be known as Your righteous child. Thank You for helping me bend with the storms. May I be planted in Your house, on You, my Rock. Whatever the storm, I trust You to get me through it. In Jesus' name, amen.*

# IN GOOD HANDS

*The Lord reigns.*

*He is clothed with majesty;*

*The Lord is clothed,*

*He has girded Himself with strength.*

*Surely the world is established, so that it cannot be moved.*

*Your throne is established from of old;*

*You are from everlasting.*

--Psalm 93:1-2

AT LEAST ONCE a year I had my class (whatever the age) do a writing assignment where students looked for common advertisements and paraphrased them to honor God instead of the product. For instance: "You're in good hands with … God;" "God … has a better idea;" "Things go better with … God." The children always found more appropriate ads than I did and often continued looking for them throughout the year.

I can see such an ad campaign in Psalm 93. What a comfort to know that the God of the universe, who loves us, is clothed with majesty. The evidences of that majesty abound on earth but they are only glimpses. I long to see Him in His full majesty.

I love the word picture that He has girded Himself with strength. First of all, no one but God could gird Himself with strength. He is the omnipotent (all-powerful)

One. I need that strength, and He will use His power to care for me. As a token promise of this, He says the world (which He created) is established so that it cannot be moved. Yes, it will all disappear one day, and God will make a new heaven and earth, but the one we're on right now will not be moved. That's good news for me: I live in California, where earthquakes are a fact of life. God is in control.

It's all been established from eternity past. God was there then. He's here now. He'll be there in eternity future. How's that for stability? Majesty … strength … duration. I'm in good hands with God.

*Heavenly Father, so often I need to read again about Your great majesty, power, and eternality. Remind me when I am overwhelmed that nothing is too hard for You. I love You, Lord. I am in awe of Your loving me. In Jesus' name, amen.*

# SOME THROUGH THE FLOOD

*The floods have lifted up, O Lord,*

*The floods have lifted up their voice;*

*The floods lift up their waves.*

*The Lord on high is mightier*

*Than the noise of many waters,*

*Than the mighty waves of the sea.*

--Psalm 93:3-4

I'M A MOUNTAIN girl myself. When I get those notices from the insurance companies that I might want to add flood coverage to my policy, I chuckle. The water would have to get pretty high to flood my little house on the side of the hill.

However, for about thirty years, I lived in the Sacramento area. During that time there were numerous years when floods occurred. The weekend Larry and I got married, it rained so much that Sacramento was cut off from the rest of the world by floods. We lived in the suburbs, but we had to drive many miles around our normal route coming home from our short honeymoon. Larry's youngest son had spent the time with my daughter and, when we called home to report our progress, I could hear the worry in his voice. Floods are a real danger. There's no shame in being afraid of one.

This is not a safe world. Earthquakes, floods, fires, accidents – we read about them, see them, maybe even experience them ourselves. What comfort to rest in the Lord on high, who is mightier than the noise of many waters. That doesn't mean we won't face physical dangers or go through hard times. It does mean He is there with us and He is more powerful than anything we have to face.

Where I live, rainbows often follow storms. They always remind me of God's promises. I'm glad I'm on the mountaintop with God, knowing He is in control.

*All powerful God of the Universe, thank You for Your promise to care for Your own. Thank You for making me one of Your children. Use Your power in my life to bring hope to others. In Jesus' name, amen.*

# THE HOUSE OF HOLINESS

*Your testimonies are very sure;*

*Holiness adorns Your house,*

*O Lord, forever.*

--Psalm 93:5

"Holiness, holiness, is what I long for.

Holiness is what You want from me."

I CAN SING that now but, as a new Christian, the thought of holiness scared me. I thought it must be some mystical thing that made a person act weird.

The great thing about being a teacher is that it forces you to learn. As I researched the meaning of "holy" it gradually became clear: to be holy is to be perfect in goodness and righteousness (something impossible for me) *or* to be devoted to God – who is the perfect and righteous One. I can do that.

I want to be devoted to God and, when I am, some of His righteousness is bound to "rub off" on me. So when I sing "holiness is what I long for," and "holiness is what You want from me," I'm telling God I want to be pure and righteous, like He is. I'm setting myself apart from the world to devote my life to Him.

So what does this have to do with caregiving? Just this: the more I am devoted to God, the more "godlike" I become, the better I will be able to do the job God called me to do – which is to care for this one God Himself put in my life.

The psalmist said, "Holiness adorns Your house, O Lord, forever." Let me be one of those adornments.

*All righteous God, I can never attain to Your holiness, but I want to grow more and more like You every day. May others see Jesus in me, Lord. Keep my thoughts and actions pure. Protect me from the evil one. In Jesus' name, amen.*

# GOD HEARS

*Understand, you senseless among the people;*

*And you fools, when will you be wise?*

*He who planted the ear, shall He not hear?*

*He who formed the eye, shall He not see?*

*He who instructs the nations, shall He not correct,*

*He who teaches man knowledge?*

*The Lord knows the thoughts of man,*

*That they are futile.*

--Psalm 94:8-11

WE DIDN'T KNOW where we were going. We knew we were finished with the ministry in Vallecito. Larry was waiting on the Lord to show him a new place of ministry. I was waiting on the Lord to show Larry his preaching days were over and to show us where to move.

Days turned into weeks. Weeks into months. It seemed like forever. We drove forty miles to attend Rail Road Flat Bible Church, not wanted to interfere with the Vallecito work from which we had resigned. Larry researched other churches that were without pastors, but did not follow up on them. I served in the RRF children's church. But we were unsettled – living where we were not wanted, not knowing where to go. And God didn't answer.

Until the day I attended the RRF ladies' Bible study and God showed me the house He had prepared for us. It was perfect, meeting all our needs, including a run for our likes-to-run-away dog, parking for my dad's RV, and rooms big enough to house Larry's considerable library.

Had God's ears been stopped? Or His eyes closed? No, He was just waiting on His own perfect timing. Lesson learned: He sees and hears and is already answering, even when it seems to us like He doesn't care.

*Thank You, Father, for planning my life. I know I can trust You to lead me to the next place of service or rest. I don't have to know the future, because You are already there and You care for me. Remind me of how You have taken care of us in the past so that I trust You always for the future. In Jesus' name, amen.*

# THE TEACHABLE MIND

*Blessed is the man whom You instruct, O Lord,*

*And teach out of Your law,*

*That You may give him rest from the days of adversity,*

*Until the pit is dug for the wicked.*

*For the Lord will not cast off His people,*

*Nor will He forsake His inheritance.*

*But judgment will return to righteousness,*

*And all the upright in heart will follow it.*

--Psalm 94:12-15

I WAS BORN with a curious mind, and it hasn't left me yet. Sometimes it has been a burden. As a young Christian, I longed to be able to understand the Bible better. I despaired of ever knowing enough to teach from God's Word, because I am also a teacher at heart, and my greatest joy is to share what I have learned about God in His Word.

I tried different methods of Bible study. I had learned to increase my understanding of college textbooks by outlining, so I tried that. I actually outlined the entire Bible in about three years. I gleaned many facts that way, but found the relationships of Bible people confusing.

So I researched the relationships of all the people in the Bible: how they were related to one another. I started on file cards and, after I got a computer, moved my results to floppy disks. The study helped me see how Bible people influenced one another, either for or against God and His commands.

Later I attended Sacramento Bible Institute. There I learned more ways to study the Bible. More importantly, I learned to apply what God was saying to me personally as I read His Word and prayed.

That was my privileged background as I became a caregiver. We don't have time for in-depth Bible study, but God will instruct us, whatever our previous Bible knowledge, if we come to Him with a teachable spirit. Those lessons minister to the heart.

*All knowing God, thank You for teaching us out of Your Word. Thank You for showing me the facts of history are not as important as the direction You give. Thank You for allowing me to teach Your Word to others as I share with them what You have been doing in my life. In Jesus' name, amen.*

# MY DIVINE HELPER

*Unless the Lord had been my help,*

*My soul would soon have settled in silence.*

*If I say, "My foot slips,"*

*Your mercy, O Lord, will hold me up.*

*In the multitude of my anxieties within me,*

*Your comforts delight my soul.*

--Psalm 94:17-19

I ONCE TAUGHT in a Christian day school where the pastor/principal acted like he knew more than God did. He began one staff devotional by saying God was not our helper. It was up to us to get busy and help God. Fortunately, I had made enough progress in the Christian life to know I could research that concept in my own Bible, and I found the principal to be totally in error. God says He is our helper in many places of the Bible. Just looking them up makes a great word study.

Of course, that statement put me on alert that this man's words could not be trusted. It also made me start looking for a different school. Those were the immediate results.

However, there were long-range, positive results as well. A few years later I found myself needing help to make decisions for the care of my loved ones. Because I had researched the subject so thoroughly, I knew that when I made errors, God was right there with me, lifting me up. As Psalm 94:19 says, "In the multitude of my anxieties within me, [His] comforts delight [ed] my soul." My God has power to help (see 2 Chronicles 25:8)!

*Almighty God, I am so thankful You condescend to help Your needy creation. I am in awe that You even want to be a part of my life. Thank You for showing me Your power. Thank You for Your ever-present help. In Jesus' name, amen.*

# HE OWNS IT ALL

*Oh, come, let us sing to the Lord!*

*Let us shout joyfully to the Rock of our salvation.*

*Let us come before His presence with thanksgiving;*

*Let us shout joyfully to Him with psalms.*

*For the Lord is the great God,*

*And the great King above all gods.*

*In His hand are the deep places of the earth;*

*The heights of the hills are His also.*

*The sea is His, for He made it;*

*And His hands formed the dry land.*

--Psalm 95:1-5

TAKING CARE OF a loved one is usually an expensive undertaking. I'm talking about money, this time. I am not even considering the expense of time and emotions. When a loved one becomes ill, there are medical bills, often beyond what insurance will pay. There are the added costs of a different diet, incontinence needs, transportation to doctor's offices, prescriptions, therapy, and that's just at the beginning. Eventually there are the heavier expenses of providing care, from respite care to round-the-clock or nursing home care.

It's easy to fall into the trap of worrying about money. I recommend getting good counsel on how to pay for these needs, and to use any resources available. However, depending on human resources will not shut off the worry button when you try to sleep at night.

What takes away the worry? It's not an easy fix, but here's where you learn to trust God. Spend time reading Scripture that reminds you of God's resources. Bring your needs to God and leave them there. Every time you find you have picked up the worry bag again, drop it back at God's throne. Stand still and watch God work for You. Then give Him the praise.

An old chorus says it well: "He owns the cattle on a thousand hills … I know that He will care for me."

*Gracious Father, You are my king. Once again I place our needs in Your hands, knowing You will take care of us. Help me just rest in Your promises. Remind me of how You have taken care of us in the past, so I can praise Your name wherever I go. In Jesus' name, amen.*

# SHEEP? OR SHEPHERD?

*Oh, come, let us worship and bow down;*

*Let us kneel before the Lord our Maker.*

*For He is our God,*

*And we are the people of His pasture,*

*And the sheep of His hand.*

*Today, if you will hear His voice:*

*"Do not harden your hearts, as in the rebellion,*

*As in the day of trial in the wilderness,*

*When your fathers tested Me;*

*They tried Me, though they saw My work,*

*For forty years I was grieved with that generation,*

*And said, 'It is a people who go astray in their hearts,*

*And they do not know My ways.'*

*So I swore in My wrath,*

*'They shall not enter My rest.'"*

--Psalm 95:6-11

LARRY GREW UP on a farm in Idaho. His mother kept a vegetable garden close to the farmhouse. His father planted wheat and kept sheep. In the summertime, he hired migrant workers to take the sheep out to fatten up on the nearby hills. At least one summer Larry went with the migrants. He told me how they would "brand" the sheep with creosote, in case any wandered into other flocks. He said the worst part of the summer was never being able to get clean.

During the WWII years my family kept sheep for a soldier who had raised his flock as a 4-H project and did not want to give them up when he was drafted into the military. Our sheep occupied a fenced half-acre beyond my mother's garden. My early memories are of abandoned lambs bedded down behind our kitchen stove. I thought it was fun to bottle feed them. My mother's memories were not so pleasant: chasing the adult sheep out of her rose garden.

God calls us His sheep. That's not very complimentary, for sheep are smelly, irresponsible, mindless followers and wanderers, incapable of defending themselves. Complimentary or not, that pretty much describes me too. I'm just thankful God Himself is the Good Shepherd who loves and cares for His sheep, and that He made me one of His.

Sometimes I get to be an under-shepherd, taking care of ailing sheep. Sometimes I'm just a needy sheep myself. Many days I'm both.

*Gentle Shepherd, thank You for bringing me into Your fold. Help me care for other sheep with the same tenderness You care for me. Let me trust in Your choices for my feeding and rest. In Jesus' name, amen.*

# TELLING YOUR STORY

*Oh, sing to the Lord a new song!*

*Sing to the Lord, all the earth.*

*Sing to the Lord, bless His name;*

*Proclaim the good news of His salvation from day to day.*

*Declare His glory among the nations,*

*His wonders among all peoples.*

--Psalm 96:1-3

ALL I SAID to the young man was, "I'm praying for your mom and your family." That was the first time his mother had been seated at the same table as Larry in the nursing home dining room. There followed several weeks in which various family members of this lady came to encourage her to eat her lunch, just as I did with Larry.

We exchanged polite questions: Where do you live? What do you do for a living? How is your loved one doing? When I told them Larry had been a pastor, the daughter became very excited and announced the news to her mother. The mother smiled and reached her hand out to us, the first time I had seen her react in any way. Her children told us she had always been active in her church and had great respect for pastors. Our presence seemed to comfort her despite the fact that there was really nothing we could do for her except pray.

Each day she ate less. Her family brought treats to tempt her appetite. She was dying with cancer, and the day soon arrived when she no longer came to the dining room. When I asked, the aides told me her family continued to gather with her for her meals, but now they stayed in her room.

One day the son came to our table to tell me how blessed his family was by my faithfully encouraging Larry every noontime, by our story of serving God, and by my statement that I was praying for them. His mother had passed into eternity the night before, and he wanted to let me know I had helped ease their burden.

The young man's words of appreciation surprised me and encouraged my heart. I realized that watching his family's faithfulness to their mother had lightened my burden as well. God is good.

*Lord of our hearts, thank You for using us to bless other lives, especially when we don't even know we're doing that. Thank You for sending others to bless our lives and help lift the burdens. May we who love You continually be Your hands and arms to lift Your children up to You. In Jesus' name, amen.*

# OUR SOURCE OF STRENGTH AND BEAUTY

*For the Lord is great and greatly to be praised;*

*He is to be feared above all gods.*

*For all the gods of the peoples are idols,*

*But the Lord made the heavens.*

*Honor and majesty are before Him;*

*Strength and beauty are in His sanctuary.*

--Psalm 96:4-6

YOU DRAG YOURELF out of bed after a night of very little sleep. When you walk by the bathroom mirror, you groan. Not a pretty sight. Caregiving drastically ages a person. Whatever happened to that cute little "chick" that went to college because the guys in the café wouldn't leave her alone? You already look older than your mother.

No time to think about yourself. Your loved one already needs your help. You pray for an easy day, but you can already detect a contrary spirit that you know you will have to deal with all day. Many more days and nights like this and you'll be looking older than your grandmother.

Fortunately, through the years, you've come to realize the truth of some proverbs concerning beauty. Beauty is only skin deep. Beauty is a beauty does. Beauty is in the eye of the beholder.

In the few minutes you have alone (even if it is just in the bathroom) God whispers His encouragement. Both strength and beauty are found in Him. Stay close to His side. He'll not only get you through the tough days, His beauty will show through your life.

How beautiful is that!

*Father, help me remember my source of strength. Although I don't like the marks of age I find on my face, thank You for shining Your love through my life. That's the most beautiful expression of all. In Jesus' name, amen*

# WHAT DO I HAVE TO GIVE?

*Give to the Lord,*

*O families of the peoples,*

*Give to the Lord glory and strength.*

*Give to the Lord the glory due His name;*

*Bring an offering,*

*And come into His courts.*

*Oh, worship the Lord in the beauty of holiness!*

*Tremble before Him, all the earth.*

--Psalm 96:7-9

EVERY SO OFTEN we need to take inventory of our assets, make budgets, and determine the best way to take care of our resources. For the child of God, this must include our giving, and that usually means assessing our tithes and offerings. I am grateful when I have enough money to tithe and give to missions. But is that what God wants from us? Is it *all* He wants from us? Sometimes I haven't been able to even do that, which I consider to be the minimum. Does that mean God is not happy with me?

Psalm 96 talks about giving to God. We are to give Him glory and strength. How can we do that? He already has all the glory and strength. I think it must mean we are to praise Him and tell others about His glory and strength. That's an offering of our time and testimony. Worship is the bottom line.

What can I give as an act of worship? If you are a caregiver, you are probably already giving. If your actions for your loved one are done out of a love for God, whether or not you always feel loving toward your charge, those duties are acts of worship. It becomes an attitude thing, and many attitude adjustments are necessary in the life of the caregiver.

Christina Rosetti (1830-1894) wrote a poem that has become a children's Christmas song: "What can I give Him, poor as I am? If I were a shepherd, I would bring a lamb. If I were a wise man, I would do my part. Yet what can I give Him? Give Him my heart."

Jesus said, "Inasmuch as you did it to one of the least of these My brethren, you did it to Me" (Matthew 25:40).

*Beautiful, holy Lord Jesus, I have nothing better to give You than my heart. Help me remember that my gift is most precious on the days it is hardest to give. In Jesus' name, amen.*

# GOD'S LIGHTNINGS

*The Lord reigns;*

*Let all the earth rejoice;*

*Let the multitude of isles be glad!*

*Clouds and darkness surround Him;*

*Righteousness and justice are the foundation of His throne.*

*A fire goes before Him,*

*And burns up His enemies round about.*

*His lightnings light the world;*

*The earth sees and trembles.*

*Her mountains melt like wax at the presence of the Lord,*

*At the presence of the Lord of the whole earth.*

*The heavens declare His righteousness,*

*And all the peoples see His glory.*

--Psalm 97:1-6

OMINOUS CLOUDS REFLECTED my mood as I followed the ambulance. After two weeks in a local hospital, my husband Larry was sent to UC Davis Medical Center in Sacramento for surgery on his shattered hip. This was a new venture for us, and I knew I had to rely on God's leading to make all the upcoming decisions.

The afternoon filled with admitting Larry into a hospital room and then multiple visits by doctors, nurses, and other medical staff. Each participant wanted exhausting amounts of information, and I had to speak for Larry as he had no idea what was going on. After each visit I attempted to calm him and keep him from removing his IV and catheter. I dared not leave until he was settled for the night.

I had arranged to stay at my stepson Paul's home while we had to be at UCD. I arrived there late in the evening, just as huge raindrops began to fall and thunder rolled.

This was the first time I had visited Paul's house since he had finished remodeling it. I admired the new kitchen and enjoyed a snack at the dining room table while updating Paul's family on Larry's condition. Just then a huge flash of lightning illuminated the adjoining great room that I had not yet noticed. I turned to look and realized one whole side of that room was two stories of windows.

The lights flickered on and off, but for about an hour we sat spellbound, watching Gods power exhibited in mighty lightning strikes and thunder crashes. Conversation changed from the problems of the day to the power of God. My mountains of fear melted like wax before His presence.

*Almighty God, we are weak, forgetful humans. Thank You for the reminders of Your power. Help us lean on You and not be overwhelmed by anything. In Jesus' name, amen.*

# SHARE THE SUNSHINE

*You who love the Lord, hate evil!*

*He preserves the souls of His saints;*

*He delivers them out of the hand of the wicked.*

*Light is sown for the righteous,*

*And gladness for the upright in heart.*

*Rejoice in the Lord, you righteous,*

*And give thanks at the remembrance of His holy name.*

--Psalm 97:10-12

I WROTE THIS on the last Monday in January. The TV news just said this is the most depressing day of the year for the following reasons: credit card Christmas bills are due, New Year's resolutions have already been broken, and the weather is gloomy at best.

Whatever day you are reading this, you can probably find excuses for depression. Those reasons, like the ones the newscaster gave, are all circumstantial. As long as we base our happiness on our circumstances, Satan will point out all the things that could make us sad or angry.

Trust God with a timely solution. My Sunday school material that same week included a statement I underlined: "Happiness is an inside job." In other words, happiness is a choice.

An old hymn tells us where to look. "Turn your eyes upon Jesus. Look full in His wonderful face, and the things of earth will grow strangely dim in the light of His glory and grace."

Rejoice with the psalmist. God preserves our souls. He delivers us. He gives us light and gladness. So we can rejoice and give thanks every time His holy name comes to mind.

Whether or not you have bills to pay, you are disappointed with your own resolve, or the weather isn't the best, none of these can dictate your mood without your permission.

Happiness *is* an inside job.

*Tender Father, thank You for rejoicing my heart. Keep me centered on You and Your grace. Help me share the hope and sunshine. In Jesus' name, amen.*

# PRAISE FOR VICTORY

*Oh, sing to the Lord a new song!*

*For He has done marvelous things;*

*His right hand and His holy arm have gained Him the victory.*

*The Lord has made known His salvation;*

*His righteousness He has been revealed in the sight of the nations.*

*He has remembered His mercy and His faithfulness to the house of Israel;*

*All the ends of the earth have seen the salvation of our God.*

--Psalm 98:1-3

CAREGIVING IS A burden. I know, we are admonished to think of it as a joy, a delight, an opportunity to show our loved one and our God how much we care. But the day-to-day, 24/7 work of caregiving is definitely a burden.

The weariness that accompanies caregiving can keep us from thinking rationally. So many times I would end the day wondering if we had made any progress at all. It just felt like we were always losing ground.

A loved one afflicted with Alzheimer's Disease does lose ground. It may be gradual, or there may be sudden drops in ability, but over time the loss is obvious. That in itself can be depressing.

Then it's wise to realize our own helplessness. People who think they must be in control find it particularly hard to be caregivers. God is the only one in control in any situation, but it is especially obvious for us.

Psalm 98 brings a ray of hope. We can sing to the Lord a new song, because He has already done marvelous things, so we can rest assured that He will keep on doing wonders. I love the verse that reminds us, "His right hand and His holy arm have gained Him the victory." I don't have to feel like a winner. He's already won the battles for me. My right hand and arm don't have much strength, but His are all powerful. He can and will do for my loved one – and for me – whatever is right and best.

*Almighty God, thank You for the assurance that we will win in You. Help me look to the ultimate future with hope, knowing that all will be well. Help me rest in You to take care of the here and now. In Jesus' name, amen.*

# GOD – WHO – FORGIVES

*Moses and Aaron were among His priests,*

*And Samuel was among those who called upon His name;*

*They called upon the Lord, and He answered them.*

*He spoke to them in the cloudy pillar;*

*They kept His testimonies and the ordinance He gave them.*

*You answered them, O Lord our God;*

*You were to them God-Who-Forgives,*

*Though You took vengeance on their deeds.*

*Exalt the Lord our God,*

*And worship at His holy hill;*

*For the Lord our God is holy.*

                                        --Psalm 99:6-9


I LED A women's Bible study on the Book of James. James is a practical book. Every time I study it, it convicts me of the sins of my tongue. It is my tongue that gets me into the most trouble.

As caregivers, the tongue gives us more trouble than anything else we deal with. We end the day wishing we had been more patient, sorry for our short answers and grouchy tone of voice, knowing we might have gotten more cooperation from our loved one if we had spoken more kindly, and praying we will do better tomorrow.

How thankful I am that God is the God-Who-Forgives. He is the God of the second (and third, and fourth – you get the picture) chance. Lamentations 3:23 says His mercies are new every morning. And every morning I start the day asking for control over my tongue, knowing it will simply display what is in my heart. I pray for God to keep working in my heart.

We try, and we fail. That doesn't mean we should give up trying. It helps to look back over months and even years to see how far God has brought us. And when we fail again, confess our need for God's help again; and thank Him for being the God-Who-Forgives.

*Awesome, forgiving God, thank You for understanding how weak we are. Change our hearts, Lord. May our tongues show that change by blessing those around us. In Jesus' name, amen.*

# GOD'S WORK

*Make a joyful shout to the Lord, all you lands!*

*Serve the Lord with gladness;*

*Come before His presence with singing.*

*Know that the Lord, He is God;*

*It is He who has made us, and not we ourselves;*

*We are His people and sheep of His pasture.*

--Psalm 100:1-3

JUST WHO ARE you working for? I've asked myself that question many times.

In college I worked at many jobs. I was willing to clean houses, iron clothing, baby-sit, tutor, proctor tests, or just about anything legitimate to make enough money to complete my degree. Every summer I sorted fruit on a pear belt. Occasionally I realized my employment might be service to God as well as to myself, but I must admit the emphasis was on doing a good job so that the employer would ask me to work for him/her again. It was all about me most of the time.

When I taught in Christian elementary schools, I was more apt to consider my work a service to God. After all, I was teaching children not just life skills but a biblical worldview. I served those children and their families, but I primarily aimed to please my Lord Jesus Christ. However I didn't always consider the time outside of the classroom as work for anyone, and I surely used that time to advance my own agenda.

In the midst of this lifestyle, I gradually had to take on more and more of my husband's care. Whenever I thought about who I worked for at this stage of life, I considered my vows to Larry and my duty as a wife. I served Larry, and not always joyfully. This increasing difficulty continued for several years, until one day a discussion with my daughter opened my eyes to the One for whom I really worked. God had given me the privilege of taking care of one of His servants. What an awesome responsibility! What a joyful privilege!

Do we automatically serve the Lord just because we belong to Him? It's an attitude thing again. I could have been serving God my whole life, and sometimes I did. But not always. When I purposely serve Him, He gives the joy.

*Loving Father, You are so patient with my slow learning. Thank You for loving me and giving me the awesome privilege of serving You. I do it with joy. May the joy be contagious. In Jesus' name, amen.*

# GOOD INTENTIONS

*I will sing of mercy and justice;*

*To You, O Lord, I will sing praises.*

*I will behave wisely in a perfect way.*

*Oh, when will You come to me?*

*I will walk within my house with a perfect heart.*

*I will set nothing wicked before my eyes;*

*I hate the work of those who fall away;*

*It shall not cling to me.*

*A perverse heart shall depart from me;*

*I will not know wickedness.*

--Psalm 101:1-4

IT STARTED WHEN I was a child. I felt convicted of my bad behavior, and I promised God I'd do better. As a teenager I understood enough of God's grace to ask Him into my life as my Lord and Savior. What a surprise when I discovered my sinful nature was still with me. My tender heart promised God I would do better — at least every month when taking communion, often weekly after a convicting sermon, even nightly as I prayed at the end of a day in which my all too human emotions had gotten the better of me.

Caregiving is stressful. Stress causes me anger or depression. I still find myself ending a day confessing my wrongdoing and promising to do better.

Doesn't God get tired of my same old confessions and promises? Won't He eventually say, "Enough, already! I've heard it all before and I'm all out of forgiveness?" No! Praise the Lord! His mercies are new every morning. His mercy is everlasting and His truth endures to all generations.

When David wrote Psalm 101, I am sure he had equally good intentions. He promised to behave wisely and walk perfectly. We can read David's story in the Old Testament and realize he wasn't able to live up to his promises any more than we are. Maybe that's why he started this psalm by reminding us of God's mercy and justice.

*Thank You, loving Father, that Your grace is enough. I'll keep trying to serve You with a perfect heart, but I need Your help to do it. Help me lean on Your Holy Spirit within me to accomplish to work You have given me to do. In Jesus' name, amen.*

# HOLDING BACK THE TEARS

*Hear my prayer, O Lord,*

*And let my cry come to You.*

*Do not hide Your face from me in the day of my trouble;*

*Incline Your ear to me;*

*In the day that I call, answer me speedily.*

*For my days are consumed like smoke,*

*And my bones are burned like a hearth.*

*My heart is stricken and withered like grass,*

*So that I forget to eat my bread.*

*Because of the sound of my groaning*

*My bones cling to my skin.*

*I am like a pelican of the wilderness;*

*I am like an owl of the desert.*

*I lie awake,*

*And am like a sparrow alone on the housetop ...*

*For I have eaten ashes like bread,*

*And mingled my drink with weeping.*

--Psalm 102:1-7, 9

MY WRITING CRITIQUE group members all agreed. None of them realized the difficult times I endured while caring for Larry. I hid it well – perhaps too well. I explained that God gave me the ability to live in the "now." As a teacher, I left my home each morning, dropped my children off at their classrooms, and concentrated on the children or faculty that God sent me to minister to that day. I did not pick up the home concerns until the family gathered at the end of the day. I accepted that I couldn't be with my children and husband all day, but God was there. I trusted Him to take care of them.

That long-engrained attitude continued with Larry's care. I left him under the charge of a caregiver and God. I did not think about home problems until I arrived at my driveway in the evening, whether I had spent the day in the classroom, a home-schooler's kitchen, or a Write Bunch meeting.

That does not mean I did not feel Larry's pain or worry about decisions I needed to make on his behalf. I grieved over losing him years before his actual passing. Our troubles seemed overwhelming many times.

I read Psalm 102 and bow in awe. The psalmist describes my life exactly. What can I add but that our compassionate God does answer our prayers. His timing may not be what we desire, but it is always right.

*Loving God, thank You that You hear our groaning and You're there with us through the sleepless nights. I may think I am as isolated as a pelican in the wilderness, an owl in the desert, or a sparrow on a housetop, but I'm not. You're right there with me every step. Open my eyes to Your presence. Help me wait on Your answers. In Jesus' name, amen.*

# FOR OUR PROGENY

*My days are like a shadow that lengthens,*

*And I wither away like grass.*

*But You, O Lord, shall endure forever,*

*And the remembrance of Your name to all generations ...*

*He shall regard the prayer of the destitute,*

*And shall not despise their prayer.*

*This will be written for the generation to come,*

*That a people yet to be created may praise the Lord.*

--Psalm 102:11-12, 17-18

YOU HEARD THE advice: you just have to be strong. Be strong for your family. Be strong for the loved one you are caring for. Just show the world how strong you are.

I don't know what that kind of advice does for you, but it makes me realize how weak I really am. I did all the "strong" stuff. Only I wasn't really strong. I was falling apart inside. But I had to look strong – for the family's sake, for the children, because I said I was a Christian.

Then I had to deal with the guilt that follows when we live a lie. My strong performance was just that – a performance. I was putting on an act to make others think I was strong, hoping that they would be stronger because of it.

It doesn't work that way. An act – a lie – is not going to help anyone, particularly the watching younger generations. If we take time to analyze the effect of our lives on our children, what do we really want them to learn? God reminds us we are weak, and that He is the strong one we can lean on. Don't we want our children to learn that?

They learn it by watching us learn to lean on God, acknowledging our weakness and need of Him. In writing or telling the stories of my life, I need to be clear about who the Strong One is and how He got me through the hard times. May my story cause "the people yet to be created" to have hope and to praise the Lord.

*Almighty Father, thank You for showing me my weakness so that I learn increasingly to lean on Your power. What a mighty God we serve. Remind me to tell my story truthfully, giving You all the glory. In Jesus' name, amen.*

# THE "GO-TO" PSALM

*Bless the Lord, O my soul;*

*And all that is within me, bless His holy name!*

*Bless the Lord, O my soul,*

*And forget not all His benefits:*

*Who forgives all your iniquities,*

*Who heals all your diseases,*

*Who redeems your life from destruction,*

*Who crowns you with lovingkindness and tender mercies,*

*Who satisfies your mouth with good things,*

*So that your youth is renewed like the eagle's.*

*The Lord executes righteousness*

*And justice for all who are oppressed.*

--Psalm 103:1-6

WHERE DO I go for comfort? It depends on my immediate need. If I am cold, I am comforted when I walk into my warm house, or snuggle up to a blazing fireplace. If I am really hungry, almost any food will fill the bill. If I am lonely, I gravitate toward friends or family, in person or on the phone, or even Facebook. If that doesn't do it, chocolate!

If my feelings have been hurt, I need one or more of the special friends who help me put my damages in perspective. Overwhelmed? I look for distraction. Overtired? I seek rest. Frustrated? I want answers.

But in all these cases, and more (needing forgiveness, sick, general dissatisfaction), Psalm 103 is my favorite. It reminds me of all God's benefits. There is not an area of my life that God does not want to fill. I need Him to tell me of His love and care because, in the busyness of life, I forget. God doesn't forget. He's there waiting to meet my needs – and He is the only one who can -- if I will just rest in Him.

*Omniscient, omnipotent God, thank You for being there to meet all my needs. Thank You for the comfort I find resting in You. Remind me early and often that You are but a prayer's length away. Help me step back from the mess I live in and watch You work. Bless the Lord, O my soul. In Jesus' name, amen.*

# WHAT DID I DO WRONG?

*The Lord executes righteousness*

*And justice for all who are oppressed.*

*He made known His ways to Moses,*

*His acts to the children of Israel.*

*The Lord is merciful and gracious,*

*Show to anger, and abounding in mercy.*

*He will not always strive with us,*

*Nor will He keep His anger forever.*

*He has not dealt with us according to our sins,*

*Nor punished us according to our iniquities.*

*For as the heavens are high above the earth,*

*So great is His mercy toward those who fear Him;*

*As far as the east is from the west,*

*So far has He removed our transgressions from us.*

--Psalm 103:6-12

I WATCHED THE family take care of their mother, noticing how they fought to get her the best care, even demanding therapy that would no longer benefit her, special attention that she could not enjoy, requesting she be moved to a better room or in with a more agreeable roommate. After the mother's death, family members outdid each other to provide a lavish memorial ceremony and the most expensive coffin. I wondered whom they were trying to impress as I suspected each son and daughter was dealing with guilt feelings.

Had they maintained a loving relationship with their mother throughout her life, they would not have felt compelled to "make it up to her" in her final months and after. I doubt this family learned from their experience, but I did. I vowed I would do my best to keep family relationships loving so that I would not go through the wrenching time of guilt added to grief.

I have observed other families deal with declining parents and search their souls for anything they might have done to cause their pain. Sometimes I have even asked, "What did I do wrong?" But I know from reading God's word that He doesn't deal with us that way. Life and death happen. Decline and death are a part of God's circle of life. God is not using my loved one's illness to punish me.

Satan accuses us of our shortcomings in our weakest moments. He will suggest God is punishing us. The answer to that is keeping short accounts with God. We all sin every day. First John 1:9 says, "If we confess our sins, He is faithful and just to forgive us our sins and to cleanse us from all unrighteousness," Knowing we are forgiven gives us power and banishes guilt.

*Gracious Father, thank You for assuring me of Your forgiveness in Your Word. Help me keep short accounts with You. Help me genuinely love my family members and commend them daily to Your care. In Jesus' name, amen.*

# GUARDIAN ANGELS

*Bless the Lord, O my soul!*

*O Lord my God, You are very great:*

*You are clothed with honor and majesty,*

*Who cover Yourself with light as with a garment,*

*Who stretch out the heavens like a curtain.*

*He lays the beams of His upper chambers in the waters,*

*Who makes the clouds His chariot,*

*Who walks on the wings of the wind,*

*Who makes His angels spirits,*

*His ministers a flame of fire.*

--Psalm 104:1-4

I LOOKED IN the rearview mirror as I moved into the exit lane. Oops! A small car that had been in my blind spot took up the space I intended to use, so close I knew we would collide – but we didn't. One of God's guardian angels doubtless kept us from tragedy. I breathed a "Thank You, Lord," watched the other car fade back and, rattled, took my exit ramp.

How many times has God saved me on the road or in places where I am not even aware of His help? Who are these angels who protect His children from harm? Can we trust them to always be there for us?

I am saddened when a friend tells me she knows her departed husband is now an angel who watches over her. Nowhere in the Bible does it say people become angels when they die. Angels are specially created beings who serve God in ways people cannot. A word study on "angels" will clarify who they are and what are their missions. Billy Graham wrote a good book on the subject, for those who don't like doing their own research.

I now have two husbands in heaven. I loved them both dearly, and I'm sure they loved me too. I don't exactly know what they are doing (other than praising God) but if they are at all interested in what's still going on down here on earth, I know they are not able to do anything about it. No matter. God has given his angels the power to work whatever miracles are necessary to bring His will to pass. That's more than enough for me!

*Lord Jesus, thank You for Your angels. I don't worship them, for they are not God, but I thank You for them and the power You have given them to work Your will. Help me live cautiously but trusting You to be there for me in the things I cannot control. Thank You for the multitude of times Your angels have saved me from disaster that I didn't even know about. In Your own precious name, amen.*

# NIGHT WORKERS

*He appointed the moon for seasons;*

*The sun knows its going down.*

*You make darkness, and it is night,*

*In which all the beasts of the forest creep about.*

*The young lions roar after their prey,*

*And seek their food from God.*

*When the sun rises, they gather together*

*And lie down in their dens.*

*Man goes out to his work and to his labor until the evening.*

--Psalm 104:19-23

PEOPLE CAN BE classed either as "night-owls" or "robins" and the owls and robins are frequently married to each other. In this psalm God contrasts the lions, who work at night, with man, who works by day. Even if you are a "night-owl," you probably don't really enjoy working all night. It is against the God-given rhythm of our bodies.

When something upsets this natural rhythm, it can cause distress not only for that person, but also for family members. In the case of Alzheimer's Disease, the so-called sundowner's syndrome is a major force to reckon with. The patient becomes restless as the day draws to a close. Further, he/she gets up frequently during the night.

The caregiver has already spent the day in exhausting duties and needs to rest. He/She needs sleep to get ready for the challenges of the next day. After a few weeks the caregiver learns to sleep so lightly the patient's slightest move awakens him/her. He/She may resort to naps during the day when the patient appears to be napping, but that too becomes a risk for one who can no longer be left unattended.

Larry was at this stage that my children convinced me I needed to find full time care for him. When he walked up to the busy highway during one of my exhausted naps, I realized I could no longer safely care for him.

No person can be on duty 24/7. I am thankful for the multitude of medical and aide personnel who cheerfully work their shifts in the middle of the night. For many of them it is a sacrifice, for our bodies are not geared to this routine. At least most of them can go home and sleep during the day, whereas an at-home caregiver cannot.

God set our body clocks. Sometimes, in order to take care of the work He has given us, we have to violate the natural setting. He gives grace and strength to His workers.

*Gracious Father, thank You for the night workers who care for Your children. Bless them and their families for the sacrifices they make. Protect and strengthen them. In Jesus' name, amen.*

# SEEKING GOD'S FACE

*Oh, give thanks to the Lord!*

*Call upon His name;*

*Make known His deeds among the peoples!*

*Sing to Him, sing psalms to Him;*

*Talk of all His wondrous works!*

*Glory in His holy name;*

*Let the hearts of those rejoice who seek the Lord!*

*Seek the Lord and His strength;*

*Seek His face evermore!*

*Remember His marvelous works which He has done,*

*His wonders, and the judgments of His mouth,*

*O seek of Abraham His servant,*

*You children of Jacob,*

*His chosen ones!*

--Psalm 105:1-6

SOMETIMES I THINK I was born at the wrong time. Women's Liberation became a big thing in my lifetime. Although I taught school most of my married life, I did not feel like I wanted to "have it all." I found juggling work, family, and church participation to be overwhelming much of the time. I did not want to add "equality" with my husband Bud. I more than appreciated letting him make the decisions. It helped that he only occasionally expressed concern that I carried a huge load.

When Bud died, I suddenly realized I had used what I considered my position as a submissive wife as a buffer against responsibility. God led our family by leading Bud. My part was to follow Bud's understanding of that godly leadership. I recognized I had allowed Bud to actually come between God and myself.

Because of this I could have felt forsaken at his death, but God was still there for me. As I crawled into bed the night Bud passed into eternity, I turned to God and said, "It's just You and me now, Lord. Like it always should have been." I felt the warmth of His embrace. He understood my confusion and He had been waiting for me to turn to Him all along.

God wants us to seek His face – evermore – as the psalm says. Nothing good, bad, or indifferent should get between us and that close relationship He desires with us. It is never too soon to seek Him. He waits with open arms.

*Father, Abba, God: thank You for Your patience in waiting for me to turn to You. I come with thanksgiving as well as with requests for my needs. I crave Your presence in every part of my life. You are the joy of my life, even on the most difficult days. I love you, Lord. Amen.*

# JOURNALING

*Praise the Lord!*

*Oh, give thanks to the Lord, for He is good!*

*For His mercy endures forever.*

*Who can utter the mighty acts of the Lord?*

*Who can declare all His praise?*

*Blessed are those who keep justice,*

*And he who does righteousness at all times!*

*Remember me, O Lord, with the favor You have toward Your people.*

*Oh, visit me with Your salvation,*

*That I may see the benefit of Your chosen ones,*

*That I may rejoice in the gladness of Your nation,*

*That I may glory with Your inheritance.*

--Psalm 106:1-5

I WAS UPDATING a friend on the status of my book about caregiving. She remarked about how helpful it would be, and then asked, "How did you remember all the things your wrote about? Did you keep a journal?"

Yes, I am a journalist – in the generic sense of the word. In writing my book, much came from my memory as I mentally relived the journey. However, when I could not remember specific details, the journal saved the day.

During an earlier time when a daughter faced danger from her angry spouse, my journaling came in handy again. Faced with a court trial, we could remember traumatic events but not exact dates. We found them all in my journal.

Journals are great for such details. However, my favorite way of journaling is to write prayers to God as I am reading through the Bible. As I look back on these journals, I praise the Lord again for His mighty acts and favors to me. They remind me to rejoice in His benefits and glory in His inheritance.

*Gracious Father, thank You for the gift of writing. My brief notes may never bless anyone else but You, but I can rejoice in my progress, for it is all because of You, Lord. I love You. In Jesus' name, amen.*

# TRAPPED

*Nevertheless He regarded their affliction,*

*When He heard their cry;*

*And for their sake He remembered His covenant,*

*And relented according to the multitude of His mercies.*

*He also made them to be pitied*

*By all those who carried them away captive.*

*--Psalm 106:44-46*

SOMETIMES LIFE'S CIRCUMSTANCES make us feel trapped. As a child I felt I would never escape from an abusive family situation. I remember the freedom I felt when I accepted God's forgiveness and became part of His family. The knowledge that God loved me enough to die for me freed my mind from the fear of living in conflict.

I learned to pray about decisions, particularly life-changing decisions. If God were going to rescue me from my captivity, I needed Him to lead me. College and marriage brought freedom, and I reveled in that. Good Bible teaching led me to use that freedom to serve God in a church.

However, marriage and children bring a measure of captivity with them. No marriage is perfect. No children raise themselves without difficulties. The added stress of teaching often brought back those trapped feelings. Had I not responded to God's hold on my life, I might have become another divorce casualty. As it was, I occasionally retreated to my car and drove away from my home in tears only to have God remind me of how foolish I was to let "them" drive me from my place of refuge.

Caregivers frequently feel trapped. The sameness of difficult day following difficult day made me long to escape. Sometimes I just needed someone to listen to my problems. Often my only recourse was to take it all to God, who promised His mercy. Knowing He knew what I endured and that He promised to take me through it was enough. I don't want any pity except God's. Only He can give us the strength to endure.

*Faithful, merciful Father, thank You for pitying me in all my captive situations. Thank You for promising never to leave me nor forsake me. Thank You for sending Your messengers, my brothers and sisters, to help me carry the load and endure the isolation. Help me reach out to others with the same mercy. In Jesus' name, amen.*

# SAY SO

*Oh, give thanks to the Lord, for He is good!*

*For His mercy endures forever.*

*Let the redeemed of the Lord say so,*

*Whom He has redeemed from the hand of the enemy,*

*And gathered out of the lands,*

*From the east and from the west,*

*From the north and from the south.*

*They wandered in the wilderness in a desolate way;*

*They found no city to dwell in.*

*Hungry and thirsty,*

*Their soul fainted in them.*

*Then they cried out to the Lord in their trouble,*

*And He delivered them out of their distresses.*

--Psalm 107:1-6

I GREW UP in a formal, mainline church. The only worship services I ever attended were quiet, pompous, slow-paced, Sunday morning rituals. Even then I felt drawn to God, but I did not find Him in that church.

As a teenager, God worked in my life through Christian friends who were not afraid to talk about spiritual things and who invited me to their church. I accepted Christ as my own Savior one night after a prayer meeting in which I realized these earnest people had something I lacked, but desperately wanted, in my life.

Then I began attending all the church services of the week. I had never even heard of people going to church on Sunday evenings, but that became my favorite time. Ordinary people actually got to their feet and spoke about what God had been doing in their lives. They called it a testimony service.

Our pastor often started the meeting by quoting, "Let the redeemed of the Lord say so." Surely this is what God wants us to do. I had been taught (mostly by example) that "religion" was too private a matter to talk about. What a revelation to find out God tells us to spread the Word. Matthew says to go into all the world and spread the gospel. Paul's letters urge us to share our faith. Even here in the psalms God says to "let the redeemed of the Lord say so."

I am sure that God wants me to share what He has done throughout my caregiving journey. Your testimony can also be a blessing and encouragement to others who may be struggling with the same problems you have. Just say so.

*Gracious Father, thank You for encouraging others with what You have done in my life. May I never get tired of sharing Your good news and giving You all the glory. In Jesus' name, amen.*

# JUST CRY OUT

*Those who sat in darkness and in the shadow of death,*

*Bound in affliction and irons –*

*Because they rebelled against the words of God,*

*And despised the counsel of the Most High,*

*Therefore He brought down their heart with labor;*

*They fell down, and there was none to help.*

*Then they cried out to the Lord in their trouble,*

*And He saved them out of their distresses.*

*He brought them out of darkness and the shadow of death,*

*And broke their chains in pieces.*

*Oh, the men would give thanks to the Lord for His goodness,*

*And for His wonderful works to the children of men!*

*For He has broken the gates of bronze,*

*And cut the bars of iron in two.*

--Psalm 107:10-16

THIS PSALM IMPLIES that some afflictions come as a result of rebellion against God and despising His counsel. As a parent I found letting a child suffer the natural consequences of bad choices was usually punishment enough and most instructive.

God deals with us that way too. If I spend my money foolishly, I won't have what I need at the end of the month. If I don't take care of my health, I will suffer for it later. If I involve myself in sin, my confession will bring God's forgiveness, but I'll still pay the price of natural consequences.

However, we don't cause all of our own troubles, particularly if we are taking care of a loved one. Illness and death are inevitable on this earth. We didn't ask for it, but we have to experience it.

Whether we bring our troubles on ourselves or take them up as "part of the job," God still promises to save us out of our distresses. Just cry out to Him. He's only a prayer away.

*Heavenly Father, thank You for caring for us. Thank You for Your grace and forgiveness, Your wisdom and strength. You have all the answers when we have none. Bring relief from suffering. Break the chains that bind. You are our hope. Let Your light overcome the daily darkness that I feel. In Jesus' name, amen.*

# LIFE'S STORMS

*Those who go down to the sea in ships,*

*Who do business on great waters,*

*They see the works of the Lord, and His wonders in the deep.*

*For He commands and raises the stormy wind,*

*Which lifts up the waves of the sea.*

*They mount up to the heavens,*

*They go down again to the depths;*

*Their soul melts because of trouble.*

*They reel to and fro, and stagger like a drunken man,*

*And are at their wits' end.*

*Then they cry out to the Lord in their trouble,*

*And He brings them out of their distresses.*

*He calms the storm, So that its waves are still.*

*Then they are glad because they are quiet;*

*So He guides them to their desired haven.*

*Oh, that men would give thanks to the Lord for His goodness,*

*And for His wonderful works to the children of men!*

--Psalm 107:23-31

I HAVE NEVER been in a storm at sea, but sometimes daily life can seem like the storm the psalmist describes here.

I remember the "storm" of taking care of my dad. We had a slow, frustrating climb to the top where I commiserated with his pain and disability every day and put up with his anger and ingratitude. That was followed by the crash of his trying to take his life. Another quick rise in his move to a hospital where he had better care. Down the trough of complaint and anger that he still had to deal with life. Move up to a compassionate nursing home and good reports, followed by the news that his aggressive behavior necessitated another move to a more secure place set up for dangerous patients. On and on to the end of his life.

I learned it's never forever. I learned I may be at my wit's end but God never is. I learned I may stagger with fatigue but God will give rest. I learned to cry out to God in my trouble. And, even in the midst of the storm, God calms the willing soul. At the end of the storm we look back and see that He was with us all the time.

The Rail Road Flat Community Church choir always did a beautiful rendition of "Master, the Tempest Is Raging." As their director, I sometimes had trouble getting them to follow the dynamics of songs, but this anthem resonated in their hearts. They made the verses loud and crashing, and skillfully brought the chorus to a calm, "Peace, be still." God had brought each member through levels of life-storms. Their singing gave credence to His care.

*Master, the tempest is always raging to some extent. But You are always there in complete control. Help me trust You. In Jesus' name, amen.*

# DRAMATIC CHANGES

*He turns rivers into a wilderness,*

*And the water springs into dry ground;*

*A fruitful land into barrenness,*

*For the wickedness of those who dwell in it.*

*He turns a wilderness into pools of water,*

*And dry land into water springs.*

*There He makes the hungry dwell,*

*That they may establish a city for a dwelling place,*

*And sow fields and plant vineyards,*

*That they may yield a fruitful harvest.*

*He also blesses them, and they multiply greatly;*

*And He does not let their cattle decrease.*

--Psalm 107:33-38

I LIVED IN a mobile home park and, because it was in the foothills, my home was perched on the side of a hill. I enjoyed the feeling of privacy. My southern windows looked out on a neighbor's rooftop. My northern neighbor looked out on my rooftop.

However, when I first moved here, I wasn't happy with my northern view: a dry, red dirt hillside, so steep nothing would grow on it except weeds. Because my kitchen and dining room windows faced that bleak sight, I decided to make some changes.

First, I had to hire a landscaper who dug, filled, and boarded up the sides to make three wide planting tiers with room for plants and walking. Then I had to research and plant flowers and vegetables suited for the local climate. This was a new experience for me, but I love to learn new things so I really had fun with it. I'm sure I drove my friends and family crazy with my amazing gardening discoveries (of things they've known their whole lives)!

What did it take to make this apparent desert yield fruitful harvests? Money, hard work, research and water. It didn't just happen.

I can see applications to my spiritual life as well. What did it take for God to turn my empty life into a productive one? The water of His Word, cultivation of trials, and mostly God's miraculous love and care.

In the dry times of our lives, look to God for nurture and refreshment. He's the only one who can turn fruitful lands into barrenness and barren lands into lush pools of refreshment.

*Heavenly Father, thank You for stirring up my life to bear fruit for You. Help me remember that I am just Your tool to bring about Your harvest either in my yard or in my spiritual life. How awesome to be used by the God of the universe! May I honor You in all I do. In Jesus' name, amen.*

# SLEEP PATTERNS

*O God, my heart is steadfast;*

*I will sing and give praise, even with my glory.*

*Awake, lute and harp!*

*I will awaken the dawn.*

*I will praise You, O Lord, among the peoples,*

*And I will sing praises to You among the nations.*

*For Your mercy is great above the heavens,*

*And Your truth reaches to the clouds.*

--Psalm 108:1-4

THE TELEPHONE AWOKE me that morning – at 9:15! At first I was annoyed that anyone would call the early and wake me up just to ask a question about the ladies' Bible study. Then I looked at the clock, and became annoyed with myself instead. I'm not usually such a late riser, but the Olympics were on TV until midnight, and I love to watch them, so my sleep pattern was totally off for these two weeks.

I used to be a late riser any time I could get away with it. I loved to stay up late reading or visiting with friends, even practicing the piano. I suffered through early morning classes in college because of my late hours.

Marriage and children changed my sleep patterns temporarily, but taking care of a husband with Alzheimer's Disease made the final adjustment. I had to sleep whenever sleep was possible, and that so lightly as to be awakened by the creak of a bedspring. Sometimes worry about Larry's personality changes or decisions that I needed to make would keep me awake even when I felt exhausted. Many mornings I found myself awake long before I needed to get up.

Facing a day without adequate sleep is daunting. It is easy to greet the sunrise with a snarl. However, David suggests we awaken the dawn with singing, praise, our own glory (such as it is), lute, and harp. When I follow his directions I am able to begin the day on a positive note in spite of circumstances.

Maybe you can't think of anything to praise God for under your trying load. David says to praise God for His mercy and truth. Think about it!

*Yes, Lord, Your mercy and truth are everlasting and they even reach me. Times may be tough but I am never without Your grace. Fill my mind with remembrances of Your blessings. Let me praise Your name. In Jesus' name, amen.*

# DOING VALIANTLY

*Be exalted, O God, above the heavens,*

*And Your glory above all the earth;*

*That Your beloved may be delivered,*

*Save with Your right hand, and hear me ...*

*Who will bring me into the strong city?*

*Who will lead me to Edom?*

*Is it not You, O God, who cast us off?*

*Give us help from trouble,*

*For the help of man is useless.*

*Through God we will do valiantly,*

*For it is He who shall tread down our enemies.*

--Psalm 108:5-6, 10-13

WHAT IS IT that makes us feel like losers? Satan convinces us that if we don't win every battle, we don't win at all. He uses our lack of sleep, overwork, frustrations with whatever system we're dealing with, and negative people (sometimes even the news on TV) to pull us down.

How do we counteract the "loser" feeling? I've tried pulling myself up by my own bootstraps. Guess what? It doesn't work. I've tried positive thinking. It doesn't go far enough, although associating with positive people lessens the effect of the negatives.

God says His beloved will be delivered. Hallelujah! I am one of His beloved! He promises to deliver me. When it seems like God has cast us off (tossed us away), He hasn't. He will give us help from trouble.

David (the writer of the psalm) endured many troubles. He spoke from experience: the help of man is useless. But through God we will do valiantly. He's the only one who can and will tread down our enemies – including Satan.

Will we win every skirmish? Definitely not. Will we win the war? Oh, yes. Our valiant mighty God will give us the victory.

*Almighty God, thank You for Your power and Your care for Your beloved. Thank You for making me one of Your children. Help me look beyond the immediate battle to the end of the fight. Help me be a positive influence on my fellow soldiers. In Jesus' name, amen.*

# DEALING WITH WELL-MEANING ATTACKERS

*Do not keep silent,*

*O God of my praise!*

*For the mouth of the wicked and the mouth of the deceitful*

*Have opened against me;*

*They have spoken against me with a lying tongue.*

*They have also surrounded me with words of hatred,*

*And fought against me without a cause.*

*In return for my love they are my accusers,*

*But I give myself to prayer.*

*Thus they have rewarded me evil for good,*

*And hatred for my love ...*

*I will greatly praise the Lord with my mouth;*

*Yes, I will praise Him among the multitude.*

*For He shall stand at the right hand of the poor,*

*To save him from those who condemn him.*

*--Psalm 109:1-5, 30-31*

IN MY RESAERCH on remedies available for my husband's Alzheimers Disease, I learned of many experimental drugs and herbs. I read the dismal test results and iffy testimonials, prayed, and determined I would not allow Larry to become a guinea pig for research.

That should have settled the question. It did not. Well-meaning friends and relatives stepped up with suggestions for his care. None offered a cure. Most friends suggested miracles that would ameliorate the symptoms. My e-mailbox was stuffed with websites that offered hope, I wanted to scream, and "There is no hope with Alzheimers Disease."

I actually felt attacked by some friends. When I went to church, several friends encouraged me to try ginkgo biloba, St. John's wort, or some other herbal treatment. We did try ginkgo for a while, with no effect. I thought that might stop the attacks, but no: I had to report the results. When I quit giving it to Larry, I was accused of not trying it long enough. They had no idea how hard it was to get him to take any pill, let alone one that had no effect.

Doctors strongly suggested we try different new drugs. Each time we tried one, I waited in vain for results. The one that was supposed to slow AD's progress gave me double worry. If it didn't work, we were wasting a lot of money on it. If it did, was I only prolonging the agony of his symptoms?

Thank God for the faithful few friends and family members who encouraged me to do what I thought was right. Thank God for Himself who gave me peace about the decisions I had to make for someone else's care.


*Yes, Lord. In return for my love, they are my accusers, but I give myself to prayer. Thank You for Your peace. In Jesus' name, amen.*

# IT'S NOT ALL ABOUT YOU

*The Lord said to my Lord,*

*"Sit at My right hand,*

*Till I make Your enemies Your footstool."*

*The Lord shall send the rod of Your strength out of Zion.*

*Rule in the midst of Your enemies!*

*Your people shall be volunteers*

*In the day of Your power;*

*In the beauties of holiness, from the womb of the morning,*

*You have the dew of Your youth.*

--Psalm 110:1-3

IN THE MIDST of caregiving, our focus can become very limited. Because of all the decisions we have to make, for ourselves and for our loved one, we are compelled to focus our attention on whatever legal or medical matters affect us personally. It's not too big a step to begin thinking the rest of the world needs to pay more attention to our needs. Family and friends when we might expect to at least be sympathetic, if not actually helpful, often fail us, unable or unwilling to share our burdens.

When I realize I have once again made myself the center of my life, then I need to step back and try to see things from God's viewpoint. Many people even in my own circle of influence may be affected by what happens to my patient and me. It's not all about me, or him, or them. As the song says, "It's all about You, Jesus."

I would like to be a take-charge person. I certainly won't allow myself to become a victim. But the truth is that God is the only One in charge. I acknowledge that I need Him for the least provision of my life. I am as dependent on Him as my helpless patient is. What a blessing to know that He is worthy of our worship for Who He is as well as all that He can and will do for our condition.

God rules!

*Almighty God, thank You for reminding me of who You are. Thank You for Your awesome power and gracious love. Help me remember where I fit in Your plan. May I be a carrier of Your grace to the ones around me. In Jesus' name, amen.*

# THE ASSEMBLY OF THE UPRIGHT

*Praise the Lord!*

*I will praise the Lord with my whole heart,*

*In the assembly of the upright and in the congregation.*

*The works of the Lord are great,*

*Studied by all who have pleasure in them.*

*His work is honorable and glorious,*

*And His righteousness endures forever.*

*He has made His wonderful works to be remembered;*

*The Lord is gracious and full of compassion.*

*He has given food to those who fear Him;*

*He will ever be mindful of His covenant.*

*He has declared to His people the power of His works,*

*In giving them the heritage of the nations.*

*--Psalm 111:1-6*

I WORRY ABOUT my friend who says she belongs to God but refuses to attend any church. I have a problem with that. How can you say you love God, but not want to be with God's people? She says she watches "church" on TV on Sunday mornings. But how could she not want to join with other worshipers praising the Lord with people she knows?

Many people substitute TV church for the real thing. There are good Christian programs on TV, but one has to be discerning and check out whether truth is being taught. My concern for my friend is that she has no place to show her gratitude to God by serving Him. Furthermore, she has no godly group of people to hold her accountable. I am sure my involvement with a group of believers has kept me from sin many times. They have encouraged me when I was troubled and prayed for me through a multitude of trials. She's missing out on all of that.

God knows how good it is for us personally to praise Him in the assembly of the upright and in the congregation. He delights in our praise. For our pleasure and His, He admonished believers not to forsake assembling together (see Hebrews 10:25).

I'll keep inviting my friend. Maybe one day she'll find the joy of fellowship in the congregation of the righteous.

*Heavenly Father, You alone are worthy of my praise. Thank You for loving me and drawing me to Yourself. Thank You for a voice to sing Your praises and fellow believers to share in that worship. May I never cease to tell of all Your wondrous works. In Jesus' name, amen.*

# WHERE TO FIND WISDOM

*The works of His hands are verity and justice;*

*All His precepts are sure.*

*They stand fast forever and ever,*

*And are done in truth and uprightness.*

*He has sent redemption to His people;*

*He has commanded His covenant forever;*

*Holy and awesome is His name.*

*The fear of the Lord is the beginning of wisdom;*

*A good understand have all those who do His commandments.*

*His praise endures forever.*

*--Psalm 111:7-10*

MY SISTER JOANNE and I were suddenly confronted with decisions that had to be made concerning our mother. Because Joanne and Mother lived together, I assumed Joanne knew how Mother was doing and would let me know if there was a problem. That proved to be a false notion. Mom went into the hospital with pneumonia, and that precipitated worsening dementia. It became necessary to place her in a convalescent home after her stay in the acute care hospital. Later Joanne told me of Mom's worsening dementia.

Joanne was a licensed practical nurse. I expected to rely on her health care knowledge. Fortunately, the hospital's liaison person helped us through the placement and healthcare decisions. I noticed Joanne seemed to have as many questions as I did. That concerned me.

Then we had to make financial and legal decisions. Joanne was nine years older than I was. I expected her to have enough knowledge of these matters to at least discuss them with me. Again, that proved to be false.

Where to turn? My expertise is in elementary education, not medicine, finances, or law. All I knew to do was to pray, and pray I did. The only possible reason for the wise choices we made was that God led us.

For many years I taught my students to memorize Psalm 111:10. Caregivers need to just live it.

*Omniscient God, thank You for sharing Your wisdom with me. Thank You for teaching me to lean on You for all things. May I never get so worldly wise that I don't think I need Your direction. In Jesus' name, amen.*

# THE DESIRE FOR WISDOM

*The fear of the Lord is the beginning of wisdom;*

*A good understanding have all those who do His commandments.*

*His praise endures forever.*

--Psalm 111:10

IT DIDN'T HELP matters that my first husband was 19 years older than I, but most brides probably feel inadequate whatever the age difference. I cannot blame Bud for making me feel that way. He never treated me like a child. Still, many nights I cried myself to sleep wondering if I would ever attain the wisdom I needed to be a competent wife and mother.

One breakthrough came early in our marriage when we attended a family Bible conference. Bible verses marked our places at the lunch table and we were encouraged to memorize them throughout the week. It is no accident that my verse was James 1:15: "If any of you lacks wisdom, let him ask of God, who gives to all liberally and without reproach, and it will be given to him."

What a promise! I needed it. I not only memorized that verse, I claimed it, and God showed me that godly wisdom didn't come from the world's philosophy (I had recently graduate from a secular college so I knew that for sure), but from time spent in God's Word.

I didn't instantly become a great guru, but I began to mature in my Christian life. By the time I needed wisdom for child-rearing and (much later) caregiving, I no longer feared making difficult decisions. My greater fear of displeasing my Savior gave me confidence that He would guide my choices. "Great peace have those who love Your law, and nothing causes them to stumble." (Psalm 119:165)

*All-knowing Father, I pray for all those caregivers who fear making decisions. I pray they will fear to displease You more than they fear the outcome of their choices. Make them aware of Your presence. Help them rest in Your love. In Jesus' name, amen.*

# YOUR LEGACY

*Praise the Lord!*

*Blessed is the man who fears the Lord,*

*Who delights greatly in His commandments.*

*His descendants will be mighty on earth;*

*The generation of the upright will be blessed.*

*Wealth and riches will be in his house,*

*And his righteousness endures forever.*

*Unto the upright there arises light in the darkness;*

*He is gracious, and full of compassion, and righteous.*

*A good man deals graciously and lends;*

*He will guide his affairs with discretion.*

*Surely he will never be shaken;*

*The righteous will be in everlasting remembrance.*

--Psalm 112:1-6

PASTOR SAM TOLD the story of his father's passing. The father had spent his last months living with one of Sam's brothers. After the funeral, the brother called Sam and asked him to come and pick up the things their father had left. On the way there, Sam wondered if he had enough room in his car to carry it all away.

When Sam received his father's possessions, he was overwhelmed. Everything his father had left was contained in a small cardboard box. None of it had any monetary value.

But was that all Sam's father left? No. He left eleven children with memories of growing up in a Christian home. He left a treasury of godly responses to the problems of growing up in poverty. He left lifelong habits to follow: basing decisions on God's Word, waiting on God for answers, spending time in prayer, walking with God through good and bad times.

Sam's dad may not have appeared mighty to the casual onlooker, but he was mighty in God's sight. His generation and those that followed after are blessed. His spiritual wealth far outweighed any money or jewels that we often mistake for riches.

I want to have that kind of everlasting remembrance.

*Eternal Father, thank You for the legacy of godly men and women that I have known or read about. Help me remember that the spiritual legacy I leave my offspring is far more important than any physical thing they might inherit from me. Help me guide my affairs with discretion for your honor and the edification of my children. In Jesus' name, amen.*

# FEAR OF BAD NEWS

*Unto the upright there arises light in the darkness;*

*He is gracious, and full of compassion, and righteous.*

*A good man deals graciously and lends;*

*He will guide his affairs with discretion.*

*Surely he will never be shaken;*

*The righteous will be in everlasting remembrance.*

*He will not be afraid of evil tidings;*

*His heart is steadfast, trusting in the Lord.*

*His heart is established;*

*He will not be afraid.*

--Psalm 112:4-8

OH, NEVER TO be shaken! I don't know how good I must be to get to that degree of security. My first response to bad news is to worry that it will get even worse.

I look back on a year in which I now realize only God could have sustained me. My sister Joanne asked me to be her guardian because she was no longer able to take care of her finances. I got her settled in our mother's home with my daughter Laura as her caregiver. Laura coped with her idiosyncrasies, but often had to call me for advice.

A month later my father had to be hospitalized, and his episodes of rage became an ongoing problem. The convalescent care facility called me frequently and warned me he might not be able to stay there. My research turned up no other nearby nursing homes that were equipped to deal with him.

Meanwhile, my mother endured the final stages of Alzheimer's Disease along with osteoporosis that caused her vertebrae to disintegrate. I answered frequent phone calls from her care facility reporting one fracture after another.

Who could blame me for cringing every time the telephone rang. At least daily someone called with a problem or bad report about one or the other of my responsibilities. I rebelled at the position I held. This was not fair. The family is supposed to take care of the baby (that's me). The baby should not have to make all the decisions for the other family members. I guess God didn't know that rule. Maybe I made it up?

I soon realized I had a choice. I could tense up every time the phone rang, or I could breathe a prayer for God to get me through whatever crisis it brought. The right response was obvious.

*Almighty Father, help me rest in You. There is so little I can control, but You have total control. Thank You for loving me enough to get me through every trial. Thank You for lowering my stress as I lean on You. In Jesus' name, amen.*

# STABILITY

*The righteous will be in everlasting remembrance.*

*He will not be afraid of evil tidings;*

*His heart is steadfast, trusting in the Lord.*

*His heart is established;*

*He will not be afraid ...*

*He has dispersed abroad,*

*He has given to the poor;*

*His righteousness endures forever;*

*His horn will be exalted with honor.*

--Psalm 112:6-9

THE LIFE OF the caregiver often feels like walking on shifting sand. Few people like change, but negative changes happen frequently with people who need care. We long for stability: a day or two to relax in some measure of sameness.

Outwardly, that probably won't happen – at least not for many days in a row. However, inwardly, we can still experience the stability of leaning on our unchanging God. Psalm 112 gives a couple of hints about how to make this happen: fear the Lord and delight greatly in His commandments.

How can that help? Just resting in God's control gives us the ability to deal graciously with problem people. It enables us to relax about the use of our resources, knowing God will supply all our needs. Our trust in God helps us run to Him for comfort and direction when we hear bad news. Acknowledging God's control calms our fears. We can react with righteousness instead of anger.

The more time I spend with God in prayer and in His Word, the more I am fortified for the caregiving job He has given me.

*Almighty God, thank You for being totally in control. Help me remember that every day. Show me times when I can learn more from Your Word and be better fortified for the task at hand. In Jesus' name, amen.*

# "YOU RAISE ME UP"

*He raises the poor out of the dust,*

*And lifts the needy out of the ash heap,*

*That He may seat him with princes –*

*With the princes of His people.*

*He grants the barren woman a home,*

*Like a joyful mother of children.*

*Praise the Lord!*

--Psalm 113:7-9

I AVOIDED READING what I considered depressing biblical books when I was in the midst of caregiving. Not Ecclesiastes. Not Jeremiah or the minor prophets. And certainly not Job. I stayed in the Psalms and New Testament for my own encouragement.

I may not have read Job during that time, but often I felt like him. Job's response to all the bad news in his life was to park himself in an ash heap and scrape his sores with a chunk of broken pottery. Kind of like a dog licking his wounds. Have you been there?

Job's fickle friends even joined him at the ash heap. They "counseled" Job by trying to figure out what he had done wrong to bring all this trouble on himself. If I were job, I would have been trying to figure out what I had done wrong to attract these poor "comforters."

Fortunately, we know the end of the story. God doesn't want us hanging out in an ash heap feeling sorry for ourselves. Back to the Psalms. God raises the poor out of the dust and lifts the needy out of the ash heap. He doesn't tell us to pull ourselves up, because He knows we can't do that. God Himself lifts us.

One of my favorite modern day songs is "You raise me up." Tears come to my eyes whenever I hear it sung. I know it is talking about my relationship with God. He is the only One who raises me up and makes me be "more than I can be."

*Loving Father, thank You for raising me from the pit of despair and the ash heap of worry. Thank You for setting my feet on the solid rock of faith in Christ. Thank You for the daily strength You give me to serve You. In Jesus' name, amen.*

# BETTER, NOT BITTER

*Not unto us, O Lord, not unto us,*

*But to Your name give glory,*

*Because of Your mercy.*

*Because of Your truth.*

*Why should the Gentiles say,*

*"So where is their God?"*

*But our God is in heaven;*

*He does whatever He pleases.*

--Psalm 115:1-3

LIFE'S EXPERIENCES TAKE us in one of two ways: we become better, or we become bitter.

God has given me a grateful heart (most of the time), so even as a child I was shocked to observe the bitterness of a family member. She apparently thought that refusing to conform with respect showed her independence. At a parade, she would embarrass the family by being the only person not standing at attention when the flag passed. In her later years she even decided no one, nor any thing, could tell her what to do – not even traffic lights. Embarrassment turned to fright as we had to physically hold her back from walking into traffic against the red light.

I found it even more shocking when she refused to bow her head during prayer at church. When I bravely asked her about her attitude, she replied, "Why should I? What did God ever do for me?"

What indeed? I was too dumbfounded to reply that every breath she took came from Him. Because of His mercy she still lived. Because of His truth she had the freedom to be bitter and disrespectful. How sad.

We all go through tough times – some more and some less. Tough times bring us to the fork in the road: will I allow this to make me bitter? Or will I give it to God and allow Him to use it in my life to make me better? It is our choice.

*Merciful, truthful, all-wise God, thank You for offering Your mercy and truth to us. Use the trials of the past and the choices of today to enrich my life. Open my eyes to Your presence in my life. Help me share what You teach me. In Jesus' name, amen.*

# COMFORT FOR THE TERMINAL

*I love the Lord, because He has heard*

*My voice and my supplications.*

*Because He has inclined His ear to me,*

*Therefore I will call upon Him as long as I live.*

*The pains of death surrounded me,*

*And the pangs of Sheol laid hold of me;*

*I found trouble and sorrow.*

*Then I called upon the name of the Lord:*

*"O Lord, I implore You, deliver my soul!"*

*Gracious is the Lord, and righteous;*

*Yes, our God is merciful ...*

*Precious in the sight of the Lord*

*Is the death of His saints.*

--Psalm 116:1-5, 15

DEATH IS THE hardest part of life, but it definitely is a major part. We don't like to talk about it. We put off making arrangements for the distribution of possessions because family members fear that discussing it will be too upsetting. We tend to delay making arrangements for power of attorney and other legal matters until the dying loved one is no longer capable of making those decisions. The looming specter of death scares us away from responsible acts.

But death is not a fearful scourge to the person who has placed his/her trust in the Son of God for eternal life. Death to that person offers blessed, everlasting relief from the pain and suffering of this life. My question, during what some have called "the long, slow good-bye of Alzheimer's Disease," has been, "Why does one have to suffer so long before that glorious moment when God says, 'Enough!'?"

When my husband Larry finally went home, as he had yearned to do for so many years, I felt grief. But in that same moment of loss on my part, I felt even greater relief for myself and joy for Larry. I could visualize him dancing around the throne of God, singing at the top of his voice. He who had been silent for months and wheelchair-bound for years, now danced in the presence of the King of kings and the saints who had gone before him. How could I grieve at that?

Larry has finally experienced what he had lived to hear from his Lord, "Welcome home, good and faithful servant. Now enter into the joy of your Lord." And the joy goes on.

*Father, I would despair if You had not clearly given us glimpses of our eternal state with You. The older I get, the more of my friends and family are already partying with You. Thank You for the assurance that when I step from this life I will be instantly in Your presence. Give me strength to live for You until the day You say, "Enough!" In Jesus' name, amen.*

# INCLUDED

*Praise the Lord, all you Gentiles!*

*Laud Him, all you peoples!*

*For His merciful kindness is great toward us,*

*And the truth of the Lord endures forever.*

*Praise the Lord!*

*--Psalm 117:1-2*

WHEN I ATTENDED grammar school (that's what they called it then), one year we had a program to commemorate the month of February. The idea we presented was that February, though the shortest of all the months, was special because of all the wonderful things that happened in it. We mentioned its snowy benefits as the center of winter, and the holidays: Valentine's Day, Lincoln's Birthday, and Washington's Birthday. We also portrayed other family people with February birthdays.

I look at this little psalm the same way. It is short – one of the shortest in the Psalter. But we learn some great truth in it.

There are not many places in the Old Testament that speak well of Gentile nations. The Old Testament was obviously written to God's chosen people, the Jews. But this little psalm calls out to the Gentiles to praise the Lord too. It implies God is merciful to all peoples, Jews and Gentiles. He is merciful to us, and His truth is available to us as well.

If we had only the Old Testament, we might not be able to find that truth, for God sent His Son to reveal it to us, and that story is told in the Gospels of the New Testament. Jesus is the revelation of God's merciful kindness. He declared Himself to be the Way, the Truth, and the Life. What a comfort to find little hints throughout the Old Testament that God loves all people and wants them all to accept His kindness and salvation.

*Gracious Father, thank You for loving us and encouraging our hearts through Your Word. Thank You for sending Your Son Jesus to die on the cross for our sins so that we could spend eternity with You. Thank You for revealing Your truth to us. In Jesus' name, amen.*

# GOD'S DAY

*I will praise You,*

*For You have answered me,*

*And have become my salvation.*

*The stone which the builders rejected*

*Has become the chief cornerstone.*

*This was the Lord's doing;*

*It is marvelous in our eyes.*

*This is the day the Lord has made;*

*We will rejoice and be glad in it.*

--Psalm 118:21-24

ONCE LARRY'S CONDITION became known, caring friends and relatives habitually asked how he was doing. I learned to answer, "He has good days and bad days." Then I might say which category I thought that particular day was. It was up to the inquirer to ask for more information. Otherwise, I left it at that.

Maybe you are thinking your care situation has bad days and worse days. Sometimes I felt like that when we were going through a time of setbacks or declining cognizance. Good days were few and far between.

Still, every morning I met with God for prayer and Bible reading and I asked Him to bless the day ahead of me. Was there a disconnect there? Was God not answering my prayers by sending difficult days instead of easy ones?

I began the practice of ending each day by thanking God for at least ten things. That helped put the day's activities in perspective. In the middle of the day – surrounded by arguments and frustrations and all that goes with caregiving – we may lose sight of God's purposes. It is good to look back and see how God has led.

Then we can adopt the attitude that each day truly is one the Lord has made. It is for our good, whether easy or hard. We must determine to rejoice and be glad in it.

*Gracious Father, thank You for making each of my days. Thank You for giving me a grateful heart. Help me keep Your ways before me, for acknowledging Your control brightens even the most difficult circumstances. Remind me You are there, Lord. In Jesus' name, amen.*

# THE LONGEST CHAPTER

*How can a young man cleanse his way?*

*By taking heed according to Your word.*

*With my whole heart I have sought You;*

*Oh, let me not wander from Your commandments!*

*Your word I have hidden in my heart,*

*That I might not sin against You.*

*Blessed are You, O Lord!*

*Teach me Your statutes.*

--Psalm 119:9-12

HERE IN THE very center of the Bible we find 176 verses wherein each contains a synonym for Scripture. How awesome is that!

It is as if God is saying, "Keep my word central and your life will be in balance." It is for young people (verse 9) and those nearing life's end (verse 33), princes and servants (verse 23).

There is a special verse for those of us going through hard times. "This is my comfort in my affliction, for Your word has given me life" (verse 50). When we find ourselves sleepless, "I remember Your name in the night, O Lord, and I keep Your law" (verse 55). And "At midnight I will rise to give thanks to You, because of Your righteous judgments" (verse 62).

When we need wisdom, verse 66 says, "Teach me good judgment and knowledge, for I believe Your commandments." There is also an explanation of why God allows us to go through difficulties. Verse 67 says, "Before I was afflicted I went astray, but now I keep Your word." Verse 75 says, "In faithfulness You have afflicted me."

It's a long psalm, but a rich one. I recommend you return to it often just to read and reflect on God's goodness through His Word. If you are attempting to read through the Bible by reading a chapter a day, consider this psalm to be 22 chapters and take that many days to read and meditate on it. God will make His Word a delight to you.

*God of the Word, how awesome You are. You created the universe by just speaking the word. You comfort our hearts with Your words. We, who are created in Your image, communicate with words. Your Word is powerful. May we use that power and learn from it. May we – like You -- minister grace with our words. In Jesus' name, amen.*

# THE PRINCE OF PEACE

*In my distress I cried to the Lord,*

*And He heard me.*

*Deliver my soul, O Lord, from lying lips*

*And from a deceitful tongue ...*

*My soul has dwelt too long*

*With one who hates peace.*

*I am for peace;*

*But when I speak, they are for war.*

--Psalm 120:1-2, 6-7

FROM MY OFFICE window in my foothills home I see a variety of beautiful birds. Because of my busy schedule and the fact that I'm often away from home, I don't have a bird feeder. That does not matter to the birds. There are plenty of trees and flowers that provide for their nutrition.

Birds are fascinatingly beautiful. I have a Peterson's *Field Guide to Western Birds* handy for those times when a bird shows up that I don't recognize. Once in a while the bird stays around long enough for me to identify it. I love their infinite designs.

I don't love their attitudes. All the birds I observe demonstrate total selfishness. The blue jays are the worst. Any bird (or small animal) fool enough to invade their territory is instantly attacked. The smaller birds don't stand a chance of finding food until the blue jays move on.

Apparently, size doesn't matter either. Hummingbirds are just as feisty as the jays. They attack each other, as well as any other creatures that appear to threaten them. Cats beware: the hummers are armed and dangerous.

Sometimes I watch the beautiful birds and relate their lives to mine. I just want to go about my business taking care of what God has given me to do without controversy. However, my loved ones often want to fight me over every act I need to do in their behalf. There are days when it seems no one is on my side and they all want me to know it. I am for peace – but they are for war. They may look good, but they are not working for my good.

The psalmist must have felt this way too. His answer was to cry to the Lord, and he knew God heard and would answer. I can rest in that same assurance.

*Father, I get weary in the battles. Thank You for the birds that display what I feel. Give me your inner beauty, Lord. Help me keep Your agenda primary in my life so that I don't feel that I have to fight for what I think I need. I don't want to be a birdbrain. In Jesus' name, amen.*

# THERE IS REAL HELP

*I will lift up my eyes to the hills –*

*From whence comes my help?*

*My help comes from the Lord,*

*Who made heaven and earth …*

*The Lord shall preserve you from all evil;*

*He shall preserve your soul.*

*The Lord shall preserve your going out and your coming in*

*From this time forth, and even forevermore.*

--Psalm 121:1-2, 7-8

I WAS A member of an Evangelism Explosion group that traveled to Eurasia to teach Christian leaders how to train other Christians how to share their faith. Part of getting ready for the trip involved sending out letters to inform friends and relatives of our mission and to ask for support donations. I pictured those who gave like fellow climbers who held the ropes for those of us who were privileged to actually go and conduct the training clinics.

I was thrilled with the responses from most of the ones who received my letters. The notes enclosed with the donations blessed my heart. Some were surprised. I was, after all, no longer a youngster. Some wondered if I'm ever going to "slow down." (No – not until God slows me down.)

A few were concerned for my safety. Georgia and Ukraine had recently made negative press. So my friends wanted to know if I was going into dangerous territory. How big was the group I would be traveling with? How secure were the groups to whom we would minister? Did I not understand there are evil people out there?

I was surprised that my prayer supporters didn't embrace the fact that the safest place on earth is the center of God's will. There *is* danger in Eurasia. There is also danger fifty yards from my house on Highway 49.

In either instance, I could roll my eyes and look to the hills expecting help. But I know better. I learned to trust God for safety for myself and my loved ones during long days of caregiving. My faith rests on the Lord who has promised to preserve me from all evil – my going out and my coming in – forever.

*Loving Father, how good to rest in Your safety. How good to know I am doing Your will, either at home or wherever You send me. How awesome that You choose to use me in Your great plan of the ages. Help me focus on Your purposes every day, wherever I am. Bless others through me. In Jesus' name, amen.*

# WHY GO TO CHURCH?

*I was glad when they said to me,*

*"Let us go into the house of the Lord."*

*... For the sake of my brethren and companions,*

*I will now say, "Peace be within you."*

*Because of the house of the Lord our God*

*I will seek your good.*

-Psalm 122:1, 8-9

ONE OF MY fond memories from childhood is attending vacation Bible school each summer. Having a natural inclination for loyalty, even at a young age I was sure the church I attended was the only right one. One VBS day my allegiance was shaken when *my* church's pastor introduced the pastor of the church across the street and asked him to teach us a Bible verse.

My mind became a tumble of confusion. Did they even use the same Bible over there, across the street, in that other church? What verse could he possible teach us that would apply to kids of both congregations? Would he come off as the arrogant impostor that I expected? I didn't recognize my own prejudice, of course.

So I was amazed as this humble minister led us in memorizing Psalm 122:1. "I was glad ... when they said ... unto me ... 'Let us go ... into the house ... of the Lord.'" As I dutifully repeated those phrases my mind whirled. I thought of my church building as the house of the Lord. Could this pastor's church building be the Lord's house as well?

I doubt our pastor had any idea the amount of deep thinking his guest pastor caused me that day. Some prejudices began to break down. That verse became impossible to forget. Many years in the future I would see the peace Sunday morning services brought to my husband in the midst of his Alzheimer's Disease journey, and I would reflect again on how glad I was to take him into the house of the Lord.

*Lord God, thank You for speaking to my heart. Thank You for providing places for us to worship You. Thank You for leading men and women to lead Your people. Thank You for Your peace. Continue to break down our prejudices, Lord. Give us both discernment and grace. In Jesus' name, amen.*

# DEALING WITH CONTEMPT

*Unto You I lift up my eyes,*

*O You who dwell in the heavens.*

*Behold, as the eyes of servants look to the hand of their masters,*

*As the eyes of a maid to the hand of her mistress,*

*So our eyes look to the Lord our God,*

*Until He has mercy on us.*

*Have mercy on us, O Lord, have mercy on us!*

*For we are exceedingly filled with contempt.*

*Our soul is exceedingly filled*

*With the scorn of those who are at ease,*

*With the contempt of the proud.*

--Psalm 123:1-4

WE WERE GROCERY shopping during the month just before I placed Larry in a care facility. He had become increasingly belligerent and tended to engage in unacceptable behavior, especially when we were away from home. On this occasion he kept lagging behind me and removing items from the shelves, sometimes carrying them and sometimes placing them on different shelves.

When I returned to find him busily rearranging the store shelves, he argued with me about each of the items. We both became frustrated. He did not understand that what he was doing was inappropriate. I could not convince him to let me put the items back. This increased in intensity over several times while I tried to hurry and finish my shopping.

The last time I retraced my steps to find him, it became necessary to speak sharply to him to get him to give up his collection. A passing shopper heard us and stopped to admonish me about how I should talk to him. She had no idea what I was dealing with, and my immediate impulse was to tell her off as well. Thankfully, I had dealt with ignorance and contempt so many times before that I could just lift my eyes to God and pray for his mercy. I managed to just respond with, "You have no idea." Then I silently prayed that the interfering shopper would never have to deal with a situation like the one she was trying to mediate.


*Father God, thank You for showing me it doesn't matter if other people don't understand our situation. Thank You for helping us live above the contempt of the ignorant – or even of the informed. It just doesn't matter, Lord. You are all that matters. Help us live above the troubles of life. In Jesus' name, amen.*

# WHO IS ON THE LORD'S SIDE?

*"If it had not been the Lord who was on our side,"* ...

*Our soul has escaped as a bird from the snare of the fowlers;*

*The snare is broken, and we have escaped.*

*Our help is in the name of the Lord,*

*Who made heaven and earth.*

--Psalm 124:7-8

AS LARRY'S ALZHEIMER'S disease developed, he became increasingly argumentative and childish. Unfortunately, anyone dealing with childish behavior is apt to be drawn into making similar responses. I learned early that I had to watch out for that. It was always best to refuse to argue, but sometimes it became very difficult to distract him from what he considered an important issue.

Many days we argued about his driving. In one sense it was important to win him over to my opinion for safety's sake and the issue of abiding by the law, especially since his driver's license had been revoked. I remember a day when the argument became heated. He declared loudly that he knew how to drive and they couldn't tell him what to do.

My voice escalated as I tried to get him to listen to reason. He no longer had a driver's license. He could be jailed for driving without one. We would be sued if an accident occurred with him behind the wheel.

"Whose side are you on?" he shouted at me.

I didn't expect that question, so I answered, "Whose side are *you* on?"

"I'm on God's side," he growled, and stomped out of the room.

I breathed a sigh of relief that the argument was temporarily over, but I had to wonder. We both think God is on our side, all the time. Are we really on God's side?

The psalmist mentions calamities that might have occurred if God had not been on his side. I could worry forever about what might happen to us if He were not on our side. We need to make sure we are really speaking for God, even when we have to confront difficult loved ones. He is on our side – both the caregiver and the care recipient – for He gives His best to both.

Often, making sure God is on my side has more to do with my tone of voice than the words I say. My good intentions must channel through my heart. God blesses that.

*Gracious Father, thank You for standing guard over my life situation. Help me keep close to You so I can honestly rest in the fact that I am on Your side. Thank You for being there for me. In Jesus' name, amen.*

# THE BENEFITS OF TRUSTING GOD

*Those who trust in the Lord*

*Are like Mount Zion,*

*Which cannot be moved, but abides forever.*

*As the mountains surround Jerusalem,*

*So the Lord surrounds His people*

*From this time forth and forever.*

--Psalm 125:1-2

I JUST READ a Facebook lament by one of my friends. She wondered if she would ever be able to see evidence of God in her life. I wanted to write her a whole sermon, but, of course, there's not room enough to do that on Facebook. However, I gave her my mini-sermon: Try looking back a year or two and compare what you see today with what you were then. Acknowledge that it is God who has made those positive changes in your life.

So it is with trusting God. As a young believer, I marveled at the faith of elderly Christians. How were they able to depend so completely on God? Was that just a natural talent of theirs? Would I ever be able to trust God that way?

Only when the trials began to come did I realize how it is that God grows faith in us. He is a gentle, patient teacher, giving us small steps to take and then larger and larger as we learn He can be trusted.

Sometimes He lets us learn by listening. Wise is the child of God who hears (or reads from the Bible or biographies) the stories of God's faithfulness and looks for similar ways to depend on God personally. I learned of God's faithfulness from hearing about my great-grandmother.

Sometimes we learn by watching. Without even knowing it, I picked up care suggestions from watching my mother care for my grandmother. I observed how God answered her prayers.

So armed, I entered the decision-making part of caregiving when my mother became a victim of Alzheimer's Disease. From hearing and watching, it was but a series of baby steps to trust God for her.

By the time I got to the most difficult steps, trusting God daily – hourly, minute-by-minute – became almost second nature. Even on fearful days I knew He was there surrounding us with His care.

*All loving Father, teach us to rest in You first. Grow our trust. Make us aware of the times we are resisting Your leading and thus shutting off our growth and Your comfort and peace. As I look back, I see Your love and how it has changed me. Thank You for that change. Keep it coming, Lord. In Jesus' name, amen.*

# GRIEF AND RELIEF

*Bring back our captivity,*

*O Lord,*

*As the streams in the South.*

*Those who sow in tears*

*Shall reap in joy.*

*He who continually goes forth weeping,*

*Bearing seed for sowing,*

*Shall doubtless come again with rejoicing,*

*Bringing his sheaves with him.*

--Psalm 126:4-6

THERE'S CERTAINLY A lot of weeping in this world, especially in the area of caregiving. Maybe you are the stoic type who doesn't actually shed tears, but inside you are as torn up as the more demonstrative of us is. When we are emotionally bound to a suffering loved one, tears can come at unexpected moments. I have a friend who says she was doing all right after her husband's death – that is until she walked through the produce section of the market and came upon broccoli, her husband's favorite. There she stood, embarrassed by tears, in front of the broccoli display. Only those of us who have been in a similar situation would understand.

During much of Larry's illness I didn't have time for tears. Even when I finally lay down for the night, I was usually too tired to cry. However, the last couple of years of his life, tears ran down my cheeks during most of my trips home from the nursing facility. Without even voicing the facts, my heart knew I had already said good-bye to the love of my life. I learned to schedule other errands before my visits so that I would not be crying when I tried to take care of business or shop.

I am still driven to tears, particularly by songs that express my heart. One of my first thoughts at Larry's passing was that now he was dancing around God's throne. There are a few contemporary Christian songs that speak of dancing in God's presence, and I tear up whenever I sing them. Our heartstrings are still attached.

Aren't you grateful for God's Word that tells us there will be no tears in heaven? We live in a world of tears, but that's not God's program for eternity. Hallelujah!

*Lord, thank You for tears, for they cleanse the soul. Thank You for heartstrings that reach from here to heaven. Thank You for love, even though it often hurts. Thank You for Your love, that assures us fulfilled, eternal life. Help us share it, Lord. In Jesus' name, amen.*

# THE FOLLY OF "DO-IT-YOURSELF"

*Unless the Lord builds the house,*

*They labor in vain who build it;*

*Unless the Lord guards the city,*

*The watchman stays awake in vain.*

*It is vain for you to rise up early,*

*To sit up late,*

*To eat the bread of sorrows;*

*For so He gives His beloved sleep.*

--Psalm 127:1-2

THERE'S AN OLD campfire chorus that goes, "Why worry when you can pray?" My husband Bud's mother was such a worrier that he gave her a note to put up in her kitchen window: "Why pray when you can worry?" Maybe turning it around helps us to recognize our lack of dependence on God.

We talk about it, but the worries still come back. I realized just a few days ago that once again I felt tension in my neck brought on by my concern over a lack of finances. As I prayed about it, I accepted the fact that there isn't a thing I can do about my financial situation. I'm not going to starve, although I may not get to indulge in Baskin Robbins this month. Once again I asked God to forgive my lack of faith and to remind me that He is in charge.

My parents each took on too much independence. Their motto seemed to be, "If you want the job done right, do it yourself." When Mother could no longer manage her own affairs, her struggles made it much more difficult for me to untangle than if she had asked for someone's help when she first needed it.

Dad surrendered more dramatically. When he needed me to care for him, he turned everything over to me: his trailer, his pickup, access to his bank accounts, and power of attorney. He told me He trusted God to use me to take care of him.

We need to trust God to use whatever means He chooses to take care of us. As the psalm says, "It is vain (useless) for you to rise early, to sit up late," and basically fret about our needs. He wants to give us peaceful sleep.

*Gracious Father, You have told us to trust in You for everything. Help us remember that we do not have the power to take care of anything unless You give us that power. Help us rest in You and watch You work in our behalf for ourselves and those we care for. In Jesus' name, amen.*

# THE BLESSING OF CHILDREN

*Behold, children are a heritage from the Lord,*

*The fruit of the womb is a reward.*

*Like arrows in the hand of a warrior,*

*So are the children of one's youth.*

*Happy is the man who has his quiver full of them;*

*They shall not be ashamed,*

*But shall speak with their enemies in the gate.*

--Psalm 127:3-5

I AM BLESSED with children and stepchildren who have supported me and even prodded me on the caregiving journey. I thank God for the lack of arguments and quarreling when we had to distribute deceased family members' belongings. What a blessing to have my stepsons tell me they appreciate my enabling their father to pursue his dream of full-time ministry. How encouraging to have them share in decision-making and for them to tell me to do what I thought was best. I know from observation that this is a rare blessing indeed.

As a pastor's wife and a caregiver I have watched many families dealing with the care of parents. It seems to me that guilt often causes children to try to outdo each other in the decisions made about care or even about funeral arrangements. Jealousies frequently erupt over who will care for the aging parent. One child feels overburdened and the others may seem to be carefree. Wise is the family that sits down together to discuss care options before they are needed.

Are my children perfect? No, it's an ongoing endeavor to keep relationships strong. In their growing up years we certainly had our disagreements and frustrations. But I still know they are my heritage, my reward. I thank God for each of them, and they know I am delighted to share any part of their lives.

*Heavenly Father, You know all about being a parent. You sent Your Son to die so that I and my children (and all others) could be part of Your great family. Help me extend that wondrous grace, to my offspring especially. In Jesus' name, amen.*

# THE BLESSING OF GRANDCHILDREN

*Blessed is every one who fears the Lord,*

*Who walks in His ways ...*

*The Lord bless you out of Zion,*

*And may you see the good of Jerusalem*

*All the days of your life.*

*Yes, may you see your children's children.*

*Peace be upon Israel!*

--Psalm 128:1, 5-6

WHEN LARRY FIRST entered the nursing facility, I worried about bringing my granddaughter, Cami, to visit him. Would she feel frightened in a place where there were only disabled, older adults? Would a kindergardener be a bother to the residents there? I often took care of her while her mother worked, so the day soon came when I had to take her with me to visit her grandfather.

Cami is a family-oriented child. If a family member is missing she usually laments that she misses that person. She had been saying she missed her grandpa, but I didn't know whether she really missed him or just said that out of habit. After all, her grandpa hadn't been very nice to her in the few months before he moved into a care home.

What a surprise! On her first visit Cami hung back at first, like she would in any new situation. But she soon warmed up to the outstretched arms of the many elderly folks who didn't remember seeing their own grandchildren for a long time. They all wanted to talk to her and even play with the doll she had brought with her. Her very presence brightened the lunchroom.

While Larry ate, Cami sat with us at the table and quietly asked questions about her grandpa and the other residents. She tried unsuccessfully to talk to him, and looked wistful when he didn't respond.

On the way to the car after our visit Cami sighed, "I don't think Grandpa remembers me."

We talked about how sometimes he didn't even remember me, but that was because of his disease, and how sad that was. She said she wanted to keep coming to visit him and I told her what a blessing her visits would be, not only to her grandpa but to other people's grandparents too. Her conclusion, "I'm sorry he doesn't remember me, but I'll always remember him. I love him."

I could only concur in my heart: me too.

*Father God, thank You for grandchildren and all that they teach us. Give me that same forgiving spirit and complete trust in Your love. Help me continue to love the people You have put in my life, however the circumstances change. In Jesus' name, amen.*

# GOD'S MERCY

*Out of the depths I have cried to You, O Lord;*

*Lord, hear my voice! Let Your ears be attentive*

*To the voice of my supplications.*

*If You, Lord, should mark iniquities,*

*O Lord, who could stand?*

*But there is forgiveness with You,*

*That You may be feared.*

--Psalm 130:1-4

"OUT OF THE depths." I wonder what the psalmist was referring to. Was he a sailor who, like Jonah, cried out to God as he came close to drowning? Was he a miner, trapped in an underground mining accident?

The only other depths I can think of are my own: the depths of despair that come with the daily care of a loved one who will never recover physically or mentally. If you are a caregiver, you've either been there or have that to look forward to.

Often our depression is exacerbated by guilt. Romans 3:23 says, "All have sinned and fall short of the glory of God." So it's not the false guilt psychologists try to soothe us with. It's real guilt. But that's all right, because we're all guilty and, better news than that: God forgives. Even in the Old Testament the psalmist knew that God was the only source of forgiveness.

The depths of caregiving will remain for as long as God's purposes determine. But we don't have to make them more depressing than necessary, for out of those depths we can cry to God and receive His forgiveness for past and daily errors.

He hears us – out of the depths!

*Forgiving Father, thank You for hearing us, even as we make our way through the shadow of death (see Psalm 23). In the midst of my darkest hours, help me cling to You and be aware of Your forgiving arms around me. In Jesus' name, amen.*

# WAITING FOR MORNING

*I wait for the Lord, my soul waits,*

*And in His word I do hope.*

*My soul waits for the Lord*

*More than those who watch for the morning —*

*Yes, more than those who watch for the morning.*

--Psalm 130:5-6

MY FRIEND BILL suffered with many disabilities that increased as he aged. He showed his servant's heart by helping people as long as he was able. Whenever I had computer problems, Bill would willingly come and help me find the answers. We had many long talks while waiting for technical support.

Bill mentioned how exhausted he became by the end of a day. As early as mid-afternoon he often longed for nightfall so that he had an excuse to go to bed. However, when bedtime came, long before his body found real rest, it began to ache and he found himself longing for daybreak to start another day.

That's not an unusual scenario for ill or disabled people. Even the psalmist knew about those long, dark hours of waiting for morning. They're painful and slow. Bill found he could help the minutes go by faster by spending time reading his Bible or listening to gospel music on the radio. When I have experienced sleepless nights I sometimes take the opportunity to pray for people I've been too busy to think about during the day.

The psalmist endured the same. He talks about painful delays. I take that to mean waiting for God to answer specific prayers, and we all know how that stretches our faith. We endure, or watch our loved one endure, months of suffering, while we wait for God's timing.

During his last days, I know Bill was praying and waiting for God to take him home. His family and friends grieve his loss, but God has finally brought morning to Bill – morning without suffering and disability – and that will go on for eternity.

*Lord, thank You for the promise of that glorious morning. Help us wait for You to act while we are still here serving You on earth, and to anticipate that final morning of eternity. In Jesus' name, amen.*

# CALMING YOUR SOUL

*Lord, my heart is not haughty,*

*Nor my eyes lofty.*

*Neither do I concern myself with great matters,*

*Nor with things too profound for me.*

*Surely I have calmed and quieted my soul,*

*Like a weaned child with his mother;*

*Like a weaned child is my soul within me.*

--Psalm 131:1-2

I WAS DRIVING with my eight-year-old granddaughter, and we were talking about some of my friends and relatives who always seem to be worried. I called them my frantic "little old lady" friends, and Cami interrupted with her sister's name. Her sister, Rachel is certainly not a little old lady. She was only twelve at the time. It reminded us both that worry is not confined to a particular age.

Mothers who could best be described as "worrywarts" raised both of my husbands. Their sons tended to be worriers too. I don't think that means the tendency to worry is inherited, but it probably means that the way we face life is apt to be copied by others, particularly our children.

Worry actually shows a lack of faith. For that reason God calls it sin. As with any sin, we don't want our offspring to continue it. Hebrews 11: 6 says, "without faith it is impossible to please [God]." In Psalm 131 the psalmist gives us a couple of hints for controlling worry.

First, verse one describes humility. Pride makes us think we can control matters. The writer says he does not concern himself with big problems, things that are above his ability.

Second, we must calm ourselves. Picture a small child, snuggled up in the lap of his/her mother. We are to recognize that our Heavenly Father will take care of all the details. Just rest in His lap and let Him do His job. What a beautiful scene of calm and quiet!

*Abba, Father, give us the faith to just rest in You, trusting You to take care of anything that would harm us. Calm our spirits. Quiet our souls. Grant us peace. In Jesus' name, amen.*

# GOD'S DWELLING PLACE

*Lord, remember David*

*And all his afflictions;*

*How he swore to the Lord,*

*And vowed to the Mighty One of Jacob;*

*"Surely I will not go into the chamber of my house,*

*Or go up to the comfort of my bed;*

*I will not give sleep to my eyes*

*Or slumber to my eyelids,*

*Until I find a place for the Lord,*

*A dwelling place for the Mighty One of Jacob."*

--Psalm 132:1-5

I AM THE substitute teacher for the adult Sunday school class this week. The Scripture is the passage in 2 Samuel where David decides to build a house for God and God tells him that's not his plan. Instead God wants to build David's household forever.

While preparing this lesson, and deciding what parts were apropos to my class, I was also making plans to take a road trip to visit friends in Washington, and friends and family along the way there and back. The day after notifying everyone involved, I received two major bills that must be paid this month. I had forgotten about them.

Immediately, I began trying to figure out a way to get around the financial problem and still go on the trip. Then it hit me. Isn't this just what the Sunday school lesson is about? Do I live what I teach, or do I try to manipulate God? Oops! The road trip was my plan, but obviously not God's plan.

I am embarrassed to have to go back to each of the people I intended to visit and tell them I miscalculated and can't afford to take this road trip after all. I am disappointed, of course, but God's timing is perfect. It really helps to be able to respond in obedience, recognizing God's leading. There will (probably) be another time for the road trip.

I don't know David's motivation for building God a temple. I do know that 1 Corinthians 6:19 says my body is the temple of God. He lives *in* me. I don't know God's reason for canceling my long-anticipated trip. I do know I can trust His leading.

Sometimes in the midst of caregiving, we get busy and don't see God's leading. He may bring us up short with changes in our circumstances. How good to be able to trust His leading there too. How good to humbly follow without kicking and screaming about what we don't see as fair. He has our best interests at heart – His heart!

*Loving Father, how good to trust You. Thank You for the peace You give as we submit to Your will. Thank You for protecting us through Your leading. In Jesus' name, amen.*

# FAMILY UNITY

*Behold, how good and how pleasant it is*

*For brethren to dwell together in unity!*

*It is like the precious oil upon the head,*

*Running down on the beard,*

*The beard of Aaron,*

*Running down on the edge of his garments.*

*It is like the dew of Hermon,*

*Descending upon the mountains of Zion;*

*For there the Lord commanded the blessing —*

*Life forevermore.*

--Psalm 133:1-3

IF ANY TIME in a life can precipitate disharmony, it is around the dying of a loved one. Sons, daughters, and grandchildren, for whatever reasons, can turn on each other in their quest to see their elderly relative cared for the way they think they should be. After the loved one's death, another round of fighting may ensue concerning the distribution of treasures. Those felt slights and rude comments can divide a family for years, even forever. The departed loved one would be grief-stricken at the results.

I thank God my family has not reacted this way in the passing of any of our loved ones. Even when my mother left several different lists of the way she wanted her treasures distributed (all undated!) we had no trouble deciding who should receive which memento of their parent's or grandparent's life. Praise the Lord!

However, it may not be so when I die. I have one grandchild who frequently tells me what she would like to inherit from me, and the list is growing. I think it includes just about anything of real or even sentimental value. I will have to list what she can choose from and keep teaching all my grandchildren about families dwelling together in unity.

Often an outside counselor can help with caregiving concerns. Caregiving is admittedly a heavy burden and it is rarely shared equally. Ideally, all adult children should help as they are able. It is better to get good counsel than to fret about perceived unfairness.

With all end-of-life considerations, planning is the key. It is a great help when the ailing loved one makes an inheritance list or marks names on favorite items or sets up a system where family members will choose items in turn. The time that he or she has to leave the home might be a good time for giving away precious things. That way the gifts can be acknowledged and promises made to care for them.

*Lord, God, You want us to honor You by living in unity. What a beautiful picture of how unity permeates our lives with fragrance. What a testimony to other families that You make a difference in our lives. What a comfort for our loved ones to enjoy. Help us plan ahead and work toward this peace that only You can give. In Jesus' name, amen.*

# MY FAVORITE NIGHT

*Behold, bless the Lord,*

*All you servants of the Lord,*

*Who by night stand in the house of the Lord!*

*Lift up your hands in the sanctuary,*

*And bless the Lord.*

*The Lord who made heaven and earth*

*Bless you from Zion!*

--Psalm 134:1-3

LARRY AND I always served in churches that had Sunday morning worship services and evening "evangelistic" services, although the "evangelistic" services were usually testimony and Bible study times with a lot more singing than we did in the mornings. I loved the evening gatherings, and Larry did too. He obviously expected every church to have that schedule. When we became part of a church that did not hold evening services, he had a hard time understanding that. I began driving us fifty miles to evening church just so that he would not stress over why we were not attending one.

As a new Christian I learned to put aside my fears and actually stand to my feet during those testimony meetings and tell about something God had done in my life. I am sure our singing and praises blessed the Lord. They certainly strengthened my spiritual life.

However, my favorite night for getting together with God's people and praising Him is Christmas Eve. Hearing the old, old story once again as the last advent candle is lit, warms my heart anew each year. Joining my voice with my Christian brothers and sisters as we sing the annual carols, fills my heart with love as I am reminded again of God's gift to us. Watching the wonder in my grandchildren's eyes as the darkened room brightens with each passing candle, helps me pray that we will all see how our "lights" can make a difference in this dark world, especially as we work together.

On this holy night I pray that we have blessed the heart of God, and that we'll go out to bless the hearts of those people He places in our paths. It's my favorite night.


*Lord, I don't know whom the psalmist had in mind when he wrote about those who stand in Your house at night. I thank You that You are in my house every night – and every day. I pray that, night or day, I may bless You with my words and my actions as I serve You by serving the people You have given into my charge. Thank You for the awesome privilege of doing Your work. In Jesus' name, amen.*

# IDOLS OF SILVER AND GOLD

*The idols of the nations are silver and gold,*

*The work of men's hands.*

*They have mouths, but they do not speak;*

*Eyes they have, but they do not see;*

*They have ears, but they do not hear;*

*Nor is there any breath in their mouths.*

*Those who make them are like them;*

--Psalm 135:15-18

CAREGIVING IS EXPENSIVE in money and time. Medical procedures come with astronomical bills that are rarely covered fully by insurance. My friend Selma says she fears going to the mailbox, for the dread of receiving another bill for her or her husband's medical services.

Most of us can relate to that. I remember having gall bladder surgery and being shocked by the bill I had to pay, even though my insurance covered 80 percent of the total. That still left me with several months of payments plus the cost of co-payments for my prescriptions.

My mind defaults to worry about money. It is as though money will bring the answer to all my needs. Money has become my idol. Silver and gold seem to be the answer to all my problems.

When I remember to bring my needs to God, even then my prayer is frequently all about money. Eventually I stop fussing long enough to hear God tell me He's still there. He still has my best interests in mind. He is God. He will take care of me in His own way and time.

Someone once told me an idol is anything that comes between you and God. There are certainly many things that can become idols in our lives, but for me, as a caregiver, the devil uses financial needs to try to shake my faith in God. At least I'm finally learning to recognize the temptation early and to bring it back to God.

*Father God, You are so patient with us. We are so prone to look for answers in our own resources instead if trusting You. Remind us early that our hope is only in You, Lord. Help us keep from any form of idolatry. We love You, Lord. In Jesus' name, amen.*

# GOD'S REPETITIONS

*Oh, give thanks to the Lord, for He is good!*

*For His mercy endures forever.*

*Oh, give thanks to the God of gods!*

*For His mercy endures forever.*

*Oh, give thanks to the Lord of lords!*

*For His mercy endures forever.*

*Oh, give thanks to the God of heaven!*

*For His mercy endures forever.*

--Psalm 136:1-3, 26

"YOU JUST HAVE to keep telling him the same thing every day." I was trying to help a friend learn how to deal with her husband who has Alzheimer's Disease.

"It's like dealing with a child," she moaned.

"No, you can't even look at it that way," I answered. "A child will learn from what you tell him. An AD patient will not remember that you even told him. You just have to pretend this is the first time you're telling him. It does no good to fuss about having to repeat yourself all the time."

God repeats things to us too. Like a parent, He repeats what is important for us to remember. We find multiple verses that teach His principles for godly living.

We find psalms that repeat verses, or parts of verses, over and over. When we realize that the psalms were actually songs the Jews sang, we can see a pattern, much like modern musical compositions. There may be a verse of instruction or praise followed by a section that is repeated throughout the psalm, like a hymn or chorus.

In Psalm 136 we find a different kind of repetition. Every verse concludes with the same praise phrase: "For His mercy endures forever." I imagine the temple choir divided into two groups. One sang the first half of each verse, and the other replied with, "For His mercy endures forever."

I don't know if the musicians added variations or dynamics to the performance. I do know that God's forever enduring mercy is worth repeating and meditating on. God said it, and repeated it, so we would get the message.

*Merciful Father, thank You that You never give up on us. Your mercy is available whenever we turn back to You. You even allow us to live like You by extending mercy to the people who offend us. Thank You for repeating the things that are important, so that we have no reason not to "get it." In Jesus' name, amen.*

# JUST DO IT ANYWAY

*By the rivers of Babylon,*

*There we sat down, yea, we wept*

*When we remembered Zion.*

*We hung our harps*

*Upon the willows in the midst of it.*

*For there those who carried us away captive asked of us a song,*

*And those who plundered us requested mirth,*

*Saying, "Sing us one of the songs of Zion!"*

*How shall we sing the Lord's song*

*In a foreign land?*

--Psalm 137:1-4

THERE'S DEPRESSION CAUSED by chemical imbalances in the body and there's depression that results from overwhelming life circumstances. Unfortunately, there's no easy fix for either kind.

I recognize when my daughter has too much to deal with. She retreats to her bed and doesn't attempt to deal with any of it. I recognize it because that's the way I used to deal with overload myself. As an onlooker, it's easy to just say, "Get up. Get going. Nothing will be accomplished by pulling the covers over your head."

But, if you've been there yourself, you know those words don't motivate. We are like those captive Israelites by the rivers of Babylon. We can't sing. We only want to weep.

Is there a way out of this great sadness? Caregivers actually benefit from the fact that they must get up in the morning and take care of things: otherwise "things" will surely take care of themselves in a detrimental way. So we have to "just do it" whether our hearts are in it or not.

We do have tools to use that will help bring back the joy. God gave us music. I think those captive Israelites who sang the songs of Zion probably found their hearts lifted. Praising God is the first step to seeing His hand in our situation. You may not be where you want to be, or doing what you want to do, but it's obviously where and what God wants for you. Praise Him for bringing you through your dry valley. Put one foot in front of the other and see if it doesn't help to sing the Lord's songs.

*God of all comfort, thank You for Your direction in my life. Many days I just feel like running away, but I cannot run away from You. I don't want to run away from You. So help me do what You've put me here to do, and to sing Your praises while I'm doing it. In Jesus' name, amen.*

# GOD'S WORD ABOVE HIS NAME

*I will praise You with my whole heart;*

*Before the gods I will sing praises to You.*

*I will worship toward Your holy temple,*

*And praise Your name*

*For Your lovingkindness and Your truth;*

*For You have magnified Your word above all Your name.*

*In the day when I cried out,*

*You answered me,*

*And made me bold with strength in my soul.*

--Psalm 138:1-3

WE DIDN'T TALK much about God in the home where I grew up. My mother took my sister and me to church frequently, but she gave the impression that religious or devotional thoughts were private matters, not to be shared.

However, one summer day when I was in the eighth grade, I was left home alone. I enjoyed the solitude and spent the time designing and making doll clothes and reading. I was startled by my mother's accusation when she got home. Something had broken off a favorite plant that graced the back door. She asked me what I had done to it.

I hadn't even been out the back door all day. So I denied having anything to do with the broken flower. Mother did not believe me. Her statement: "Well, God knows."

I think that was supposed to shame me into admitting my guilt. But I wasn't guilty. It did cause me to wonder about God. Did He know everything? How could I get to know more about God? How could I get to know Him?

I didn't ask Mother those questions. I realized the family member most likely to know the answers was my grandfather. I knew this because I noticed he kept his Bible near him most of the time. Sure enough, when I asked him how I could know more about God, he suggested I read the Bible, and that is just what I began to do.

I don't recommend an unbeliever or even a new believer begin in Genesis and read straight through to Revelation, but that's what I did. Somewhere along the way, about a year and a half later, God revealed Himself to me through godly friends, circumstances, and His Word. I received His gift of eternal life by trusting in Jesus' payment for my sins.

How important is the Word of God? The psalmist says He magnifies His Word above His name. I think that's because it is only through His Word that we can come to know Him.

*Almighty Father, even on the caregiving journey it is still true that we get to know You better by spending time reading Your Word. Help me rest on what I know and add to my knowledge each day. In Jesus' name, amen.*

# HE REGARDS THE LOWLY

*All the kings of the earth shall praise You, O Lord,*

*When they hear the words of Your mouth.*

*Yes, they shall sing of the ways of the Lord,*

*For great is the glory of the Lord.*

*Though the Lord is on high, yet He regards the lowly;*

*But the proud He knows from afar.*

--Psalm 138:4-6

CAREGIVING IS A humbling experience. In the early days of Larry's Alzheimer's Disease I constantly worried about what other people were thinking about him. He had been a pastor, dignified as well as humble. I watched in horror as his personality changed and my gentle, inoffensive husband turned into an argumentative, profane stranger. I felt I should explain his confusion and abnormal behavior to store clerks, flight attendants, seatmates — anyone who talked with him. Frankly, he embarrassed me, and I didn't know how to handle that.

Prayer and heeding good advice from other caregivers and support groups gradually helped me learn to step back and let people figure out what they needed to know. When Larry wanted to do things for himself, I let him go as far as he could on his own. He would never take advice or help, especially from me, until he came to the end of his own resources and asked. If I waited until asked, he would respond with gratitude. If I interfered while he still thought he could handle the situation, I was met with hostility and anger.

God waits for us to ask Him for help too. Many times we think we can manage the situation or don't think our problems are big enough to warrant God's help. We get cocky and may even tell God (by word or action) that we can handle this one. This is *so* dangerous. God will let us go as far as we want to without His help, but that's the way to trouble. Verse six says He knows the proud "from afar."

He regards the lowly. He wants to help us. He delights in our coming to Him with our problems, big and little. I'm learning to ask for help early, before I get too far away from where He wants me.

*Heavenly Father, thank You for always being there waiting for us to turn to You for help. Help me stay so close that I never get into trouble. Thank You for making my way clear, the closer I walk with You. I am Your child. I need You. I love You, Lord. In Jesus' name, amen.*

# GOD'S PERFECTION

*Though I walk in the midst of trouble, You will revive me;*

*You will stretch out Your hand*

*Against the wrath of my enemies,*

*And Your right hand will save me.*

*The Lord will perfect that which concerns me;*

*Your mercy, O Lord, endures forever;*

*Do not forsake the works of Your hands.*

*--Psalm 138:7-8*

I USED TO be a perfectionist. Getting all A's in first grade set me up for a lifetime of striving to keep that standard. At first it was to keep my parents from being disappointed in me. I don't know when it became a driving obsession just to please myself.

Keeping a 4.0 grade point average was easy in elementary and high school. It assured me of a scholarship to continue my education. I expected it to be just as easy to maintain the 4.0 in college, even when I doubled up on classes in order to finish the four-year course in three. I did all right until my sophomore/junior year, when my U. S. History teacher announced that he never gave A's. Then he qualified that by saying he had actually given an A once – to a student who had gone on to MIT and graduated summa cum laude. I feared that the B I got in his class would cause me to lose my scholarship and I continually battled my anger toward him as well as my inability to meet his standard.

All this to say that it took me nearly twenty years to figure out that I wasn't perfect, not in a single area of my life. That didn't keep me from trying, but the result was stomach ulcers and migraines, not perfection.

I began to realize that it was all right to be less than perfect. God accepts us as we are. He made us. He makes up the difference when we fail. However, it wasn't until I came to those caregiving years of my life that I really gave up and just learned to do the best I could and leave the rest to God. There's something about the stresses and strains of caring for a loved one that points out your own limitations and directs you to rest on God's grace.

Do you long for perfection? The psalmist says, "The Lord will perfect that which concerns me." He goes on to remind us that God's mercy endures forever and we are the works of God's hands – not our own.

*Merciful Father, thank You for perfecting whatever is needed in my life. Thank You for taking care of my loved one in spite of my feeble attempts. You have made us. You know how we work and what works for us. Help us do our best but leave the rest to You. In Jesus' name, amen.*

# WHO KNOWS ME?

*O Lord, You have searched me and known me.*

*You know my sitting down and my rising up;*

*You understand my thoughts afar off.*

*You comprehend my path and my lying down,*

*And are acquainted with all my ways.*

*For there is not a word on my tongue,*

*But behold, O Lord, You know it altogether.*

*You have hedged me behind and before,*

*And laid Your hand upon me.*

*Such knowledge is too wonderful for me;*

*It is high, I cannot attain it.*

--Psalm 139:1-6

FOURTH-GRADER TYLER HAD never played chess before. I introduced it on a winter day during recess, hoping to give the students something fun to do when we had to stay inside because of rain or cold weather. In just one game, Tyler caught on to the various moves different chess pieces could make. How exciting to see the astonishment on his face as he realized his thinking was way ahead of any other student (or teacher) in this complicated game. I could tell he formerly had no idea of his chess ability, but it was no surprise to me. I had observed his strategy mentality the whole school year.

Many times we don't understand ourselves. We have no idea about our strengths and weaknesses until they are tested. But God already knows. He doesn't test us so that He will find out what we will do. He tests us so that we will find out about ourselves. Especially in the phases of caregiving, as God brought me through trials that looked impossible, I emerged totally surprised by my own strength and wisdom, and humbled because I knew it all came from God.

Is there anything God does not know about us? No, He knows the when, where, what, why, and how of our every action and reaction. He knows what we will speak and in what tone of voice, and when we will refrain from speaking and thus avoid trouble. He's there to encourage us in our wisdom and protect us from our foolishness. As the psalmist said, "Such knowledge is too wonderful for me."

*Omnipotent Father, thank You for caring about me. Thank You for making me just the way I am. Thank You for stretching me, causing me to grow, and protecting me from myself. Thank You for teaching me what I need to know to do Your will each day. In Jesus' name, amen.*

# NO HIDING PLACE

*Where can I go from Your Spirit?*

*Or where can I flee from Your presence?*

*If I ascend into heaven, You are there;*

*If I make my bed in hell, behold, You are there.*

*If I take the wings of the morning,*

*And dwell in the uttermost parts of the sea,*

*Even there Your hand shall lead me,*

*And Your right hand shall hold me.*

*If I say, "Surely the darkness shall fall on me,"*

*Even the night shall be light about me;*

*Indeed, the darkness shall not hide from You,*

*But the night shines as the day;*

*The darkness and the light are both alike to You.*

--Psalm 139:7-12

BUD LIKED TO tell stories about when he was in the army. One of his favorites showed how his platoon buddies once helped him volunteer for a job he didn't want to do. When the sergeant asked for volunteers to step forward, everyone but Bud took a step backward, leaving him standing out in front "volunteering." He wanted to hide, but he was exposed.

On difficult days I have wanted to hide. I have felt like someone volunteered me for a job I had no intention of doing. And on days I have not done my best, I have even wanted to hide from God.

Apparently the psalmist had those days too, but he contemplated the fact that there is nowhere we can go to hide from God. He's everywhere, in the broad daylight or pitch black of night. However, we have a merciful God who desires a loving relationship with us. We know that if it is sin that separates us, 1 John 1:9 tells us we need only confess those sins and God forgives and cleanses us so that we are comfortable in His presence once again.

Pastor Jessup used to say, "The good news is that God is watching you. The bad news is that God is watching you." What a truth! And really, it's all good news. We don't need to hide from God; we need Him as our hiding place from anything that would cause us fear.

*Heavenly Father, You are my hiding place. You are my Redeemer. You are the merciful God who enables me to serve You. Thank You for forgiveness and strength, day after day. May I never want to hide from You. In Jesus' name, amen.*

# OUR DAYS ARE NUMBERED

*For You formed my inward parts;*

*You covered me in my mother's womb.*

*I will praise You, for I am fearfully and wonderfully made;*

*Marvelous are Your works, and that my soul knows very well.*

*My frame was not hidden from You,*

*When I was made in secret,*

*And skillfully wrought in the lowest parts of the earth.*

*Your eyes saw my substance, being yet unformed.*

*And in Your book they all were written,*

*The days fashioned for me,*

*When as yet there were none of them.*

--Psalm 139:13-16

WHY DOESN'T GOD do something? Why does He allow my loved one to suffer? Or why did God take my mother from me? (Or my husband, wife, or child?) Why, why, why? This question occupies the minds of most people who must watch a loved one suffer and ultimately die.

Could God change the circumstances? Yes. He made us and He can certainly repair us. Our congregation recently celebrated the recovery of two men who went through lymphoma and are both declared cancer-free. We praise God for these clear miracles of healing.

Could God keep us from any affliction at all? Yes, "there is nothing too hard for God." However, I can't imagine any spiritual growth in the life of such an individual. We might like fewer and less-intense trials, but God knows what grows us best.

In a practical sense, what if no one ever died? What if sin had never happened back there in the Garden of Eden? What if death never became part of mankind's experience? In the thousands of years of this earth, how many people would live here? That's a mind-boggler!

Suffering and death are the result of sin, but God brings good out of them. Romans 8:28 still says that all things work together for good to His called ones. He has measured our strength and numbered our days for our good and His glory.

*Loving Father, help us to trust Your wisdom during our suffering and loss. Thank You for going through the dark valleys with us. You know us; You made us; our times are in Your hands. In Jesus' name, amen.*

# GOD'S THOUGHTS

*How precious also are Your thoughts to me, O God!*

*How great is the sum of them!*

*If I should count them, they would be more in number than the sand;*

*When I awake, I am still with You ...*

*Search me, O God, and know my heart;*

*Try me, and know my anxieties;*

*And see if there is any wicked way in me,*

*And lead me in the way everlasting.*

--Psalm 139:17-18, 23-24

WHEN I WAS a child, I rarely could figure out what my father was thinking. Mother said he had a "poker face." I realized that meant he didn't register his thoughts by facial expressions. In his later years he became more transparent, but many times, in my growing-up years, I would worry about what Dad was thinking, fearing his wrath, but hoping for his sense of humor.

Sometimes I have wondered what God was thinking. When my husband and I had decisions to make about a large purchase, like a home or vehicle, we would pray for God to reveal His will for us. Even now, when confronted with a ministry opportunity, I have learned to ask God about it before saying "yes" or "no." I want to know God's thoughts, particularly concerning my life.

We do have access to God's thoughts. He has given us a huge book of them. The Bible reveals God's opinion on any general principle we need to know.

For the specifics, God is still ready to reveal His plan to us. We spend time in the Bible learning His ways. Then we spend time talking to Him about the impending decision. We ask Him to search us, know our hearts, try us, know our concerns, reveal any sin, and then lead us in His way. The hardest part is waiting quietly for His answer.

His thoughts are precious, and they are for us.

*Wise Heavenly Father, thank You for revealing Your thoughts to us through Your Word. Thank You for caring about our every decision. Keep me pure so You can use me. Stop me the moment I start to stray from Your direction. In Jesus, name, amen.*

# JUSTICE FOR THE POOR

*I know that the Lord will maintain*

*The cause of the afflicted,*

*And justice for the poor.*

*Surely the righteous shall give thanks to Your name;*

*The upright shall dwell in Your presence.*

*--Psalm 140:12-13*

CAREGIVING TAKES A toll on the family in all ways, but often it is felt most financially. Only the wealthy are able to adequately prepare for the end-of-life financial burden. Even with government help, the patient's family is confronted with huge bills for medicine, doctor's visits, special diets, ambulance fees, and nursing home care. I purchased long-term care insurance for Larry (and myself) years before it was needed. To my amazement, even the good protection I bought ran out in just a few months. Fortunately we were poor enough to qualify for Medi-Cal.

God taught me practical lessons about conserving finances when I took care of my mother's affairs. Mother frugally balanced her income and savings so that she would have money to pass on to my sister and me. She saved her money instead of spending it on improvements we felt she needed to make to her home. I don't think she ever considered that she would one day have to leave that home for better care in a convalescent facility. When that happened, we had to use the money she had planned to give us to pay for her care. We were required to "pay down" her finances until she qualified for Medi-Cal benefits. She would have been saddened to know the result of her thrifty living.

Illness can impoverish a family. Each time I had to take over the decision-making and bill-paying for my parents and spouses, I was tempted to despair. Where would the money come from? How could these bills be paid? I had nowhere to turn but to God, which, after much practice, eventually became my normal response to any crisis. I can honestly say I relied on God to maintain the cause of my afflicted loved one and give justice to me, his poor child. I don't know how all the bills got paid. God used various sources, but I know He is the ultimate source of strength in every area of my life, including finances.

*Almighty God, thank You for taking care of our needs every day. Thank You for giving us guidance to make wise decisions as we call on You for help. Thank You for the miracles that sustain us. In Jesus' name, amen.*

# SEAL THOSE LIPS

*Lord, I cry out to You;*

*Make haste to me!*

*Give ear to my voice when I cry out to You.*

*Let my prayer be set before You as incense,*

*The lifting up of my hands as the evening sacrifice.*

*Set a guard, O Lord, over my mouth;*

*Keep watch over the door of my lips.*

*Do not incline my heart to any evil thing,*

*To practice wicked works*

*With men who work iniquity;*

*And do not let me eat of their delicacies.*

--Psalm 141:1-4

I HAVE SAID before, it's not so much what I do as what I say that gets me into trouble. As a child I was constantly admonished for talking too much in class. My parents would lecture me on self-control, and then I was left to continue the same pattern. At home, they were more concerned with my tone of voice when I answered them. I worked at keeping the sass level down, but it didn't occur to me that my real problem was attitude. The mouth just expresses what's in the heart.

Even as adults, when we are tired and frustrated our mouths give us away. Early in my marriage my husband and I argued a lot. At a women's conference I learned the secret of not arguing: shut your mouth. Clamp your teeth firmly together and don't open them until there are kind words waiting to be let out.

That's a pretty simple remedy and it worked – when I remembered to apply it. It especially worked well when Larry developed Alzheimer's Disease and wanted to argue about everything. I mentally joked to myself about the foolishness of having a battle of wits with an unarmed man. It was not a put-down, and I would never have said it to Larry, but it helped me avoid wrangling over pointless things. Close the lips until I could think of something to distract him and move away from the argument.

My friend Betty passed away at the age of ninety. In the last Bible study she attended, she once again mentioned that it was her mouth that still got her into trouble. Most of us agreed it was the same for us. To my dying day I may struggle with my tongue. That doesn't mean I'm going to quit asking God to help me control it.

*Merciful God, thank You for teaching us right principles. Thank You for helping us control the habits of our lives. Thank You for Your forgiveness and for giving us the strength and wisdom to continue the work You have given us to do. Make us wise and gentle. In Jesus' name, amen.*

# NO ONE CARES

*I cry out to the Lord with my voice;*

*With my voice to the Lord I make my supplication.*

*I pour out my complaint before Him;*

*I declare before Him my trouble.*

*When My spirit was overwhelmed within me,*

*Then You knew my path.*

*In the way in which I walk*

*They have secretly set a snare for me.*

*Look on my right hand and see,*

*For there is no one who acknowledges me;*

*Refuge has failed me;*

*No one cares for my soul.*

--Psalm 142:1-4

MY PASTOR'S WIFE had a beautiful alto voice. She especially favored us with missionary songs. One of the first that I heard her sing was "No Man Careth for My Soul." It is a poignant reminder that millions of lost souls despair because no one has taken the gospel to them.

Often in the busyness and weight of caregiving it seems that we are going it alone. Our cry can be, "No one cares for my soul: my needs, my problems, my inability to make all these decisions by myself." I know. I have been there. Caregiving can be a lonely life.

However, a few minutes in God's Word and in prayer usually restored my sense of reality. I might feel alone because there was no friend or family member with whom to share my burden, but I had the greatest burden-bearer of all beside me and within me. He cared for me even more than I care for myself. He could do for me what no earthly person, ever, could do. I am truly blessed.

If God's very presence and promises are not enough. He even goes beyond that. Look around you. Take advantage of the network of God's people He has provided for your comfort and direction. No man cares for your soul? That's the devil's lie!

*Merciful Father, thank You that You not only care about our problems, You have the real answers to them. Help us get our eyes off ourselves and our problems and raise them to You, our Salvation in this world and the next. Help us to reach out and comfort others who feel alone. In Jesus' name, amen.*

# WHEN IT'S OKEY TO LOOK BACK

*I remember the days of old;*

*I meditate on all Your works;*

*I muse on the work of Your hands.*

*I spread out my hands to You;*

*My soul longs for You like a thirsty land.*

--Psalm 143:5-6

I REMEMBER THE first time I realized Larry's forgetfulness was more than normal loss of memory. It suddenly dawned on me that he was no longer capable of doing the very thing he most loved to do: deliver a scriptural sermon with a logical application. His reasoning simply caused him to repeat his thoughts in a circular pattern. He found it difficult to bring his sermon to a conclusion. He finally just broke off his speech in the middle of numerous repetitions.

My next memory is the panic I felt. How would God take care of him? What would happen to us, especially to our ministry? Fear filled my heart for the changes I knew were coming. Once I recognized the symptoms pointed to Alzheimer's disease, my mind filled with devastating scenes from caring for my mother, who was even then in the final stages of that same dread disease.

Fortunately, along with the frightening and sad scenes came the remembrances of all the times God had gotten me through the decisions and emotions involved with her care. Instead of focusing on the problems I knew would arise with Larry's disease, I focused on God's answers to prayer in past caregiving.

We always have choices. We can look back with regret and sadness, thus coloring our future with fear. Or we can look back with gratitude and joy, anticipating how God is going to work. He has promised never to leave or forsake us (See Hebrews 13:5). We can trust that whatever we go through, He is there with us and will only allow what is best for us (see 1 Peter 5:7).

Look back, and rejoice!

*Loving Father, thank You for walking with us all the way. Thank You for caring for us with Your everlasting love. Help me to dwell on remembrances of the triumphs You have brought in my past. I look to the future with hope and joy in the knowledge that You are already there. In Jesus' name, amen.*

# HAPPY PEOPLE

*Blessed be the Lord my rock …*

*My lovingkindness and my fortress,*

*My high tower and my deliverer,*

*My shield and the One in whom I take refuge …*

*Lord, what is man, that You take knowledge of Him?*

*Or the son of man, that You are mindful of him?*

*Man is like a breath;*

*His days are like a passing shadow …*

*I will sing a new song to You, O God;*

*On a harp of ten strings I will sing praises to You …*

*Happy are the people who are in such a state;*

*Happy are the people whose God is the Lord!*

--Psalm 144:1-4, 9, 15

I REALIZE KING David wrote Psalm 144 and it refers to specifics about his enemies and his kingship. However, isn't it fun to read through the psalms and glean little treasures that apply to us as well as to the great King David?

David did not delay to ask God for help whenever he found himself in trouble. We can learn from that. If Israel's great king could put aside his pride and ask for

God's rescue, surely it is not beyond us to do the same. And we will have the same results as David: perfect rescue from Almighty God.

David ends this psalm by looking at God's provision for him. David had problems. His family, his enemies, and his kingdom gave him a multitude of headaches. But he did not focus on the problems. He focused on God's bountiful gifts.

We can take a cue from David here too. We have problems — no doubt about it. We may not have the bounty that God blessed David with, but we have all we need. Look around.

Notice again how God has blessed you: physically, emotionally, spiritually, and in so many other ways.

Thank God for those blessings and then you can say with David, "Happy are the people who are in such a state. Happy are the people whose God is the Lord!"

*Father God, in my weariness and frustration, I forget to look at what You provide me every day. Help me focus on Your goodness and pass it on to others. In Jesus' name, amen.*

# PASS IT ON

*I will extol You, my God, O King;*

*And I will bless Your name forever and ever.*

*Every day I will bless You,*

*And I will praise Your name forever and ever.*

*Great is the Lord, and greatly to be praised;*

*And His greatness is unsearchable.*

*One generation shall praise Your works to another,*

*And shall declare our mighty acts.*

*I will meditate on the glorious splendor of Your majesty,*

*And on Your wondrous works.*

--Psalm 145:1-5

SHORTLY AFTER LARRY and I married (second marriage for both of us) we sat down with the Will Maker software program and planned how we intended to divide up our assets when we passed from this earth. Larry moved into my house, so we rented his out for a short time. Then, when we moved to pastor the Vallecito Union Church, we sold both of our houses in order to buy a home in Vallecito. Our intention was that when we both passed away, our assets would be divided equally between his three children and my three. We expected that inflation would continue so that our children would receive a greater amount than if we divided the money from his house at the time of its sale.

We all know about the economy. Our assets have diminished instead of increasing. We went from the Vallecito home to an A-frame in Rail Road Flat, to a mobile home that I had to sell for barely enough money to cover the cost of water damage repairs. I lived for four years as a live-in caregiver until I could afford to have my own home again: another modular unit in a mobile home park. I'm still paying it off.

My will still gives one sixth of our assets to each of our children, but they are not going to get anything near what we had planned for them.

So that's obviously not the legacy we are leaving our children. What we have taught our children and grandchildren, and the godly example of their consistent preacher-dad (step-father, grandpa), is a far more valuable inheritance than any material or financial gift we could leave them. Learning how to lean on God through times in life is a valuable asset to be prized. Seeing positive praise and hearing the testimony of God's greatness in our lives has more lasting value than fleeting finances.

I would still like to be able to shower our children with material gifts, but I can't. I can and will continue to pass on our spiritual legacy.

*Loving Father, whether in prosperity or poverty, I love You. You give us the most valuable gifts because they are eternal. Help me pass these on to my children. Open their eyes to true value. In Jesus' name, amen.*

# WHERE DO YOU FIT?

*Praise the Lord!*

*Praise the Lord, O my soul!*

*While I live I will praise the Lord;*

*I will sing praises to my God while I have my being ...*

*Happy is he who has the God of Jacob for his help,*

*Whose hope is in the Lord his God,*

*Who made heaven and earth,*

*The sea, and all that is in them ...*

*The Lord shall reign forever –*

*Your God, O Zion, to all generations.*

*Praise the Lord!*

--Psalm 146:1-2, 5-6, 10

I LOVE THE ending psalms. I visualize myself joining a praise service that keeps increasing in intensity. Psalm 146 starts it all by rehearsing the ways God meets our needs.

Do you need truth? He keeps truth forever (vs. 6 )

Are you oppressed? He executes justice for you (vs. 7)

Hungry? He provides. Remember, the earth is the Lord's and all its bounty (Ps. 24:1)

Do you feel trapped, imprisoned by your circumstances? God gives freedom (Ps. 146:7)

Are you blind, physically or even spiritually? He promises to open your eyes (vs. 8)

Overburdened? He'll raise you up (vs. 8)

Anyone righteous out there – or trying to be? He especially loves you (vs. 8)

And He provides relief for the fatherless and widows (vs. 9)

Whenever you fit in this list, God has you covered. Praise His name!

*Father God, You know us and You love us anyway. You meet our every need as we allow You to work in our lives. Open our eyes to that truth. May our first response to trouble be to turn to You. Thank You, thank You, thank You. In Jesus' name, amen.*

# CATHY'S LEGACY

*Praise the Lord!*

*For it is good to sing praises to our God;*

*For it is pleasant, and praise is beautiful ...*

*He heals the brokenhearted*

*And binds up their wounds ...*

*Great is our Lord, and mighty in power;*

*His understanding is infinite.*

*The Lord lifts up the humble,*

*He casts the wicked down to the ground.*

*Sing to the Lord with thanksgiving;*

*Sing praises on the harp to our God.*

*--Psalm 147:1, 3, 5-7*

DOTTIE'S FRIENDS PRAYED for her daughter Cathy for years. Cathy spent much of her early adult years following her addictions to the point that her physical and mental health was compromised beyond medical help. One day Cathy yielded to the call of God and put her life and her eternal destiny in God's care. Cathy's addictions became controllable, but the damage she had done to her body and mind remained. Our prayers now centered on Cathy's physical ailments and a place to live where she would have the care she needed.

After her conversion experience, Cathy became a beacon of warning to anyone she saw engaging in the kind of behavior to which she had been addicted. She devoted her hours to studying the Bible, and she wanted nothing more than to honor her Savior with her life.

When Cathy passed away her family and friends gathered at her service to remember her life and grieve together over the loss of a loved one. Her twin sister asked the family members to take part in a symbolic balloon ceremony. They chose Scripture verses that they thought Cathy would want to share. These had a two-fold purpose: pointing the onlookers to Heaven and influencing anyone who found the dropped verses.

The gathered family members read the verses in turn, and then attached them to various colored balloons. Then they let the balloons escape into the air. Each person watched the balloons, particularly noting the one she had held. For a long time the balloons stayed together. Then they parted slightly and everyone noticed that Cathy's mother's balloon seemed to bump from one balloon to another until it had touched all of them. Finally, before they disappeared from sight, the balloons came back together, not as a clump but in the shape of a cross. The message to all was clear.

*Lord, You lift up the humble. You give us opportunities to work through us in ways we would never imagine. You heal our broken hearts and You bind up our wounds. You show us in creative ways that You are with us. Thank You. In Jesus' name, amen.*

# NEVER TOO OLD

*Praise the Lord from the earth,*

*You great sea creatures and all the depths;*

*Fire and hail, snow and clouds;*

*Stormy wind, fulfilling His word;*

*Mountains and all hills;*

*Fruitful trees and all cedars;*

*Beasts and all cattle;*

*Creeping things and flying fowl;*

*Kings of the earth and all peoples;*

*Princes and all judges of the earth;*

*Both young men and maidens;*

*Old men and children ...*

*Praise the Lord!*

--Psalm 148:7-12, 14

IN THE CHURCH I attend there were three centenarians who regularly came to Sunday services. Sometimes they came with walkers or canes. Usually they sat while the rest of us stood during the worship time. Only rarely could they hear the preaching enough to understand. They didn't move to the music or wave their hands to acknowledge God, but they worshiped. That's why they came: to worship

My friend Betty went home to be with Jesus early on a Monday morning. Where do you think she spent her last day on earth? In church with God's people. Praising God and reminding us that Jesus was going to return soon. She came to worship.

My friend Pat was housebound with a terminal heart condition. She had already gone through heart surgery and refused to do it again. She couldn't come to church on Sundays so we went to her house every month to take communion with her. She was overjoyed when we came to visit her, but her face really glowed during the communion time. She was there to worship.

Even when my husband Larry complained that he felt worthless because he could no longer preach, his lifetime habit continued to draw him to church every Sunday morning. He might sleep through the sermons, but the old hymns had his full attention. When he could no longer actively serve God, he could still worship.

I am inspired by the devotion of my older sisters and brothers in Christ. I pray I will never tire of my love of worshiping with God's children. I try to encourage my grandchildren to understand that worship is not just for grown-ups. God delights in all of our worship.

*Father God, I love You. You are always good. How could I not want to worship You? Keep my heart warm and receptive to Your will. Thank You for other believers to worship with. In Jesus' name, amen.*

# SINGING IN BED

*Praise the Lord!*

*Sing to the Lord a new song,*

*And His praise in the assembly of saints ...*

*Let them praise His name with the dance;*

*Let them sing praises to Him with the timbrel and harp.*

*For the Lord takes pleasure in His people;*

*He will beautify the humble with salvation.*

*Let the saints be joyful in glory;*

*Let them sing aloud on their beds.*

*Let the high praises of God be in their mouth.*

--Psalm 149:1, 3-6

SOMETIMES I ASK my preschool class to think about where they can talk to God. Children are very literal and they will actually ponder over all the places they might be when they need to talk to God. After several minutes and a huge list of "prayer places" they will simultaneously come to the conclusion that we can talk to God anywhere, any time.

The same is true of when and where we can sing God's praises. Is there any place where we cannot sing His songs?

You may be thinking that there might be places where we are supposed to be silent. We wouldn't want to belt out a gospel chorus in a hospital hallway. But I have seen sick people comforted by quietly singing familiar hymns. Even in Larry's last days he delighted in joining groups who came to minister to the elderly with their songs. He had nearly forgotten how to speak, but he could still sing along with the hymns of his childhood, and I noticed that many other residents, whom I had never heard say a word, would sing along too.

Verse five talks about singing aloud on your bed. Don't you often awake with a song in your head? Even on the most trying days I remember that happening to me. My voice is not very melodic in the morning, so I'm not apt to vocalize and scare my little dog and cat, but I may find myself humming as I think the words of praise to God or encouragement from Him.

Is there any place we cannot talk to or sing to God? None.

*Father God, thank You for filling our hearts with joy. Thank You for songwriters who give us the words to express our love to You. Waken us with joyful songs that we may start our days encouraged by You love. In Jesus' name, amen.*

# PRAISE THE LORD!

*Praise the Lord!*

*Praise God in His sanctuary;*

*Praise Him in His mighty firmament!*

*Praise Him for His mighty acts;*

*Praise Him according to His excellent greatness!*

*Praise Him with the sound of the trumpet;*

*Praise Him with the lute and harp!*

*Praise Him with the timbrel and dance;*

*Praise Him with loud cymbals;*

*Praise Him with clashing cymbals!*

*Let everything that has breath praise the Lord.*

*Praise the Lord!*

*--Psalm 150:1-6*

WHAT A CRESCENDO of praise to God! What an awesome climax to God's hymnbook. Let's look again. Where and why and how can we praise God?

- In His sanctuary
- In His mighty firmament (the heavens)
- For His mighty acts

- According to His excellent greatness
- With the trumpet
- With the lute and harp
- With the timbrel and dance
- With stringed instruments and flutes
- With loud cymbals
- With clashing cymbals

And who can enter into this noisy praise service? Let everything that has breath praise the Lord!

*Almighty God, we praise Your name. We lift up our hearts to You in love and adoration. You have brought us through many trials. You are still bringing us through difficulties. We rest in You alone for our salvation in this life and the next. Thank You, Father, for making a way for us to have a relationship with You. May we live as Your honorable children. In Jesus' name, amen.*